Thirteen Ways of Looking at a Man

Images and ideas associated with masculinity are forever in flux. In this book, Donald Moss addresses the never-ending effort of men—regardless of sexual orientation—to shape themselves in relation to the unstable notion of masculinity.

Part 1 looks at the lifelong labor faced by boys and men of assessing themselves in relation to an always shifting, always receding, ideal of "masculinity." In Part 2, Moss considers a series of nested issues regarding homosexuality, homophobia and psychoanalysis. Part 3 focuses on the interface between the body experienced as a private entity and the body experienced as a public entity—the body experienced as one's own and the body subject to the judgments, regulations and punishments of the external world. The final part looks at men and violence. Men must contend with the entwined problems of regulating aggression and figuring out its proper level, aiming to avoid both excess and insufficiency. This section focuses on excessive aggression and its damaging consequences, both to its object and to its subjects.

Thirteen Ways of Looking at a Man will be of great interest not only to psychoanalysts and psychotherapists, but also to a much wider audience of readers interested in gender studies, queer studies, and masculinity

Donald Moss is on the faculty of the Institute for Psychoanalytic Education of NYU Medical Center. Moss focuses on the elemental problem sites of masculinity—mind/body, inside/outside, heterosexual/homosexual, love/hate, singular/plural—while arguing against any settled notion of what men—and women—want.

Thirteen Ways of Looking at a Man

Psychoanalysis and masculinity

Donald Moss

Routledge
Taylor & Francis Group

LONDON AND NEW YORK

First published 2012
by Routledge
27 Church Road, Hove, East Sussex, BN3 2FA

Simultaneously published in the USA and Canada
by Routledge
711 Third Avenue, New York NY 10017

Routledge is an imprint of the Taylor & Francis Group, an informa business

British Library Cataloguing in Publication Data
A catalogue record for this book is available from the British Library

Library of Congress Cataloging in Publication Data
Moss, Donald, 1944–
   Thirteen ways of looking at a man : psychoanalysis and masculinity /
   Donald Moss.
      p. cm.
   1. Masculinity. 2. Men–Psychology. 3. Psychoanalysis. I. Title.
   BF175.5.M37M677 2012
   155.3'32–dc23   2012000721

ISBN: 978–0–415–60491–8 (hbk)
ISBN: 978–0–415–60492–5 (pbk)
ISBN: 978–0–203–10599–3 (ebk)

Typeset in Times by
Swales & Willis Ltd, Exeter, Devon

Printed and bound in Great Britain by MPG Printgroup

For Lynne, Hannah, Ivan and Isaiah,
and in memory of my father.

Contents

Foreword
On Donald Moss's style

Alan Bass

 Like drives, cultural products place a demand on the mind for work.
(Donald Moss, 2010)

Among American psychoanalysts writing today, Donald Moss has perhaps the most distinctive voice. By voice, I mean a style that is immediately recognizable. In this book, he explicitly weds his style to what he is saying about masculinity. Moss wants us not only to look at men, but to look at a man, himself, writing about men. He wants us to understand why he develops a certain style, and why, for him, having us watch the work of this style will give greater purchase on the question of what men are like. (But not, as he specifies, the question of what men are.) Most particularly, he wants to focus on what men are like from a Freudian point of view: the point of view of drives, body, mind, and work. In order to read this book as it demands to be read, to make the point Moss himself has made in the epigraph above, the reader will have to experience it as a drive stimulus: a demand for work. But what is a demand for work that is inextricable from a style?

Freud's definition of the drives preoccupies Moss; he cites it several times, and elsewhere uses it as the title of an article (Moss 2010b) (the epigraph above). It opens Chapter 4, on one of the book's central topics: homophobia. Moss wants us to think of homophobia not only as prejudice, but as a symptom, and like all symptoms, related to drives. Moss uses the quote again in Chapter 5, on the general relation of psychoanalysis and homosexuality. He is speaking of the necessary psychoanalytic search for neutrality, which always encounters what he calls a "tilt" in the analyst, a drive-related experience that seems to make immediate sensuous sense. He says that "the tilt I feel pulls my mind toward an alignment with demands emanating from my body. The mental work demanded of me is to satisfy this drive-based tilt: to provide it with theoretical cover, to adorn it with thought." Understand: the "theoretical cover," the "adornment" is the work itself, which for Moss is also the work of achieving analytic neutrality against the pull of the "tilt." In Chapter 6, "Internalized homophobia in men," Moss pursues his examination of homophobia as a symptom and writes

I am conceptualizing drive here as did Freud, as 'the demand made upon the mind for work as a result of its connection to the body.' Often, that demand is experienced as same-sex desire, which, for a multitude of interdicting factors, cannot be met. In such cases, homophobia and internalized homophobia are likely symptomatic outcomes.

To paraphrase: as a symptom, internalized homophobia works against the work demanded by the drive. Extending this possibility, in Chapter 7 Moss writes of a patient who finds satisfaction nowhere in his life. He again cites Freud's definition to conceptualize this man as a "slave to drive," a slave to a work that promises no satisfaction.

The point of these citations is to open up unexpected resources of Freud's definition of drive as work. To understand homophobia as a symptom demands a certain kind of work in the analyst. Moss conceives this as the work of thinking beyond the conventional understanding of self-hatred as internalization of societal prejudice in order to see how such internalization can produce alienation from the work of the drives. The analyst, too, is a creature of drives, and if not alienated from them, will have to perform another kind of work: the work of challenging what seems to make immediate, bodily, sensuous sense. In some people, alienation from the drives is so radical that they can only work at ensuring that the work of the drives will come to nothing. No matter how one responds, there is no escaping this demand for work.

But there is another aspect to Moss's insistence on the work of the drives. He is asking us to attend to the ways *he* seeks drive satisfaction from the work of his style. He treats this question in depth, and this is where the autobiographical aspect of the book comes in. It is full of first-person accounts: Moss the analyst at work, Moss looking at a Calvin Klein ad, Moss as a young child with polio, Moss listening to his father's war stories, Moss and his friend Ted, Moss listening to Little Richard, Moss as a boy betraying his angels. And there is another kind of autobiography here, the account of Moss telling us about how he writes, and why he writes as he does.

This account is very attentive to the tensions of writing as both an individual and as a member of a collective, for example, as a psychoanalyst among psychoanalysts and as a man among men. Two citations on this issue:

> For me, the first-person singular voice elegantly—efficiently—serves to both illuminate and obscure some of my relevant membership obligations and, more importantly, to reveal a conundrum integral to membership itself. The conundrum is illuminated the moment I begin to try to write a psychoanalytic text. Write a word and I immediately feel the presence of anxiety, an awareness of potential danger. Whatever I say may constitute a violation. Writing as a psychoanalyst, my "I" may be excessively oppositional, my "we" potentially presumptuous.

(p. 9)

> Writing psychoanalysis, then, demands caution, the wish to preserve poten-
> tially breakable bonds. But it also demands audacity, the willingness to risk
> violating those same bonds. The first-person singular voice seems to me to
> best accommodate these demands and more; it is a voice filled with overtones,
> capable of simultaneously conveying a wide range of apology, assertion and
> insistence. It speaks not in single notes, but in chords.
>
> (pp. 9–10)

In other words, and strangely, writing in the first-person singular is the best
approach to plurality. Moss is asking us to look at him writing this book, asking
us to see him in his singular multiplicity—just as he looks at himself looking at
his multiple responses to the Calvin Klein model. This is both conventionally
psychoanalytic and daring.

Conventional in the sense of following Freud: Freud, after all, writes about
himself—"The interpretation of dreams" (1900), he says, is the record of his self-
analysis—and he also tells us that the analyst must always listen to himself. For
Freud, the rule of free association for the patient must be complemented by the
analyst's attention to everything that comes to his mind while listening to the patient.
Moss is committed to this psychoanalytic perspective; self-analysis and close
attention to his own associations while listening to patients are evident throughout.

Daring in this sense: Moss goes further than Freud on this issue when he analyzes
being a man writing about men:

> Being a man means being a member of the group of men. As such, just as
> problems of voice and membership infiltrate the work of writing, so do such
> problems infiltrate the work of "being and becoming a man." That is, a "man"
> (I put this in quotation marks to indicate that we lack a clear idea of what the
> term actually signifies), like a writer, must, in order to take on the task of
> "becoming and being a man," contend with the problems presented by voice.
> In what voice will this "man" aim to speak—with what degree of idiosyncrasy,
> with what degree of integration? With what degrees of apology, of assertion,
> of insistence, will this man speak? How will his voice pass through the channel
> bounded on one side by self-abnegation, on the other by arrogance?
>
> (p. 10)

> I think that the problems associated with being and becoming a "writer" are
> congruent with the problems associated with being and becoming a "man."
>
> (p. 10)

One at first wonders: how can this be? Is there anything specific about what men
are like that is really analogous to being a writer? Moss would want us to
understand that the question is badly framed. Take his point of departure. Looking
at himself looking at the man in the Calvin Klein ad, Moss tells us that when he
looks at any man, he immediately enters an area of "blurred boundaries and endless

resemblances," or, as he memorably puts it elsewhere, a "conceptual estuary." But, he says, this is the "only reliable marker of my place." The best he can do is to attend to this unchartable place and its endless complexity, and to use simile and metaphor to say what men are like. So then to reframe the question: do Moss's tropes and his observations about what men are like, that is, the style of his writing about men, effectively bounce off each other, so that his statement about becoming a writer and becoming a man is justified?

What, then, are men like? Men, for Moss, are always pretending to be men, because they have always just missed being men. Citing a patient who says, "You can't be a man if you don't love men. You can't be a man if you do love men," Moss writes:

> Masculinity, on its face, lacks the capacity to legitimate itself. It always needs affirmation, and there, in that need, lies its delegitimating "weak point," its confession to be less than—other than—it aspires to. No matter how complete, masculinity suspects itself of pretending.
>
> (p. 7)

> This man frames an enduring, destabilizing predicament that seems to me to perpetually dog both the definition of and the aspiration toward masculinity. Since you must simultaneously love men and hate them, while also neither loving them nor hating them, you will have just missed the masculinity you're after. No matter where you land or who you love; no matter what you renounce or what you take in, you will always, always, be susceptible to the judgment that you did it wrong.
>
> (p. 8)

> So finally, since you both missed it and are missing it, as this patient so woefully says, "You can't be a man, not really."
>
> (p. 8)

The patient speaks in the voice of someone tormented by a double bind. He wants to be a man, really, but the conditions of doing so prevent him from doing so. Moss, I believe, speaks in a voice that affirms this bind, even at its most tormenting. Not only is his "I" always divided, his style always bifurcated, his clinical accounts intensely personal, his autobiographical accounts clinical, his psychoanalytic theorizing infused with social issues, and vice versa. He also is writing from a position that implies that his patient has come upon an almost unbearable truth: that one must seek to achieve an essence of masculinity that does not exist. Yes, incontestably, they are men; but they have no central, fixed core, they exist in a complex relation to irreducible, contradictory demands. Moss is then obliged to find a way to write about masculinity such that he is fully attuned to the possible tragedy of this condition, while simultaneously staying attuned to himself as man and as psychoanalyst writing about it. This demands acute observation of all the twists and turns of attempting to become what one cannot be; and it demands a style that captures these twists and turns as an affirmation of psychoanalytic theory and technique. This, I think, is the justification for Moss's claim that the problems of becoming a writer are congruent with the problems of becoming a man, and, I would add, of how he understands becoming a psychoanalyst.

Why not say the same thing about becoming a woman? Moss's first chapter (from which the citation of the patient's double bind masculinity is taken) is entitled "Masculinity as masquerade." Psychoanalytic readers will immediately hear the reference to Joan Riviere's classic 1929 paper, "Womanliness as a masquerade." And when Moss speaks of the relation of identification and object love, such that each masks the other, he says that each position becomes a kind of "drag." Here, one inevitably thinks of Judith Butler's argument in *Gender Trouble* (1990) about drag and gender performativity. I think that Moss works in the tradition of these writers, and is perhaps the first to apply some of the resources of their thinking about femininity to masculinity. But the question of style remains. Neither Riviere nor Butler addresses Moss's crucial topic about the "I" in their texts, about the kind of observation and rhetoric necessary when writing about becoming a woman/man as a woman/man.

To write about sexual difference, about homosexuality, about heterosexuality, as both psychoanalyst and sexed or gendered person, is to be compelled to describe a reality that has no essence, but that always seems to have one. From the psychoanalytic point of view, this appearance is guaranteed by the work of fantasy. This is a point at which the intrapsychic and the social intersect. Moss writes:

> "Masculinity," whatever it may signify, certainly seems grounded in the most private, personal unconscious fantasy. And yet, these fantasies themselves seem derived from elements that are in conscious public circulation. "Masculinity" seems, then, to stretch across the divide between the private and public spheres.
>
> (p. 18)

Again, the question immediately arises: is this not true for femininity as well? Moss addresses the question:

> Given the elemental status of sexual difference, our ways of looking at a woman will necessarily provide an inverted mirror of our ways of looking at a man. If we bracket out the commonalities we might find between the sexes, the contrasting remainders will constitute whatever we mean by "sexual difference." "Difference," then, inversely binds the terms "man" and "woman" no less than sameness directly does.
>
> (p. 98)

In order to tackle this difficult question, Moss says that we need to insert "the analyst's desire into the conceptual slot vacated by axiomatic heterosexuality." We will "then have the power to illuminate the radical uncertainties attached to any effort to clarify and categorize the determinants and meanings of female—and male—sexual desire." Note the emphasis on the "analyst's desire" and on "radical uncertainties." This is another place where the question of style becomes paramount. Moss wants to describe both the analyst's desire and the radical uncertainties as precisely as possible, and wants us to look at him doing so. His observation of the endless complexity of how he looks at the Calvin Klein ad, he tells us, is the "place from which this book emerges." Hence, it is also the place from which the style emerges. Moss places his readers in his own position looking at the ad: one has to read a style that itself demands to be looked at, and one has to think about the irreducibly complex responses one has to it. This is a demand for work.

There is another piece of work that I found the book demanded. Moss does not discuss the source of his title, the Wallace Stevens poem "Thirteen Ways of Looking at a Blackbird." At first I assumed that Moss was citing Stevens on irreducibly multiple ways of looking at a singular phenomenon—a man, a blackbird. On rereading the poem, I came to think otherwise. The poem comprises thirteen numbered sections, each describing a particular reaction to looking at a blackbird. Like this book, it is about looking, describing, and about the intertwining of what is being looked at and the looking itself. The first two sections immediately engage the reader in the question of the intertwining of looking at something, and looking at the looking: "I. Among twenty snowy mountains, / The only moving thing / Was the eye of the blackbird. II. I was of three minds, / Like a tree / On which there are three blackbirds." After the first sharp image of a blackbird's moving eye in a still, cold landscape, the poet says something about his mind looking at the blackbirds, about its complex responses ("of three minds"), but does so by comparing his looking mind to what he is looking at ("like a tree on which . . .").

Seemingly out of nowhere, the fourth way of looking enjoins sexual difference: "IV. A man and a woman / Are one. / A man and a woman and a blackbird / Are one." What is going on here? The first two lines—"A man and a woman / Are one"—seem conventional. Assuming equal value for each term, male and female are two halves of a whole; male and female together make one. What is the blackbird of the second two lines? A zero, such that the two halves still make one? Or have the values changed? Again assuming equality of value, is each now a third? Would that mean that man and woman could be either a half or a third of a whole? That the blackbird is something that changes the oneness of man and woman, such that there is something that is neither the one nor the other that still makes them one? There is something about "three" here. The poet is of three minds, like a tree on which there are three blackbirds; a man and a woman and a blackbird are one. Are the three minds the three of the man, the woman, and the blackbird? But what does a blackbird have to do with mind or with sexual difference? Is it not extraneous to both? Or is that the point: is there something extraneous to mind and to man and woman—that is, a nothing—that is a fraction of them both? And that can only be described by a self-reflexive simile (three minds like three blackbirds)?

Moss also speaks of a triangle whose third point is a zero. Speaking of the structure of the Freudian wish, and its relation to absence, Moss says:

> From the beginning . . . the wished-for object, when absent, is always, and necessarily, located elsewhere, "there" rather than "here" where I wish it to be. . . . Prior to its being occupied by a particular psychic representation, though, the site itself serves as the third term of a triangle. The triangle snaps into place as the product of a wishing subject. . . . Using a numerical metaphor, we could say that the third point in the original triangle is occupied by the place holder, zero.
>
> (p. 26)

Like Stevens, Moss is saying that the relation between what appears to be "two"—subject and wished for object, or, I would add, man and woman—always includes a "place holder," a zero—a blackbird—that makes each term what it is. If man and woman are one, so too are man, woman, and blackbird, that is, the zero apparently extraneous to each term that is within them as their relation to each other. One might say that the blackbird is sexual difference itself, the necessary zero of two inextricably related terms that expresses that relation. To look at sexual difference is to look at a blackbird. Or, as Moss says: "'Difference' . . . inversely binds the terms 'man' and 'woman' no less than sameness directly does" (p. 98).

If there are men and there are women, Moss's patient is right: one cannot be a man, not really, if this means achieving fixed status as half of a whole. There is always something missing from man and woman that makes them what they are. But, of course, the patient cannot tolerate why he is right. He is torn between contradictory fantasies that symptomatically conceal and reveal this knowledge. Moss's style, like Stevens's style, is designed to capture and reflect on this process, by looking at itself doing so. Both share a phenomenological passion for precise looking, and a writer's passion for precise tropes to describe the looking. But Moss, the psychoanalyst, takes on the irreducible work of looking at the unconscious processes—the realities, fantasies, affects, anxieties, defenses, and drives that inhabit the looking itself.

Which is why the book's style, its self-reflexivity, opens it to the world. All of Moss's autobiographical chapters engage his confrontation with himself and his drives in the social context. This is most poignantly so in the last chapter, when, as in the prologue about looking at a man in an ad, he tells us where the book comes from. Moss the boy has trouble sleeping, but can reliably use the lullaby from *Hansel and Gretel*, "When at night I go to sleep," to relax and to sleep. The angels of the song, "two at my right side, two at my left," etc., occupy a strange nether region:

> They were never concrete figures in my mind; they had no color, no wings, no faces; they made no sound. They never really appeared, not really. They

were neither invisible nor visible. They were out of sight, elsewhere, just on the other side, guarding the room I was in, guarding the body I was in.

(p. 139)

The angels take care of him, but never appear, not really. ("You can't be a man, not really.") And having anticipated for months singing this, his favorite song, in front of his elementary school class, Moss realizes from the looks on the boys' faces as he introduces it that he must not. He sings the "Marines' Hymn" instead. He contests the typical understanding of the story: not wanting to appear like a sissy in front of the other boys by singing a lullaby. His analysis is rather that

a boy loves boys so much that, in the name of that love, in fear of their rejection, he renounces his angels, the loves of his life. He then turns outward, now in the company of boys like himself, and searches for new "angels"—cute girls, say—melancholically aware that what he is "really" doing in that fateful turning outward is simultaneously preserving and betraying his original love of angels, affirming and denying his new love of boys; after all, now he and the boys are joined together in looking elsewhere for the angels they might have all once had.

(p. 141)

I again hear an echo of Judith Butler and her theory of the melancholia that inhabits the renunciation of same sex love, but there is more: Moss is renouncing his love for that which needs no concrete presence to care for him. Winnicott (1950) would certainly call this the transitional, and there is every reason to think that belief in an essential masculinity or femininity renounces the transitionality that inhabits both.

Echoing his prologue, Moss writes:

This book can be thought of as an extended effort to unpack that moment in front of the class and, indirectly, to apologize to the angels for my treachery. I was unfaithful to them. I renounced them in public and continued to do so for decades. Their love for me was unconditional. It remains unconditional. They ask for no explanation. They demand no apology. They are still there, those angels, I know it. My love for them is another of those that dare not speak its name. In fact, even if it dared, what name would it have, that love of protective angels?

(p. 141)

What name indeed? The love of that which could have boys love each other for their shared love of what they can't be, really? For their neither visible nor invisible angels? And how can a man, a psychoanalyst, and a writer *look* at that?

Moss's style is the answer to such questions. How many angels are there? The lyric of the Humperdinck song is unambiguous: fourteen. Moss gives it as thirteen.

A slip? A sly allusion to his own title and to the Stevens poem? Perhaps a condensation of looking at men, at blackbirds, and at angels? Or, to cite the last line of another Stevens poem ("The Snow Man"), a psychoanalytic look that "sees nothing that is not there, and the nothing that is"? To see nothing that is not there is to see what is there; but what is there might be a nothing—a zero, like an angel, neither visible nor invisible, or a blackbird that makes a man and a woman one. A real nothing, a nothing *that is*, a nothing that never appears, "not really," such that "you can't be a man, not really."

But even while we contend with torment, treachery, failure, and apology expressed in Moss's demanding style, we ought not forget that other great stylist who is one of the dedicatees of the book—Little Richard. Moss's description of himself listening to Little Richard, screaming along with the records, is unforgettable, and so too is the surprising lesson he draws from the experience: "Psychoanalysis at its best does what Little Richard did. Like Little Richard, the analyst, the man, is always out there at the edge, not screaming, but insisting with words and with silence, why stop, why stop there; come on, come on."

Prologue

On a billboard dominating a busy New York intersection reclines a gorgeous young man, naked except for his Calvin Klein briefs. Inside the briefs lurks an erection. Next to him leans a beautiful woman, her crotch barely covered by wide-mesh panties. The man has the face of a feasting lion: a mix of intense pleasure and latent ferocity. One of his hands grasps the elastic band of his briefs. He seems about to pull them off.

The image discomforts me. I am smaller and weaker than this guy. I cannot effectively compete or object. I can neither become like him nor find a woman like his. I also cannot take my eyes off of him. As I continue to look up at his image, though, I realize that I can, in fact, do one more thing—one thing only. I can buy Calvin Klein briefs.

Here I sit, then, in my fashionable suit and dignified automobile, waiting for the light to change: locked in, riveted, reduced to ogling, with my only sanctioned activity being to buy the briefs, which, on my body, would humiliatingly reveal the unbridgeable differences between this guy and me. I am simultaneously furious, provoked, competitive, disgusted, critical, engaged, thoughtful, abject, infantile, aged, superior, indifferent, captured, compliant . . . the list is long and kaleidoscopic. Its particulars shift slightly each morning as I encounter the image.

Each morning I am relieved at the green light that shortens the encounter, challenged by the red one that prolongs it.

That is, each morning I am helpless.

This is neither expected nor as I'd like it to be. After all, for over 30 years as a psychoanalyst, I have developed a wide-ranging, finely tuned appreciation of the elements that contribute to intense experiences like this one. As engines and transmissions are the focus of a mechanic's work, intense experience—particularly unwanted, repetitive intense experience—is the focus of mine. My work consists of thinking about how it comes to be that we cannot easily change our minds; that, despite whatever intention we might bring to an encounter, we confront limits—firm, merciless limits—on our capacities to realize those intentions. Reason and self-preservation prove shockingly weak allies in our ongoing efforts to reconfigure ourselves. Psychoanalytic treatment, though, has proven itself a strong ally. Minds can change; minds can be changed. Thinking clear-headedly about limits, naming them, disturbing the grounds on which they rest—this sequence works. Bring it to bear on an encounter that otherwise leaves you helpless and you are likely to find your way to effective change.

Nonetheless, no matter how frequently I have brought this sequence to bear on my own encounters with the enormous image of this gorgeous man, it has not led to effective change. Instead, the sequence has led only to a heightened consciousness and an expanded range of descriptive power. It has reduced neither my helplessness nor my disturbance.

What happens when I look at this man? What keeps me disturbed? What locks me in?

Each day, the same thing happens. The image of this man provokes a volatile, incompatible mix of emotions and impulses. At any single encounter with the image, I can name those impulses and emotions: jealousy, indifference, disgust, competition, pain, excitement; each day a different mix—different varieties, different intensities—each mix yielding a different product, a different state of mind.

If I thought it useful, I could chart each component of each state on some multidimensional grid. I could then preserve each day's grid, could compare one day's to the next's, last week's to this one's. But, since I cannot generate any thought large enough to synthesize and clarify the changing patterns, such grids would be of no use.

So, I think, maybe there are just too many dimensions for my thought—any thought—to handle. Maybe. But why, then, would this be so? What about this image, this encounter, generates such complexity?

Unlike the changing daily experience, the shifting weekly patterns, this question seems to hold steady: what about my encounters with this image generates such complexity?

This, then, is what I have: an enduring question, something to start with. I welcome this question. It serves as the immediate antidote to the poisonous prospect of buying myself some Calvin Klein briefs.

Landing on the question, feeling the solidity it provides me, I feel I have found something in the billboard that the billboard itself did not dictate. This modest finding seems like a triumph.

Here it is again, my finding: How is it that thought consistently, predictably, fails to adequately grasp, master and change the pertinent elements of my daily encounters with this image?

Standing on one question, perhaps I can then generate another.

Here goes: Yesterday's emotional cluster is not replicated today; today's will not be replicated tomorrow. I might think the billboard an offense on Monday, a hearty provocation on Tuesday, a playful seduction on Wednesday, a conceptual problem on Thursday, a crude advertisement on Friday. The next week, order and content will change. This certainty of change along with the unpredictability of the particulars that change—this too I have.

The changes seem unrelated to my mood. I may be gloomy as I approach the billboard and respond with a smile to its welcomed daring. I may be rested and raring to go and respond with gritted teeth to its disgusting aggressiveness. Something happens; this is all I know. It's unpredictable; it seems independent of all the usual precursors.

I can now generate a second question, in fact a second cluster of questions. What makes the experience of the billboard so variable, so independent of predictors? How is it that the billboard never becomes exactly familiar? What keeps it alien, new, and steadily provocative? Why does it never get boring?

Looking back on the days, on the weeks now, I come up against an enduring and unchanging awareness that I lack the capacity to bundle these momentary clusters together. I cannot find single thoughts, single notions, single strategies of interpretation that will hold up over any single reflective weekend, say, let alone withstand the new encounter with the ostensibly identical image on the next Monday morning.

The changes are too rapid, too close to random, for my thinking to grasp.

Each day, then, is more than I can synthesize and the relation between the days follows no pattern that I can discern.

I have these facts.

The image stays fixed, of course, and I, because I am a more or less sane man, stay fixed, and yet, with each encounter between these two fixed points, the outcome varies so widely, so unpredictably, that almost nothing steady and enduring can be said about it.

Learn to ride once and every experience between you and whatever bicycle you ever come upon will be predictable. You will never have to learn to ride again. But, it seems to me, learn to encounter a man one day and whatever you might have learned in that experience will have so little bearing on your next encounter with either that man or any other that, in the second encounter, you will likely not even be able to speak of having learned a thing.

I have long been accustomed to such volatility when looking closely at a man. The particular elements of the mix change, of course, depending on the man, the image, and the moment.

What doesn't change, though, what has never changed, is the fact of volatility. In looking at a man, in really looking, never do the elements of what I see and feel settle and cohere. Never do they click into place. Never do I achieve the sense that yes, now I have it, now I have him, now I know what I'm seeing.

Not every man captures my attention like the one on this billboard does. Most move through my field of vision as nondescript blurs. But, without exception, those that occupy my field of vision long enough to come into focus, to be registered— these, every single one of them, disturb me. Maybe "disturb" is not the right word here. "Remind" is more precise.

I can say with certainty that each of the men whose image I have registered, and, in fact, each act of registration, along with each return to the long list of entries already registered, reminds me of an ongoing disturbance, a continuous disturbance, that, between encounters, I can easily forget. The disturbance is somehow related to looking at men.

"Looking at men"—what do I mean by that? What am I doing when I'm "looking"?

Near the center of my experience of looking lurks a tangle of questions. The apparently innocuous question on the surface of this tangle possesses a strange urgency. What is it like to be the man I'm looking at? Its urgency derives from the latent, and pressing, questions that this one both points to and obscures. These other questions include:

- What is it like to look at this man?
- What is it like to want something from him?
- What is it like to be afraid of what I want?
- What is it like to try to expose this man, to look through him?
- What is it like to celebrate him?
- What is it like for him to be looked at by me?
- What is it like to be a straight man looking?
- What is it like to be a gay man looking?
- What is it like for this man to be looked at?
- What is it like for me when this man sees me looking?

There are more questions, and, like these, they all take the form of "what is it like?" This form of question—what is it like?—delineates a modest ambition, for no matter how thoroughgoing my inquiry, how aggressive my gaze, how well-formed my search, I will have to settle for "likeness," for similes, metaphors, and approximations. That is, even when successful, my looking will leave me only momentarily satisfied. Asking "what is it like?" I cannot reasonably expect to find out what it actually is.

The best I—and, I think, "we"—can do will be to attach our own transient and unsteady experiences of looking at this man to something else that, for the moment, we can manage to hold fixed and still. For instance, looking at this man, we might say, is "like looking in the mirror." With this, we would be trying to hold steady to a fixed notion of "mirror." This move may prove credible, productive, even generative. Using "mirror" as a fixed point—what some analysts refer to as a "dry spot"—we may have momentarily found something resembling satisfaction. But the experience will only resemble satisfaction because the moment we lean on it, the moment we might feel we have finished, we are disturbed by the unwelcomed emergence of a new question: "What is it like to look in the mirror?" Well, then, we might proceed, what *is* it like? We could respond to this second question by recalling that looking into a mirror is, say, like being looked back at by the mirror— it is as though the image in the mirror were seeing us. And with this, we may have provided ourselves with another moment resembling satisfaction. But only almost, for this moment too will not stay fixed. The unstable answer resolves itself into yet another new question: "What is it like to be looked at by an image in a mirror?"

Behind every question, behind every response, lurks another. When we ask what is it like to look at a man, we place ourselves at the head of an endless procession of likenesses.

Some questions, of course, can be answered without recourse to simile. If we ask, for example, "What is water?" we can answer clearly: water is two parts hydrogen, one part oxygen. But if we then go on to inquire about "wetness," the form of our question must change to "What is wetness like?" Certain psycho-analytic questions can be of the "what is water?" type: empirical, definitional, textual questions. Most, though, cannot. These will be responded to differently, depending on the momentarily fixed points to which they are referred. "What is anxiety?" for example, will generate a wide variety of responses, each of which, I think, actually represent a transformation of the question to "What is anxiety like?"—like a somatic event, like fear, like apprehension, like impending loss, etc.

Throughout this book, *Thirteen Ways of Looking at a Man*, all questions about "looking at a man" or "being a man" or "being seen as a man" will resemble the kinds of questions we can ask of "wetness" and not at all the kinds we can ask of "water."

One way of "looking at a man," of course, is "listening to a man." As a psychoanalyst, listening is what I steadily do. Like looking at the billboard, listening to a man consistently leaves me in states of uncertainty. On a moment-to-moment basis, my listening is organized around these interlaced questions: "What is this experience like?" "What does this experience resemble?" "What, or who, does this man resemble?" "Feeling this way while listening to this man, who, or what, do I resemble?"

Here, for example, are the words of a man to whom I was recently listening. He says:

> I had a dream last night. There was an idiot, like a village idiot, a retard. There was one I knew as a child. He was always masturbating. In my dream, there was a boy like that one. He was into sexual pleasure, the only kind he's capable of. There's another man in the dream. He is masturbating the retard. The retard can't come until the man releases his grip on his penis. The sexual tension builds up indefinitely. Then the man lets go. Sperm flies in all directions. The idiot had a childish enjoyment of his orgasm: giggling and waving his hands. He shoots sperm into his own mouth.
>
> I was to the side, observing. I felt disgust but also admiration. The retard doesn't care what others think. He's enjoying himself. He doesn't know to care.
>
> Then the dream developed into a disturbing scene. There was news in the group that someone was eaten by another. Whether the retard had been eaten or was a cannibal was unclear.

At this point I asked the man what was disturbing about this second scene.

He said: "Someone was killed, disemboweled and eaten. It was a nightmare feeling."

Here I said I could not tell whether this man felt the dream had any meaning for him.

He said: "Maybe everything in the dream has to do with me who dreamt it. If so, here's what I think: My own sexuality is like a dumb retarded thing that pays no attention to things going on around it. I'm like the retard. I want sex without being able to or wanting to think of consequence or conventions. It's irrational sexuality."

Let's pause here to look more closely at this man.

We see a man dreaming other men, looking at them, telling us what they are like, what they resemble. He further tells us that the men he is dreaming might somehow constitute an indirect form of self-portraiture as a masturbating/being masturbated village idiot.

Like the man I look at on the billboard, the man here presents me with more than I can integrate. "What is it like to be you dreaming this?" I think. What is it like to tell me this dream? What is the man like to whom you feel you are telling it? Where are the two of us—or, maybe, all of us—intersecting? What are our points of contact?

And further, I now think, in what way might your self-portrait of the masturbating village idiot resemble the portrait of the man in the billboard, or resemble me looking at both you and the man in the billboard? In what ways, then, might these three apparently dissimilar figures share the retarded, idiotic, amoral, indifferent sexuality that you advertise as yours alone?

And with that, for the moment, via a slight turn of my thought, the construction of a question, we are all joined. I bring the man in the billboard together with the man on my couch and with the village idiot of his childhood and with the retard in the dream. And I bring myself together with all of them and with the dominating figures of the dream, the cannibal and the man manipulating the idiot's arousal.

And then I think that maybe the dream is about what it's like to be in analysis with me. Maybe, I think, for this man, being with an analyst is like being a village idiot in the presence of a dominating figure controlling his arousal. Or maybe, I think, it's the inverse: being the analyst of this man is like being the helpless village idiot.

Or maybe it's both.

And, by the way, where are the women?

They're missing here. Or maybe they're present, disguised and hidden. Maybe. Maybe.

That "maybe" serves as the only reliable marker of my place, a place of blurred boundaries and endless resemblances.

And there, from that place, this book emerges.

Chapter 1

Masculinity as masquerade[1]

In the Hollywood summer flick *Nacho Libre*, the main character, the hilariously unfit Jack Black, assumes a secret identity, affecting the costumed excesses of a caped, macho street wrestler. By day a menial in a monastery, by night he wants to win matches, money, and a woman. In the film's signature moment, Black reassures his protégé, a young boy who has spotted him surreptitiously dressing up, that "it's okay because sometimes a man just goes into his room and puts on stretchy pants and has a lot of fun." This declaration is meant to mollify the boy's uncomprehending, and suspicious, gaze, to reassure him that his adored older friend, regardless of the stretchy pants and what used to be the forbidden "feminine" posturing in front of a mirror, remains what he always was: the incarnation of an admirable, straightforward masculinity.

It seems to me that many of us psychoanalysts occupy a position resembling that of the astonished boy of *Nacho Libre*. We can feel ourselves located slightly behind the advancing femininity/masculinity curve, waiting to see what's next, readying ourselves for the necessary adjustments. Over the past few decades, for example, we've been bombarded with well-warranted correctives—from heterosexual feminists, from gays, lesbians and transsexuals—to what, in retrospect, now seem outmoded ways of interpreting femininity and masculinity and the putative bedrock on which they once seemed to stand.

For the moment, let us treat Jack Black's instruction to "have fun with stretchy pants" as though it might contain a cardinal feature of all emerging masculinities—something audacious and rule-bending. What's "fun" about the "stretchy pants" is that they self-consciously defy the regulatory norms that seem integral to the boy's—and our—sense of what "masculine" means. That is, "masculinity" meant, in this case, the repudiation of "stretchy pants" as a means of fun. So here, then, Black's "masculinity" takes one step forward; it repudiates a repudiation.

This seemingly daring repudiation is the marker of what I mean by an "emerging" masculinity. As it takes this one step forward, it leaves behind a repudiating

1 A shorter version of this chapter first appeared in Moss, D. (2006) "Masculinity as masquerade," *Journal of the American Psychoanalytic Association*, 54(4): 1187–95. Used with permission.

predecessor. This predecessor, of course, had itself once left behind a repudiating predecessor of its own. Emerging masculinities, then, looking back over their own shoulders, will spot the traces of ever receding, ever surpassed, always anachronistic, old-fashioned masculinities; a historical trail, each advance marked by a repudiation of a predecessor. No longer repudiating what their predecessors had to repudiate, emerging masculinities will necessarily claim that they are, by self-definition, freer, stronger masculinities, in fact, more masculine masculinities.

Nacho Libre exemplifies and applauds an emerging masculinity that, in having fun with stretchy pants—in flirting with the marker of a once-repudiated "femininity"—is repudiating its previous repudiations. The film pokes fun at men still retrograde enough to take seriously and, therefore, to still comply with yesterday's repudiations. With this act of defiance, the film and its hero make their advance into history. They move forward; they turn themselves contemporary. This, I think, is the organizing tactic characteristic of all emerging masculinities: the repudiation of the repudiations of their predecessors. (Crucial to notice in this tactic is that the strategy of repudiation, per se, is not repudiated. Masculine identities remain tied to successful acts of repudiation; masculinity's leading edge rids itself of suddenly devalued erotic currencies while taking on suddenly valued ones—for example, stretchy pants.)

What are we to make of this emerging stretchy-panted figure—still masculine, but now the object of our uncertain gaze, and with that gaze, like Black's protégé, perhaps also of our uncertain identifications? How can we figure out a reliable way to think about this figure? More pertinent still, how can we figure out a way to listen to him, to do something other than merely believe or disbelieve him, tout court, when he says, with a wink, that our once shared problem with stretchy pants no longer exists; that he has, as they say, moved on.

The same nest of questions hovers over this delightful self-report from another man who has, apparently, "moved on." The report comes from Sebastian Junger's 2010 book, *War*. Junger lived for months with a group of American soldiers in Afghanistan. His book is a chronicle of that time and of those men. Junger writes of this man:

> Bobby claimed a kind of broad-spectrum sexuality that made virtually no distinction between anything, and as the months went by that expressed itself in increasingly weird ways . . . Bobby wasn't gay any more than he was racist, but a year on a hilltop somehow made pretending otherwise psychologically necessary. And it wasn't gay anyhow; it was just so hypersexual that gender ceased to matter. Someone once asked Bobby whether, all joking aside, he would actually have sex with a man up here. "Of course," Bobby said. "It would be gay not to."
> "Gay not to?" O'Byrne demanded. "What the fuck does that mean?"
> Bobby launched into a theory that "real" men need sex no matter what, so choosing abstinence can only mean you're not a real man. Who you have sex

with is of far lesser importance. The men knew it made no sense—Bobby's weird brilliance—but no one could quite formulate a rebuttal.

(Junger 2010: 224–225)

"No one could quite formulate a rebuttal." Indeed. Emerging masculinities leave behind a trail of puzzled witnesses in states of reluctant admiration, no one quite able to formulate a rebuttal. The power of such masculinities resides in their refusal to comply with the repudiations of their predecessors. For Bobby, only non-masculine men—men he refers to as "gay"—comply with norms that gratuitously restrict their choice of sexual object. To submit to yesterday's repudiation would not be masculine. Only "gay" men would comply with the regulation that bars heterosexual men from having sex with other men. By way of this hilarious reversal, Bobby nails a central feature of emerging—masculine—masculinities: their right, even their obligation to "have fun" with stretchy pants, or with other men. Emerging masculinities take pleasure with what their restricted predecessors had to renounce. Like Jack Black, Bobby catches masculinity's extraordinary plasticity, and, therefore, its fundamental absence of integral, authentic features.

In this play of shifting repudiations, nothing is being created; no new idea, no new form emerges. Instead, pre-existing elements emerge in new combinations. The once repudiated is now embraced. What was once outside is taken in; what was taken in is now expelled. Emerging masculinities seem to repudiate previous repudiations and to renounce the premises on which they were based. Certain definitions of the masculine are no longer defended; they are instead subverted. Emerging masculinities taunt the limitations of their predecessors.

In this they mimic emerging theories: surpassing, with an often self-satisfied backward glance, the old-fashioned constraints of their predecessors. There may well be structural links and congruencies binding our notions of the masculine and our notions of the psychoanalytic. What if, for example, psychoanalytic thought, like Jack Black, continuously aimed, in effect, to have fun with stretchy pants, to reconsider its own repudiations? And what if, in doing so, it fancied itself protecting and advancing its own psychoanalytic/masculine competency, moving stride for stride with parallel "advances" in the masculinities surrounding it? If such parallel developments were taking place, our capacities to think about the one while holding the other steady would be necessarily, and seriously, taxed. For instance, contemporary psychoanalysis has tended to repudiate its previous repudiations of homosexuality. Ostensibly less anxious than its predecessors, contemporary psychoanalysis, newly open to homosexuality, now permits itself, in effect, to wear stretchy pants rather than to interpret them. What once had to be interpreted now can be worn.

Can we be certain that this taking in of the once repudiated represents an enduring advance, that the resulting restriction on interpretation will be stable? I think not. I can easily imagine developments to come in which the original repudiation might be restored, and stretchy pants again be placed in the category of the interpretable. Such a restoration would not necessarily be regressive. It might, in fact, mark another newly emerging, stronger theory, this one insisting on its right to interpret the stretchy pants its predecessors felt compelled to wear. Just as a continuously developing masculinity's central features cannot be fixed, neither can those of a continuously developing psychoanalytic theory.

If we are to think about emerging masculinities, linked or not with our emerging theories, we need to reflect on the role of ideology as it infiltrates both of these potentially linked zones of expression.

On ideology

Much of psychoanalytic theory and practice over the past hundred years has been deformed by ideology transferring itself onto theory. There seems widespread agreement among psychoanalysts that a stabilizing, long unnoticed convergence of theory and ideology served to underwrite what, only much later, was revealed as a degraded conceptualization of gays and lesbians, of women and femininity.

By and large, the deformations in our theories of masculinity have appeared indirectly, structured as the silent complement to our more direct, and more directly deforming, theories of femininity. Masculinity has served as a strong and silent anchoring point, the presumably non-deformed referent against which all of these deformed categories meet their measure. Gays and lesbians—women in general— were thought deficient precisely to the extent that they lacked whatever "masculinity" possessed.

Our theory has made substantial advances. Across the board, we are less ready than we once were to offer up uniform standards of sexual competence and integrity. With each advance, in effect, we try on those once derided stretchy pants, hoping, in the effort, to untangle an expanding theory from a restrictive ideology. But, no matter how untangled our theory gets, we can still sense, with near certainty, the ideological critique-to-come.

Ideology invariably infiltrates theory. We need to both know and not know this. We need to not know it so that we can protect our theory from skeptics who doubt its reliability. And we need to know it so that we can join those very skeptics in an effort to dismantle and shore up its reliability.

Our first move toward including the once excluded stretchy pants will be informed by a sense that, if we want to stay current with the culture that surrounds us, this is what we ought to do. And yet, once done, we can restore the boundary that separates us from that same culture and take our own—psychoanalytic—look at the stretchy pants we're now wearing. We submit to ideological forces, taking in what we must. And with that, we buy the time, the clinical and cultural opportunities, to think psychoanalytically about what we've done and where to place what we've contingently taken in. A state of permanent flux characterizes the passage of items back and forth across the threshold joining the domains of psychoanalysis and ideology.

The following two sentences from Proust (1913) demonstrate the difficulty of separating any notion of masculinity from its imbedded ideology: "'That's no way to make him strong and active,' she [the grandmother] would say sadly, 'especially that boy, who so needs to build up his endurance and willpower'" (p. 11).

We know the grandmother is out to support the boy's masculinity, but we also know she is saturated with local ideology. In effect, she is insisting that he get out of stretchy pants.

"Strong," "active," "endurance," "willpower"—how do we chart our movement away from these masculine signifiers that give force and meaning to this ideologically loaded sentence?

Whereas we would no longer write that sentence, we would, I think, still support the grandmother in her efforts to help the boy . . . do what? To somehow become masculine, by teaching him to repudiate; in this case to repudiate "passive" forms of pleasure.

Can we theorize the grandmother's effort; can we write it, *with particulars,* in such a way that we can feel confident that those particulars are immune to a lurking ideological critique? I don't think we can, not with confidence. All the particulars that make up today's required repudiations are potential targets. The act of repudiation itself endures, in principle, indifferent to shifts in contemporary particulars.

Repudiate weakness, say, and perhaps we might join with the grandmother in an effort to help the boy *develop*, that is, become less weak, less childish, more . . . well, masculine? If so, we would be linking weakness to non-masculinity, grandparents and psychoanalysts to development. Both links are immediately troublesome. The moment we want to lead the boy from where he is to where we want him to be, we seem to be courting trouble. Or, are we? After all, isn't that the proper setup joining adults to children? The one that helps boys become men? Isn't it? Maybe, maybe not. Perhaps, instead of expelling weakness, we want to expel the grandmother here, repudiate her self-righteous norms. But isn't she looking out for the boy's long-term interests? If so, perhaps we want to keep her. Or, maybe we want to expel her and take in the boy's weakness (his version of stretchy pants). Each choice has its own coherence. The interface is vibrant with choice and vibrant with uncertainty. The choices are neither purely scientific nor purely ideological. It's like a conceptual estuary here, a mixed zone where psychoanalysis meets ideology, where regulation meets defiance, and where each element in each contesting pair assumes its own integrity.

Here's the second sentence from Proust, easier perhaps to position ourselves against, but nonetheless equally difficult to loose from its ideological moorings: "My father would shrug his shoulders and study the barometer, for he liked meteorology, while my mother, making no noise so as not to disturb him, watched him with a tender respect, but not so intently as to try to penetrate the mystery of his superior qualities" (p. 11).

We can confidently locate, and expunge, much of the ideological freight residing in "the mystery of his superior qualities." But how would we now write that moment? How would we theorize what the mother sees—some feature of the father that seems to provoke her love? She wants to maintain an attachment to this feature, whatever it is. She wants it left undisturbed. The feature seems to suggest that masculinity, no matter how ideologically saturated, is "the mystery of his superior qualities."

How would we theorize a masculinity whose cardinal feature is that it be the object of idealization? One has the sense that both mother and father share in the idea that they are living amid his unnamed "superior qualities," the mother as a believer, the father as a carrier. Might not their shared silence represent an effort to preserve a belief in these qualities, a kind of piety? Certainly here, and perhaps more widely, it seems that the very idea of masculinity might depend on a community of believers. This may be an enduring characteristic of masculinity—that it houses the unattainable—that, in that sense, it stands as both parallel and in complement to feminine "beauty." (This line of thought, by the way, is directly indebted to Lacan's theorization of the "signification of the phallus.")

No matter its particular ideologically mediated forms, then, masculinity, as an object of belief, might enduringly resist capture by reason. When cornered, say, masculinity, like beauty, would, as an integral feature of itself, repudiate reason, renounce it. Masculinity, like beauty, would stake a claim on special rights, "superior qualities." It would locate a possibility, an aspiration, a point of ongoing, and enduring, resistance to regulation. There seems something rogue about masculinity, simultaneously destructive and hopeful, our enduringly present "bad boy." Such ideologically mediated idealization of masculinity and of beauty would leave the carriers of both, especially to the extent that the carrying task was experienced as a necessity, burdened by lives of brittleness and fragility.

Clinically, our work on masculinity (and, for that matter, on beauty) aims to reframe, and thus to lighten, this burden. The burden is bundled into ideologically mediated packages. Perhaps the best we can hope for in this work is to reveal the shape and content of our predecessors' packaging and to await descendants who will expose our own.

Requirements of the masquerade

In order to think a bit further about "masculinity," let us consider for a moment the following quick, and confusing, view of another couple. A wife is speaking of her husband: "Even though he was a man, he was more like a woman. . . . He was so nice and tender. He was very feminine. I couldn't tell the difference whether he was male or female: So I never begrudged having to feed him" (*New York Times,* July 17, 2006: A4).

Here, in Marado, South Korea, in a village of women who bring in the money by diving in the sea and men who tend the house and raise the children, we hear of another man being spotted sporting another version of stretchy pants. He "was so nice and tender," says his wife of the husband who, in effect, seems to have repudiated the demand to repudiate the "feminine" qualities of niceness and tenderness.

How does this woman seem to gauge the husband's repudiation, to assess its meanings? How would we? There is no clear telling, given the scant information we have. But I think we can sense immediately that the husband's posture of apparent repudiation provokes questions, certainly in the wife and probably in us: What is he doing and why is he doing it? To what extent is his being "feminine" compulsory; to what extent masterful? What is the place—where do we look in order to find—what anyone might actually mean by "masculinity" in this ostensibly scrambled setup? What kind of framework might we need in order to think non-ideologically about this question? Can we find one?

To pursue these questions a bit, let us imagine an even more scrambled setup. Let us imagine a masculinity powerful enough to have surpassed the necessity of any repudiation; not only nice and tender, but also housing all the pertinent dualisms: assertive and submissive, penetrating and receptive, active and passive, dominating and submissive, kind and gruff.

I think that even here, in this patently fantastic vision, this endlessly plastic, inclusive version of masculinity would not necessarily satisfy us, no matter whether we were its bearer or its witness. It would instead seem merely another "version" of masculinity, an extreme one to be sure, but one that, on its face, lacks the power to convince us. This, I think, is the point. Masculinity, on its face, lacks the capacity to legitimate itself. It always needs affirmation, and there, in that need, lies its delegitimating "weak point," its confession to be less than—other than—it aspires to. No matter how complete, masculinity suspects itself of pretending.

Let us, for the moment, locate a critical, perhaps cardinal, facet of masculinity at the point where it encounters this suspicion. Here, I think, is a pointed example. A 25-year-old woman in analysis is speaking of her husband:

> He always says I look beautiful when I'm naked. But he never does anything to make me naked. He never goes after me, takes off my clothes. He respects me too much. He treats what's mine as mine. It's why I can live with him. But I want violence. Why isn't he more like that? He can't be. He shouldn't be. But I want him to be. I want him to do what I don't want him to do. It's too confusing.

This woman, I think, is struggling to assess her relation to "masculinity" and her desire for it in her husband. Whatever he's done, whatever accommodations he's made, leave her simultaneously pleased—"It's why I can live with him"—and dissatisfied—"Why isn't he more like that?"

This woman is inhabited by a suspicious shadow, an internal object, say, against whom her husband's "masculinity" (and, by the way, her analyst's "real" effectiveness) must be measured. She is dogged by the pursuit of "real" masculinity, her desire to find it as well as her desire to flee from it. As in the moment spoken of above, each time she lands on a resolution, she finds it both partial and temporary.

The "masculinity" she finds has always—and will always, I think—prove suspect: too violent, not violent enough; too gentle, not gentle enough; too respectful, not respectful enough, always only approximating what she calls "the real thing."

And what about this imaginary man who can do it all—an idea that is figured here, in the patient's fantasy, in the form of a man simultaneously violent and respectful—a man who can rise above elemental contradictions? I think she (and, like her, we) will always remain suspicious even of this imaginary figure. We will still insist that he legitimate his claim. We will insist that the term "masculinity" be pinned down. And we will invariably, I think, pin it down by having it lean on, and be measured against, its predecessors.

"Masculinity," I think, always leans on an idealized memory of men, or perhaps of one man, a kind of original. In trying to think one's way into what "masculinity" might mean, one drifts toward an image of an original figure. After that come all the rest, the followers. And because, in imagination, they are merely that—followers—they are always susceptible to the accusation that their version of "masculinity" is a masquerade.

We insist that the claimant mean what he says, do what he means. But the problem, I think, is that finally what he really means is to be like an imagined predecessor, to masquerade as an original. And he is, I think, without exception, caught in the act.

Clinical postscript

"Fuck you. I hate you."
"Fuck you. I love you."
"You can't be a man if you don't love men."
"You can't be a man if you do love men."

This nearly poetic outburst, addressed to his analyst, came during the psycho-analytic treatment of a 55-year-old, self-consciously contemporary man, a Jack Black kind of figure, a man located at what he senses to be masculinity's cutting edge, a man who recently landed the woman he yearned for, the job he never thought he'd get, and the openly expressed gratitude of long embittered sons.

This man frames an enduring, destabilizing predicament that seems to me to perpetually dog both the definition of and the aspiration toward masculinity. Since you must simultaneously love men and hate them, while also neither loving them nor hating them, you will have just missed the masculinity you're after. No matter where you land or who you love; no matter what you renounce or what you take in, you will always, always, be susceptible to the judgment that you did it wrong.

So finally, since you both missed it and are missing it, as this patient so woefully says, "You can't be a man, not really."

Chapter 2

Immaculate attachment vs passive yearning

Thoughts on being and becoming a man[1]

In *Experiences in Groups*, Bion (1961) beautifully catches the tension residing in the problem of voice, when he asks, in effect, in which voice does a member of a group speak? Bion describes an irresolvable conflict between wishes to organize personal experience privately and wishes to organize it socially. That is, membership in a group entails contending with incompatible and co-existing wishes to separate from and to integrate with the group as a whole. A member will simultaneously be drawn to the mutually incompatible satisfactions promised by speaking in the first-person singular and those promised by speaking in the first-person plural. The wish to belong—to unite with and to join the group—necessarily entails an attitude of antipathy toward one's own idiosyncratic interiority. At the same time, the wish to distinguish oneself, to preserve one's sense of personal difference, entails an attitude of antipathy toward the group's ethos of unity.

I evoke Bion here in order to underline the fact that I self-consciously wrote this chapter—and much of the book—as a member of many groups: the group of men, of writers, of psychoanalysts, of psychoanalytic writers, etc. My memberships in these groups are self-evident. What may not be self-evident, though, are the obligations and responsibilities that come with those memberships.

For me, the first-person singular voice elegantly—efficiently—serves to both illuminate and obscure some of my relevant membership obligations and, more importantly, to reveal a conundrum integral to membership itself. The conundrum is illuminated the moment I begin to try to write a psychoanalytic text. Write a word and I immediately feel the presence of anxiety, an awareness of potential danger. Whatever I say may constitute a violation. Writing as a psychoanalyst, my "I" may be excessively oppositional, my "we" potentially presumptuous.

Writing psychoanalysis, then, demands caution, the wish to preserve potentially breakable bonds. But it also demands audacity, the willingness to risk violating those same bonds. The first-person singular voice seems to me to best accommodate these demands and more; it is a voice filled with overtones, capable of

1 Some material from this chapter first appeared in Moss, D. (2008) "Immaculate attachment/intelligent design," *Constellations,* 15(8), No. 8, 2008. Used with permission.

simultaneously conveying a wide range of apology, assertion and insistence. It speaks not in single notes, but in chords.

The problem of voice comes down to, then, a problem of positioning. We employ voice in order to position ourselves in relation to our audiences, our objects, and our interiorities. By way of voice, we aim to stake out and defend our positions effectively. At base, voice offers us a means to steer between two dangerous and extreme poles: on one side the abnegated miming of the cowed loyalist, on the other the arrogant dictates of the imperial self.

Being a man means being a member of the group of men. As such, just as problems of voice and membership infiltrate the work of writing, so do such problems infiltrate the work of "being and becoming a man." That is, a "man" (I put this in quotation marks to indicate that we lack a clear idea of what the term actually signifies), like a writer, must, in order to take on the task of "becoming and being a man," contend with the problems presented by voice. In what voice will this "man" aim to speak—with what degree of idiosyncrasy, with what degree of integration? With what degrees of apology, of assertion, of insistence, will this man speak? How will his voice pass through the channel bounded on one side by self-abnegation, on the other by arrogance?

I think that the problems associated with being and becoming a "writer" are congruent with the problems associated with being and becoming a "man." "Writer" and "man" are each membership categories, and as such they each impose the problem of finding a proper voice. The difference between the two is one of register and not one of kind. Voice lends physicality to its words no less than stride, posture, and bearing lend it to bodies.

The first-person singular voice seems to me best suited to illuminate the problems inherent in speaking personally while simultaneously affirming group membership. The possibilities for the first-person singular voice—the writer's or the man's—are abundant. Its "I" is a composite "I," and so, therefore, is its voice. The first-person singular voice in this chapter, then, also will be a composite.

The first-person singular voice, whether overt or covert, offers me an optimal combination of structure and liberty. My use of the *overt* first-person singular voice indicates that I mean that same singular voice to *covertly* infiltrate the entire chapter. In using it intermittently and in switching overt voices frequently throughout the chapter, I hope to expose some of the structural mechanics, some of the labor, that I think goes into psychoanalytic writing. And, in exposing this labor, I hope to bring additional light to the congruent labor that goes into the explicit object of this chapter: the problems and labor that go into "being and becoming a man."

***

I spotted a big guy on the street sporting a tee shirt that declared in gold letters "I am a 100% pure man." Feeling provoked, I stared at him. He didn't look that smart or that self-possessed; he seemed a little nervous. For me, this short list of impurities sufficed. The guy was clearly a fraud.

Then I paused. In the moment that I judged this man a "fraud," I also must have considered the authenticity of his claim a possibility.

"Considered" exaggerates the conscious reflective dimension of the experience. The moment was more a virtual one than an actual temporal one. That is, it was one that I must have passed through while sizing the man up, a moment in which fantasy infiltrated consciousness. The fantasy, though not exactly conscious, shaped my conscious experience. I want to unpack some of the more accessible features of this fantasy.

Under its influence, for that one moment at least, what I was doing was stacking this guy up against a figure whom I could call, say, "my guy." This fantastic figure functions as a kind of presence in my mind: a kind of "guy," of whom, in fact, I felt, in the moment, that it could be validly said that he—"my guy"—is, indeed, a "100% pure man." Though "my guy" would never actually wear that tee shirt, for me he functions/ed here as the only "guy" who, were he to want to, could.

Thinking some more about this "my guy" figure, I realized that not only does he win here, against this fellow; but, more importantly, he always wins, against anybody. That's what "my guy" does; he wins. In some sense, then, "my guy" functions as the standard figure against whom, against my "better judgment," I momentarily judge claims of masculinity.

After the fact, upon reflection, "my guy" certainly seems a kind of cartoon figure. But "my guy" doesn't function "upon reflection." He appears, and thus functions, only in brief flashes, in urgent moments. He functions before "reflection" does. He beats "reflection" to the scene. He shows up in the form of an impulse. I can, and do, argue against his influence, but what I cannot do is dismiss him. He is there, a fleeting imaginary companion. Try as I might, I can't reach a mental place from which to permanently dislodge him. (Perhaps that is best. I fear that if I could dislodge him, it would only mean that I, myself, had, in that moment of victory, outdone him, and, therefore, had become "my guy"; the gap between us would have vanished. I might then, in effect, be inclined to sport the "pure man" tee shirt.)

"My guy" seems anything but an idiosyncratic figure. He is an amalgam of standard elements: strong, taciturn, handsome, ugly, clear, vigorous, alert, modest, sexy, direct, shy, brazen, rhythmic, awkward, graceful, bookish, paternal, naïve, flamboyant and conservative; the list is long, self-contradictory, and constructed entirely of elements afloat in the culture. Each element is attached, willy-nilly, to a "masculine" figure. Each element is available for the taking.

With each of his features available for the taking, in what is likely an endless range of varieties, "my guy" is a creature, then, of whose imagination? Certainly not just mine. In effect, his location is simultaneously out there and in here. Whoever or whatever "my guy" is, then, he/it does not seem properly thought of as exactly, or simply, "my" guy. More precisely, somehow, he is "our" guy, whoever "we" are. By "our" guy I mean "our" even if, whoever you are, your version of "your guy" might not match up, one to one, with my version of mine.

This point of intersection, of convergence, between "my" guy and "our" guy serves as a segue for a consideration of Freud's (1921a) "Group psychology and the analysis of the ego," a text that situates itself precisely at the point where "my" ego and "our" group are indistinguishable.

Freud's (1921a, b) text, "Group/mass psychology and the analysis of the ego/I" focuses on the dynamic movement, back and forth, between the first-person singular and the first-person plural, the "I" and the "we." He is, as always, interested in mechanisms, motives and consequences. For Freud in this text, as though by default, the voices in question, whether singular or plural, are the voices of men, particularly those of heterosexual men. Freud is interested in what happens when the ostensibly separate and singular "ego/I" of such men seems to lose its separateness by coalescing into an "artificial" (impermanent) "group/mass."

What happens when an unaffiliated man becomes a member?

Freud offers the Church and Army as exemplary groups. They are exemplary because, for Freud, membership means membership in a group organized around clearly identified leaders. The separate "ego/I" of Freud's individual man dissolves as it attaches itself to a leader. The "we" that "I" becomes is constituted by that set of men who share an attachment to the same leader.

For Freud, this vertical attachment to the leader is primary and definitive. The horizontal attachment between fellow members is secondary and derivative.

Freud is interested in the psychodynamics that facilitate or impede attachment to a leader. Regardless of direction, whether toward or away from a leader, Freud wants to theorize the wishes and satisfactions at play in the formation and dissolution of "I"s and "we"s.

Were we to follow Freud's lead—were we, as readers, to join his group—we would see before us what our leader seemed to have seen. We would have two categories about which we could think: 1) men attached to leaders, and 2) men unattached to leaders.

As members of Freud's group, what would not come into focus, what we would not see, is a third category, an apparently permanent one, invariant and ongoing. It is the category of "men," per se. This category seems to persist, unchanged, unaffected by the changing proportions of "I"/"we" of its permanent membership. Affiliated or not, men remain men. This category seems to precede, and seems somehow deeper, than the two that Freud sketches.

This permanent group, "men," also has leaders, figures to which the members are attached. The founding leadership, the originals, have vanished and are, therefore, difficult to name. The evidence of their presence is indirect. The demands they make, the requirements they set for membership, present themselves in the form of often-incompatible stories, fantasies, images, possibilities.

Whoever they are or were, we "men"—all of us, I think—get our membership bearings by positioning ourselves in relation to them. We "know" we are "men" when we "know" we are, in some way, fashioning ourselves in the likeness of a predecessor, either imagined or named. No man is entirely self-authorized to become a member of the group "men."

Even were such power claimed and put to use, I think it would be found to derive from the self-authorizing power of a predecessor; one would be becoming like that predecessor, taking him as a leader, and turning oneself into a member of the group of self-authorized, individual, men.

We "men" constitute a group/mass led by unnamed predecessors. Membership in the group comes from placing oneself in one form or another in proper relation to a predecessor. The line of predecessors is continuous and without end.

How is this long-standing, stable group of men formed and constituted?

Without naming it as such, this is the central problem taken up in Freud's chapter on "Identification."

Freud trumpets the chapter's theme immediately:

> The small boy exhibits a special interest in his father, wanting to become like him, be like him, take his place in every respect . . . This behavior has nothing to do with a passive or feminine attitude towards the father (and toward the male sex in general); in fact it is exquisitely masculine.
>
> (Freud 1921b: 5)

A little boy, then, for Freud, becomes a member of the group of men of which his father is a member by way of an "exquisitely masculine" mechanism that "has nothing to do with a passive or feminine attitude."

This pre-existing "exquisitely masculine" capacity makes the little boy, from the beginning, a proto-member of that group. The capacity for "identification" provides him with the sole, non-passive/non-feminine means for achieving full membership.

Freud does not name the source of this "exquisitely masculine" capacity.

"Identification" as the primary means of becoming a member distinguishes the permanent group of "men" from the Church, the Army, and all the artificial/temporary others. In these groups, the artificial ones, with named leaders, the only way for an "ego/I" to become a member is to employ passive or feminine attitudes.

"Identification" here, making possible the little boy's special attachment to his father, allows Freud to avert what, for him, would be a conundrum.

Without "identification," he would have us picturing the "little boy" as employing "passive and feminine" attitudes in order to become a member of the group "men." A passive and feminine posture would be the sole means to join a group whose hallmark would be its renunciation of the feminine and passive attitude.

This conundrum finds beautiful voice in the patient of whom I have already spoken, someone we might call an obligate heterosexual. To repeat, this man says:

"Fuck you. I hate you."
"Fuck you. I love you."
"You can't be a man if you don't love men."
"You can't be a man if you do love men."

I think that this man, like many others, has never been able to find access to Freud's proposed solution. He apparently lacks the "exquisitely masculine" capacity to identify with his father and, therefore, to avoid the problems posed by the feminine and passive attitudes as they relate to his efforts to, as he puts it, "be a man," or, as I put it here, to become a member of the group "men." He can't be a member if he hates the leaders; he can't be a member if he loves them. These seem to him his only choices.

Freud's proposed solution, unsurprisingly, is not a stable one. This instability heralds itself elegantly when we compare the *Standard Edition* to the new Underwood translation.

In the *Standard Edition*, we read in the run-up to Freud's chapter on identification that:

> We shall . . . turn our attention . . . to . . . being in love . . . we would like to know whether this . . . as we know it in sexual life . . . represents the only manner of emotional tie with other people, or whether we must take other mechanisms into account . . . we learn from psychoanalysis that there *do not exist* other mechanisms for emotional ties, the so-called identifications.
>
> (Freud 1921a: 102, emphasis added)

In other words, here, with this slip of the printer, Freud is presented as saying that the only kinds of emotional ties about which we learn in psychoanalysis pertain to being in love, as we know it in sexual life—that there do not exist other mechanisms, such as "identifications."

But, in the new, and corrected, Underwood translation, we read:

> Psychoanalysis does in fact teach us that there are other mechanisms of emotional attachment, [the] so-called identifications.
>
> (Freud 1921b: 55)

While the *Standard Edition* says the only form of emotional attachment that generates the ties that hold groups together resembles "being in love as we know it in sexual life," the Underwood edition says "other mechanisms, the so-called identifications" exist, and that their existence accounts for an important feature of the ties that go into group formation.

Is there or is there not an exquisitely masculine capacity for identification? Reading these two editions, we cannot find the stable yes or no that we might hope for; we find, instead, an unstable yes and no.

Freud's notion of "identification" serves as lynchpin and fuel for what might be called the myth of immaculate attachment. It is comparable to a myth of intelligent design. Little boys, as though by design, possess an intrinsic "exquisitely masculine" capacity. This capacity allows them to attach themselves to their fathers, and through their fathers, to an endless line of masculine predecessors. In turn, other little boys, also possessed of this "exquisitely masculine" capacity, will identify, immaculately, with us.

In this myth, little boys become like their fathers "in a flash." There are no monstrous transition stages, no traces, no scars that mark any "passive and feminine" passage.

For Freud here, the passive and feminine seem to occupy a position in relation to the exquisitely masculine that resembles, for the believer in intelligent design, the position occupied by the chimp or gorilla in relation to the human. Identify and you're there. And, once there, rest assured; you were, in principle, always there.

But less than two paragraphs into the chapter on identification, Freud begins a relentless backing off from his adherence to this myth. The "exquisitely masculine" mechanism of identification seems to undermine itself from within. What had been the simple flash of identification is revealed to contain component parts that not only resemble, but are, in fact, identical to identification's putative opposite, the sexualized object love of passivity and femininity.

Freud writes:

> identification is ambivalent from the outset . . . it can turn into an expression of tenderness . . . and a wish to remove . . . it behaves *like* the first oral stage of libido organization in which the coveted, treasured object was incorporated by eating . . . it may suffer an *inversion* . . . in which the father . . . in a feminine mind-set is taken as the object.
>
> (Freud 1921b: 57, emphasis added)

So, instead of an enduring and singularly "exquisite masculine" capacity, identification, upon examination, shows itself, from the beginning, to be loving and hateful simultaneously, to be tender and obliterating, to target treasured objects, to covet, to incorporate, and to be susceptible to inversion; that is, to vanish entirely, and to turn into that which it was never meant to have been, housing, in disguised form, the self-same passive/feminine mechanisms it was "designed" to oppose. With this, the self-contained integrity of the concept vanishes.

Identification loses its separate, exquisite status, and starts to seem like simply another of the many mechanisms of object love. Like each of these mechanisms, identification has the power to obscure and to substitute for the others.

This property of substitutability is important. Freud writes that identification "substitutes" for a libidinal object-attachment. That is, identification functions not so much as an exquisite masculine alternative, but rather as an exquisite masculine masquerade.

Freud writes that in identification "the father is what the child wishes to be." In object love, the father is "what the child wants to have." But, he has just pointed out that the identificatory wish to be is realized through a wish to incorporate, a wish to have. The difference between wanting to be an object and wanting to have it fades away. Each is a means for the other: being is a way of having the object, having it is a means of being it.

The wish to be and the wish to have each functions as a kind of disguise. Each contains and obscures the other. Manifest object love obscures the wish to become the object no less than manifest identification obscures the wish to have it. Each, then, is a kind of drag.

I want to conclude with some clinical material. Examples are abundant. Listened to in clinical situations, men seem to be, without exception, inhabited and accompanied by their "guy." That imaginary presence simultaneously confirms and debunks their own claims to have successfully become "men." This unstable, and differently proportioned, mix of confirmation and debunking seems an integral feature of all such claims—claims made by people trying, in ways both reflexive and ingenious, to finally and permanently figure out their relation to the tantalizing prospect of achieving permanent membership in the group consisting of "MEN."

Case I

The patient is a 55-year-old man who now, after ten years of being alone, is living with a woman. The woman has a 13-year-old daughter. Below them lives a couple and their son, a teenage boy. The couple fights loudly and often. Separation seems in the air. The son plays the drums—seriously, loudly and often—loudly enough that the police are often called. The last time the police came, they compelled the boy to come upstairs and apologize for the excess noise. The man talked with the boy. The patient describes the boy as "alone; his parents divorcing; he's interested in art; and he is ugly. Exactly like me."

The patient spoke with the boy and the following day the drumming was quieter.

The next day, the patient went to work. When he got back home, his woman friend told him that she had called the police on the boy. The drumming had been intolerable. The man felt a frightening burst of hatred toward her, and of love toward the boy. He said nothing. "I had to cut off. I had to avoid any conflict. I felt like saying 'Why the fuck did you do that to him?' The only thing that was important to me was to protect the boy. He needed me and I could give him what he needed."

At dinner, he paid no attention to his woman friend, but focused on the daughter. Her eating habits were suddenly unbearable: too noisy, too slouchy, the food too junky. He hated them both.

He told me: "I cared so much about the boy. More than I ever had about either of them. It was crazy. I don't even know him. All I know is he was exactly like me: divorce, art, ugly."

I said to the patient that he felt his own words to me were like the boy's drumming and he wanted me to do for him as he had done for the boy. He said that he and the woman friend had, the night before, gone to a movie.

> She rested her head on my shoulder. She liked me. [But it was nothing.] What I want can't come from a woman. It has to come from a man, a man like me. But it can't come from a man. If I give a man that kind of opening, he may fuck me. I can't let you fuck me. The way a man has to do it is to just show up and do it, just go to the door and knock. Give the boy what he needs and leave.

The conundrum is perfectly stated here. What he needs in order to feel like a man has to have come to him from a man. But anything of the sort that comes to him from a man signifies that he has been "fucked" by a man and that, therefore, his claim to have gotten it "exquisitely" has been invalidated. This patient's "guy," like, I think, many men's, simultaneously grants him the status "man" and takes it away, affirms it and debunks it, leaving the patient to stumble, first one way, then the other, always in excess, exaggerated and diminished, never getting it right, always pursuing it, never quite a member, always an invitee.

Case 2

The patient is a 35-year-old Indian man. He lives alone. His father died when he was five. He has had one girlfriend, from whom he split up ten years ago. He cannot get her, or his father, out of his mind. He waits for the father and girlfriend to return. Anything else will not do. The man is an athlete and sports fan. He is about to begin training for the NY Marathon. His training partner is 6'3", from the South, blond, a walk-on to his Division I baseball team. They talk about sports and women. The patient says, "Every time he talks, I feel uncomfortable. I can never be like that, sound like that." He has the feeling that there is no way to get from where he is, from who he is, to where the Southerner is, to who the Southerner is. "You're born with it or you're born without it. My dad died. Until he comes back, I'll never have what he would have given me." In order to become the man he wants to be, this patient must be given what his father can no longer give him. He waits, then, eager, open, and expectant. But this very eagerness and openness are, for him, a sign that he lacks what the Southerner has. The proper solution, then, would be to have been given that which he now wants, to have been given it, that is, and to have erased any traces of having wanted it. Wanting it is the precondition for getting it and it is also the marker of not having had it. This man cannot make himself a man nor can he find a way for another to make him a man. He waits at the group's margins, neither in nor out, both in and out. "His guy" seems to function as an oddly internal, yet nonetheless alien, presence, vetting all claims to masculinity, living inside of him, but apart from him, an entirely "masculine" internal presence whose influence is only felt as punitive and debunking. "His guy" is an internal masculine presence who declares the impossibility of my patient ever housing an internal masculine presence.

Case 3

This man stutters whenever he has to promote his own business. "I can't stand the rules," he says to me. "Why can't they just know what I'm thinking? Why do I have to tell them?" His business demands that his clients trust him, that they see in him someone with whom to identify—that they see a person like themselves. Almost all of his clients are men. "I am not a man," he often says to me. "I don't want to be one. I don't want to age. I don't want any of it." Of his stuttering, this man says:

It's awful. It's embarrassing. It costs me money. But I can feel that right behind the stuttering is a smile. It's my way of telling them I'm not like you, I'm a boy. I'm jealous of you. I hate what you have. I hate that you have what I don't. Trust me and I'll steal it from you. Better not trust me.

I hate that you have a life and I don't. I want to steal it from you. I can't stand the starting point. Give it to me. Give me everything you have. If you don't give it to me . . . I hate you . . . I will not work at this . . . I love the pleasure of hating you, of denying you the chance to get me to work with you, of making you watch as I remain a boy. The pleasure of hating you. The hatred of pleasing you.

His is the voice of a man aiming to evade the demands and requirements of "his/our guy"—"the pleasure of hating you; the hatred of pleasing you." This kind of solution to the always-unattainable demands of "pure" masculinity drives him into a deformed version of boyhood, and leaves him in a permanently brittle, fragile state, one that has already resulted in a psychotic episode. In this episode, this man "achieved" what he hoped for, became "the man" he wanted to become, and in so doing, felt himself suddenly catapulted into feeling like a god, responsible for everything on the planet, burdened without limit, crazed with the enormity of what "pure" masculinity had brought him.

***

"Masculinity," whatever it may signify, certainly seems grounded in the most private, personal unconscious fantasy. And yet, these fantasies themselves seem derived from elements that are in conscious public circulation. "Masculinity" seems, then, to stretch across the divide between the private and public spheres. Its "pure" form promises to reconcile this divide, to unify the two sides. My third patient, above, lived out a moment of such "reconciliation," where the promise of "reconciliation" brought, instead, the reality of "collapse." Here, in the unreconciled gap between the public and private, "masculinity" seems to reside, always sensing its own incapacity to eliminate this gap. Here lies its enigmatic status: simultaneously failing to realize its project of reconciliation while succeeding at realizing its own failure. The outcome is a volatile, unstable mix: success and failure, authenticity and masquerade, "my guy" and "ours."

First aside: Ted

I loved Ted. His head, always swiveling and startled, made him look as though something terrible or wonderful had just happened to him, something he was just now trying to figure out. But then another thing would happen and his chance would vanish. Time bullied Ted. Things went too quickly for him.

I thought it was me who was keeping him sane. Whenever he saw me, he would laugh with pleasure and relief, as though sighting land from a disabled boat.

Ted was a wicked guy, contemptuous of convention and of everyone conventional. To be loved by Ted was to be exceptional. He allowed me, compelled me, to feel superior. I hoarded all he gave me, treating it like currency. Ted did the same with whatever I gave him.

I was about to get married at the time. Barbara was a beauty, soft-spoken and shy, not far from a kind of craziness herself. Ted wanted each of us, I think; would have wanted the three of us to combine into some beautiful molecule, stable enough to last for years yet volatile enough to disintegrate without a trace.

Ted took a lot of acid. Maybe he was always high. He usually looked blissed-out and terrified. I took acid a few times with him. I remember the first time. We saw *2001* together and when the ape threw the bone in the air and the bone turned into a space ship, well, it seemed right, what I was doing, that there was more here, where Ted had taken me, and that coming back to it again would make sense.

Not long after my first acid trips with Ted, I started to have sexual problems with Barbara. I couldn't do it. I'd get frightened. I'd feel like I was trying to be something—a man, I thought—that I wasn't. And so one day, again on acid, again walking with Ted, who was hunched as always in an old pea coat, I told him about this, about how maybe I wasn't really man enough or masculine enough to manage sex and getting married. Ted turned to me, still slouched. He smiled, laughed, stared at me, wondering, I guess, what I might be meaning. He told me I was as manly as a person could get and that all that was happening with my woman was that, maybe, I wasn't liking sex enough and when I liked it more and wanted it more things would be fine.

I was astonished to hear this. To me, not being able to have sex had seemed a sign, likely related to punishment, perhaps the first sign of a lifetime of punishment, with whatever would follow being more intense, more punishing—no sex now and, when accustomed to that, say, maybe a debilitating illness next, and then something affecting my mind, accidents, things lining up; no sex the first plague, nine worse ones to come.

So, when Ted said this, the plague idea suddenly turned into primitive mumbo-jumbo, no more sound than had I been treating a rainstorm as a sign of the Lord about to flood the earth and rid it of humanity.

This experience added to my loving him. Suddenly, Ted showed me a power he had. In that moment, with one smiling, clearheaded phrase, he had moved me from primitivity to enlightenment. His words worked. I think it was that night that the sexual problem vanished. I had never before thought that sex had much to do with what I wanted. It had just been something I had had to be able to do.

So, Barbara and I got married. We moved away and a few months later Ted came to visit. We had heard from friends that he was becoming crazier. But I still believed I had the power to keep him sane.

Ted was entirely out of his mind when he arrived. He sat in front of the TV and spoke to it, telling us that it was speaking back. He hunched over, he laughed, he pointed, he smiled, and none of it made sense. Seeing him like this was like watching death at work in someone you loved.

Ted was a monster, turning worse by the minute. He stayed with us only one day. That night he sat outside our room and took a kitchen knife to our door. He was chipping at the door with the knife. It wasn't frightening. It was some kind of crazy signal that he wanted to be with us. We each knew that. I opened the door and screamed at him. He put the knife down and laughed his mad laugh. We couldn't keep him in the house, though. We put him in a hotel and I never saw him again.

Ten years later, he wrote me a letter in lipstick. It was addressed to me as a member of the Committee to Persecute Psychiatric Patients. He signed it Love. He had found a way to be admitted to the chronic ward of the hospital in which his mother was confined. He stayed with her there for a long time, and when he got out, he drifted to Telegraph Avenue in Berkeley: homeless, begging, and mad.

I'd hear about him every so often. He fell off the grid while I thrived on it.

I think now that what he offered me was intoxication. I found a kind of substance in Ted's suffering. I could hook on to his certainty. He was the craziest person I'd ever known. And, in that way, he was the most reliable person I'd ever known. He was broke, busted; he had nothing, and I knew it. I knew it. It was the nothing of Ted to which I tried to adhere. I wanted a dead friend. I wanted a talking dead man. Ted was it. It was like loving a ghost. I knew he would vanish. I knew it. And maybe Ted knew it, too, knew he would vanish and that when he did I wouldn't go with him. Maybe that's what the letter in lipstick was about, an accusation that each of us knew was true. There he was, writing in lipstick, mad and destitute, and here I was, all pens and pencils, shirts and ties—guilty as charged, or maybe not.

For Ted, I think, none of it was a bet. He had crossed over. Maybe this is what I spotted: a man hanging on to nothing, no safety nets, the kind of man not meant to be alive, not meant to be a citizen, a real alien, no spaceship, although he did make it back to his planet of origin, his crazy mother locked up in a hospital, "the wisest woman he'd ever known," Ted told someone later, "a woman who speaks in a language that only she and I can understand."

Ted was mad and I wasn't.

Maybe that's what the lipstick letter was about: the crazy accusation grounded in something sane. Maybe Ted knew I was, all along, hedging my bet, working against ours: getting married, becoming a doctor, buying into long-term, low-interest, low risk.

Ted, gone now, was my sacrificial lamb.

The book is dedicated to him.

Chapter 3

On neither being nor becoming a man[1]

There is a group of men who do not seem to wish. Seeming immune to the educative impact of either disappointment or pleasure, they have no use for experience of any kind. They neither pursue satisfaction nor flee from pain. Unmoved by either, they seem static. Each day is the same. They seem to instantiate Samuel Beckett's mordant remark: "The day you die will be like all the others, only shorter" (Beckett 1978: 208).

They describe their sessions, like their lives, as inert, dead and lacking in elements of interest; they move from moment to moment in a spirit of sodden compliance. Arriving on time to an appointment, they feel their work is complete—something good and transformative ought to take place right then. When it doesn't, they feel they have exposed one of reality's outrageous injustices. The analyst regularly senses a demand to provide sufficient reward, to somehow release the patient from his/her inescapable condition.

Many items on these men's to-do lists are designed to mime what "other people" do—things like "reading books," "going to museums," "traveling," but sometimes going so far as "falling in love," "having a sexual relationship," and "wanting children." They consistently make the point, though, that, regardless of appearance, they are entirely different from those "other people." Their apparent desires feel, in fact, like artificial ones. What is real about themselves, they say, is precisely this artificiality. They often claim to see through desire and glimpse its artificial core.

They are uncertain whether this sense of things marks them as superior or inferior to others. When superior, they portray people with desires as dupes and phonies, slavishly proper, "patients you see in Woody Allen movies." When inferior, the others are a source of maddening jealousy; the others have it all. "I want everything they have, everything, their clothes, books, bodies, lovers; I'd steal it all if I could; if I can't get it in a flash, though, there's no point in going after it," said one.

1 This chapter includes material that first appeared in Moss, D. (2011a) "It's Oedipal all the way down," *Fort/Da*, 17: 42–52, and material that first appeared in Moss, D. (1989) "From the treatment of a nearly psychotic man: A Lacanian point of view," *International Journal of Psychoanalysis*, 70: 275–286. Used with permission.

Time offers them nothing. Complying and thereby demonstrating the futility of compliance, there seems no useful temporal dimensionality to their lives: nothing distinguishes the past from the present from the future. As one patient put it, after seven years of four-times-per-week psychoanalysis, there will never be a "second session." These patients describe time as continuous and empty—waiting without expecting, as close to sleep as possible, although they almost never remember dreams. Commonplace activities of mind—daydreaming, wondering, hoping, comparing, imagining, thinking—have no place in their daily lives. Those lives, in fact, have been stripped of almost all activities that might have once been sources of pleasure: hobbies and the like. They seem to be serving time and want it known that, if they are suffering at all, it is because they have been unjustly sentenced to suffer like this. If you cannot offer a commutation of the sentence and massive reparations for the injustice of wrongful time served, then you cannot offer anything of value.

"The only thing I know how to do, the only thing that gives me fuel, is saying 'No.'" The "No" that these men speak is not so much a signifier of refusal as it is a signifier of righteousness and indignation. Sessions begin happily if, earlier that day, these patients may have had their privacy violated by some shill on the subway or seen a parked car sideswiped or encountered a homeless person giving offense to bourgeois order. Such experiences serve as reliable sources of excitement— these patients seem to welcome encounters with the lax and the deceptive. In sessions, you can see them regularly clenching their fists, arrogant and indignant, as though they were reformers. They get excited when they spot evidence that the world, including their analyst, is a site of wrongdoing. Outrage seems to snap these patients into temporary states of vitality. The outrage quickly fades, though, and with that, their vitality vanishes.

As with almost all available forms of "experience," these men seem to have no use for the analyst's thoughts; they often refer to whatever the analyst says as "just words." They soon make it clear that what they want instead of "just words" is the transformative impact of 7-day, 24-hour contact with the analyst. If the analyst cannot provide that, then how can the analyst expect to be useful? "If I rely on you, I disappear. Saying 'No,' I'm certain. Forty-five minutes with you and then it's over. Nothing. All I have then is my list: work, shop, etc. Maybe if I had more time. 24/7. No. Even then . . ." *Failure to dream the pain of their world*

Their aim is not triumph but rather comfort—achievable, these patients seem to think, by the elimination of difference, the turning of two people into one. Difference and separation pose what feel like insurmountable problems to these patients. "What is the point," one says. "You're there; I'm here. Now what? Say whatever you want, you'll still be there; I'll still be here. You can't deny it. There is no point in talking. You can't change reality by talking about it. It is what it is. Now, then, and always."

These patients are particularly tuned in to the limited time of each session, the limited number of sessions per week. Each interruption, each ending, each break, is seen as direct evidence of the analyst's incapacity, unwillingness to actually be of help. Outside of the sessions, these patients report that they never think of the analyst or of anything that has happened in any of the sessions. The session ends, and with that ending, the analysis ends, only to resume when the patient comes back.

"I want to continue where we left off yesterday . . ." This is often the organizing posture of these patients at the beginning of sessions. When, every single time, the impossibility of actually doing that, of "continuing where we left off," becomes clear, the patient often says, "The session's over. What's the point?" The psychic work of experiencing a session on one day, living with its mnemic residue in the interim, and returning to the next day's session in order to continue whatever was done there—patient and analyst each grounded in their particular sense of what happened last, what happened between and what might happen now—this whole process seems entirely foreign to these patients. Regarding their feeling of being in sensuous contact with their object, the quantitative falloff from physical immediacy to psychic representations is so steep as to make it seem to them that psychic representation is utterly useless, that in demanding this work of them, you might as well be asking them to find their requisite calories by remembering yesterday's meal.

This, then, might usefully be thought of as the crux of the matter for this group of men. Either out of incapacity or refusal, these men cannot, or will not, do the work demanded of them by their objects' physical absence. Such work seems to them to offer nothing. They experience the demand to do it as either a demand to join in on a fools' game—why settle for mere representation when you deserve, and can get, the thing itself—or to attempt an impossibility.

> I hate endings. You accept them and then you get whatever reality offers. I don't accept them. I have nothing to say. Never will . . . Now it's just snippets. Enough talk. I see your glasses, a coat, books, the chair. I hate it, hate it. Make something of that. Snippets. Nothing else. Nothing. So many books here. So many books all over the place. How can you possibly choose between them? No matter which you choose, you make a mistake, you limit yourself. I want all the books or none of them.

All or none—these men renounce the third ground, the one consisting of choice, of object choice, that is, and the conscious burden that choice imposes. Give it all to me, or give me nothing. The choice, these patients communicate, is ours, not theirs.

From the outside, from the analyst's vantage point, this manifest and volatile mix of incapacity and refusal presents a daunting challenge; the moment the analyst puts the one in the forefront, the other appears as the pertinent one. Interpretations, then, are likely to always be wrong. This experience of always being wrong pushes the analyst toward the patient's state of mind, diminishing the difference between himself and his patient. When the patient's state of mind begins to seem impossible to interpret, this becomes the occasion for the analyst, like the patient, to feel that his own analytic work and the entire project of psychic work that underwrites it, makes no sense, that the work of psychic representation and the possibilities for thinking that representation affords, is, indeed, either a fool's game or an impossibility, and that, as the patient feels, magical transformation might be the only medium of effective cure.

Pushed toward magic and away from his customary confidence in reason, the analyst, in what can feel like a last-ditch defense of reason, is made particularly susceptible to states of repeated exasperation. In the midst of these states, he can sense, often only out of the corner of his eye, the patient's rapt attention to the question of whether the analyst, like the patient, will, in the face of such exasperation, really give up.

These men occupy a narrow, yet densely populated, diagnostic zone. Psychoanalytic diagnosis conceptualizes the manner in which wishes are processed. The two poles of such processing are, of course, primary process and secondary process. Sketchily put, psychosis refers to the use of primary process wishing—the direct hallucinatory restoration of lost objects; perversion refers to the processing of wishes via the disavowal of their representational dimensions and the pursuit, via enactment, of their concrete realization; neurosis refers to the wishful and pained pursuit of substitute aims and substitute objects, all psychically represented, with all the originals—aims and objects—disguised beyond recognition.

The men I have in mind here do not sit easily along this diagnostic axis. They do not belong there because there is no evidence that in fact what they are doing is pursuing wishes. In this sense, then, they are neither psychotic, perverse, nor neurotic. They may seem similar to psychotic people in, say, their flagrant disregard for the educative force of reality; similar to perverse people in, say, their dogged disavowal of all pertinent psychic underpinnings; similar to neurotic people in their reflective ruminations on meanings and intentions. But, under close scrutiny, similarity is all one finds; in this sense, then, these patients are best thought of, I think, as nearly psychotic, nearly perverse and nearly neurotic.

Here is a sample of one such man's recent reflections:

> The world makes me a loser by operating in a strange irrational counter-intuitive way. There is a huge gap when I see a woman with a cute ass. If I talk to her as a sexually active man, from down below, she will think I'm desperate and maybe a sexual predator. If I talk to her from up above, just chat, I'll feel like I'm totally lying, not expressing what I really want. Failure is assured. There's no way not to fail. It's like running in the woods with your eyes closed. I was at a concert yesterday. Wonderful. Two people making the most non-musical sounds with their instruments. It was trancey and shamanistic. Later my friend said to me that they had not had formal musical training. And I thought that was ridiculous. What a roundabout way to do things. Learn the rules only to then be able to break them. Why not just give the instruments to a 7-year-old? They would make the sounds directly, spontaneously: no rules, no thinking.

"What is the point?" he seems to be saying. Why take the roundabout (secondary process) path of training (thinking), when primary process immediacy—in the form of the imagined figure of the 7-year-old—ought to and might be available?

But this man, representative of this group, is, in fact, immobilized; he can neither take steps toward training nor towards becoming 7 years old. He can neither submit to wishing via secondary process training nor can he directly realize his wishes via primary process immediacy. He is left in a state of temporarily invigorating righteous complaint.

I will offer a conceptualization of these men based on what I think of as the cornerstone of Freudian psychoanalysis: the conceptualization of wishing and of the primary and secondary processes. This cornerstone has a triangular structure: at one point of the triangle is the subject who is wishing; at the second point is the absent, psychically represented object being wished for; and at the third point is another object, represented, in the wished-for object's absence, as the "not here," the "there" to which the wished-for object has gone.

From the beginning, then, the wished-for object, when absent, is always, and necessarily, located elsewhere, "there" rather than "here" where I wish it to be. Only later does that elsewhere, that "there," get occupied by a named competitor— the representation of the father or of the mother, say. Prior to its being occupied by a particular psychic representation, though, the site itself serves as the third term of a triangle. The triangle snaps into place as the product of a wishing subject. "I," the subject, want "it," my object, and locate it, in its absence, as "there"/ "not here." From the beginning, the triangle has two named occupants—"I" and "my object"— and a third unnamed, though structurally necessary, one: "there" where my object is. There is no wishing without the experience of the object's absence. There is no experience of absence without the experience of "not here." The third point in this original fundamental triangular structure is the place, the "not here," at which the wishing subject locates its missing object.

The later arrival of a named competitor at this third point does not disturb this original structure. It simply fills it in. Using a numerical metaphor, we could say that the third point in the original triangle is occupied by the placeholder, zero. Later, this held place serves as the arrival point for the wishing subject's primary competitors. The triangle's zero predates, reserves, and makes possible the later arrival of number one, say, the first psychically represented competitor. Put yet another way, the father is present in principle, and in all of his traditional depriving effects, before he arrives in name and in body.

I turn now to a sketch of Freud's notion of wishing. The antecedent to a wish is an "experience of satisfaction," an experience in which a disturbance, a pertur-bation, is quieted. This antecedent experience of satisfaction leaves behind a perceptual trace, a memory. The next time a similar disturbance arises, the wishing subject seeks to replicate the original experience of satisfaction, to "recathect its mnemic image." That image, the residue of an earlier experience of satisfaction, is stored in memory, and is wish's first object. We turn to the storehouse, recover the image, and await satisfaction. The object's recollection, appearance, and its promise of satisfaction are immediate and simultaneous. Sometimes this process of wishing works. When it does, the subject has no experience of the object's absence. Only when it fails to work does the subject experience the object's absence. With that absence, the triangular structure of wishing snaps into place.

Freud calls this moment when the restored image fails to provide an "experience of satisfaction" "the bitter experience of life." It is precisely this bitter experience of life that then drives the wishing subject to seek satisfaction elsewhere, to turn his/her attentions outside of our own storehouse of images toward the external world. We seek there what we were unable to find here. That initial process of wishing—turning inward to find and extract an image that will provide us with an experience of satisfaction—is what Freud calls the "primary process." Turning outward, toward a world in which images are not reliably stored but in which it is objects—not images—that must be looked for, found, and apprehended, Freud calls the secondary process. Of the difference between primary and secondary process, Freud (1900: 567) writes: "All this activity of thought merely constitutes a roundabout path to wish-fulfillment which has been made necessary by experience . . . Thought is after all nothing but a substitute for a hallucinatory wish." The primary process seeks and finds identity, the absolute replication of the stored perceptual elements of the original experience of satisfaction. The secondary process seeks, and finds, substitutes. What follows is a series of reflections on the crucial difference between the identical and the substitute.

Picture it: in one direction lie internally stored perceptions/images; find the right image and satisfaction might be immediate. In the other direction lies the world. To turn toward the world, one must first turn away from the internally stored images and only then, remembering them, thinking about them, put them to orienting usage and go on to seek their likeness in the outside world.

Let us, for the moment, try to freeze the mind in its operation right here where bitterness—and with it, necessity—enters the scene. The mind is perched, poised, at a great divide. In one direction lies the promise of the image: immediate, identical, satisfying. In the other direction lies the necessity of the substitute: mediated, approximate, nearly satisfying. Bitter experience, in essence, forbids direct access to the image: it will not work, you must turn away, you must turn to the outside, you must seek a substitute.

The mind is driven by force, law, and necessity to turn away from what it most immediately desires and to seek instead an approximation, a substitute. The hallucinatory image sought by primary process occupies the traditional maternal site; the force of bitter experience occupies the traditional paternal site; the mind seeking satisfaction occupies the traditional child's site.

Let us keep the mind in question precisely where it is here: not yet moving, at the inception of "bitter experience"; let us not have it move yet in either direction—not, as in perversion and psychosis, toward perceptual identity; and not, as in neurosis, toward substitutive satisfactions. Let us leave it here, fixed in place, immobile, neither transformed by "bitter experience" nor able to renounce such experience and live in defiance.

And there, fixed in place, we can, I think, locate the psychic workings of the group of patients I here have in mind.

They are, therefore, static; their attempted solution, then, is to renounce wishing itself, renounce the consequences of primary process, of perversion and psychosis, in one direction: direct movement toward the naked body of their desired object; renounce the consequences of secondary process; deprivation from their primary object, compliance with the law, and a potentially melancholy lifetime of merely imagining what they might have once had.

They are still. Their effective vocabulary consists of one word: No. They tell us that we offer only punishing thought and depriving interpretation. Therefore, the problem, they say, as well as the wish to solve it, is ours, and ours alone.

These are men who have no interest in being or becoming men. The category "man" burdens them. "Men," they seem to think, find satisfaction in being and becoming "men." For these men, though, the project of "finding satisfaction" is of no interest. They replace this iffy project with a more immediate one, one undiluted by time and by waiting. These men do not "find" satisfaction; they do not "look for" satisfaction. Instead, renouncing the risks inherent in the pursuit of satisfaction, they aim, instead, for permanent possession of it. All it takes, they seem to imperiously say, is the renunciation of pursuit itself.

What follows comes from the long psychoanalytic treatment of one such man:

> I know what they say. This one's handsome, that one's not. It doesn't matter that sometimes they marry the ugly ones. How you look is the most fundamental thing. The rest is gloss. I really know this. I look at myself from the point of view of women. I know how they see. No doubt about it. It's like I don't really need to want any women. I don't need anything from them. I am them. Looking at me like they do makes me feel like one of them, so they have nothing to offer me. Whatever they might have had, I take by being one of them. I can't imagine one actually wanting to be with me. Wanting me. Me. Not because I tricked her, or conned her. There was N. I found out she liked to sail. That weekend I read some books on sailing. I was certain that only if I was exactly like her could she love me. There was R. She was an actress. I decided to work for an Off-Broadway outfit. As long as I'm not the same as her, there is no hope. Difference means having to think. That's what I mean by saying that consciousness is a disaster. You just become conscious of the fact that you are too ugly to ever be wanted. Forget that. I prefer this. Having what I want just because I say I have it.

This is the voice of L, in the fifth year of treatment.

L lives in a condition of near permanent vigilance. Of that vigilance he says:

> The only language I can use is one which feels like I make up all the meanings myself. Every word has to be private. The moment you use my words, it's over. You seem to be mocking me. What was once mine is gone. The words

become yours. Take them then. I can't bear having them for a while and losing them. I want silence. If I have to speak, there's no point in continuing. I want it like it was: the toaster in the kitchen—something next to me which always works. Whatever it is, it can want nothing in return.

After finishing college, L left his parents' home to work in a foreign country. There he was isolated, spending almost all of his free time alone. On a weekend bus trip to the mountains, the landscape suddenly appeared to L as unusually beautiful. That beauty, he immediately reflected, must be at least partial testimony to the beauty of he who notices it. Not only that, he continued, but he who notices must be linked to he who creates, and, so linked, might be the creator himself. Possibility turned to certainty and L suddenly felt himself not only the landscape's creator but the source of all life on earth. He was immediately terrified, certain that anything he did could topple the entire natural order. He tried to shut himself down: to remain absolutely still and to eliminate all mental activity. Suicide tempted but seemed a calamitous self-indulgence: a universe deprived of its creator might precipitously collapse.

In the midst of this, from across the aisle, came the clatter of a group of boarding peasants: pleasant and raucous. L immediately knew that these people could not possibly be the product of his own imagination. Their apparent lightheartedness, inconceivable to him, was firm evidence of the limits of his imagination's power. So limited, the "cascade" came to a halt. L's psychotic moment was over.

Back in the capital city, L found a psychoanalyst whom he knew prized American patients. The subsequent therapeutic discourse, L recalls, was founded on a mutually established grandiose conceit. The analyst likened their work to the creation of a piece of art: analyst as sculptor, patient as marble. Turn crude marble into noble figure and both the talent of the artist and the purity of the stone would be certified. The grandeur of this premise comforted L. It was a reminder of two earlier psychotherapeutic contacts in which each therapist seemed oracular. The new analyst moved to the head of this already established lineage.

Three years of treatment, however, had little obvious effect. Wanting to become "strong and wise and noble," L instead was only aloof, obsequious and without friends. He blamed himself for failing to absorb his analyst's power.

L returned home certain that he lacked the requisite boldness for a successful psychoanalysis. He joined his father's business, relieved to find clearly marked paternal footsteps to follow. His smooth progress was interrupted by the onset of a terminal malignancy in his mother. L spent many hours with her, "wanting something," he says. But, as usual, the time with his mother seemed barren: deathbed business conducted, politenesses exchanged. The mood perfunctory and dispirited, L was discontented. A few days before dying, L's mother told him that she thought her entire life had been a waste. Nothing had mattered: not herself, not her husband, not L. L heard this revelation as merely a cowardly appeal for his sympathy.

His contempt for his mother surfaced only during his adolescence. It was then that each of them seemed suddenly unable to keep to an earlier, unspoken set of what he recollects as mutual promises: he to be her brilliant, playful boy; she, his graceful, beautiful witness and inspiration. These promises betrayed, L felt duped and regularly began to wish her dead.

Mother and son had each been the other's only necessity. Father played no remembered part. L recalls his mother's devotion to him. She kept his room and his body free of the dirt and paraphernalia of childhood. She bathed him until he was a teenager. Until the age of eight, L often consciously refused to control his bowels, and remembers with pleasure being washed and wiped by his smiling mother. He speaks nostalgically of his pleasure at exciting her with his bathtub erections. While she dried him off, they often spoke baby-talk together, during which time he would frequently fondle her breasts.

When L's mother died, he wished he could have felt a "more substantial" sense of loss. He wanted to mourn, but had access to none of the necessary emotions. Still isolated and lonely, he thought again of psychoanalytic treatment.

During the prolonged opening phase, L continually alluded to an imaginary figure: a white-robed old man, pure and omnipotent, who would relieve any properly devout supplicant of his suffering. For L, the treatment would have an identical structure. The right words said, he would be redeemed and reunited with such a figure. So joined, the two would plot vengeance on all the ones who had failed L—not only his parents, but the "entire world, all four billion of you." L's idea of the "right words" was a stilted language, "from television shows, from *Ordinary People*." He awaited the moment when all these words would no longer be necessary, when speech itself would turn superfluous. "It outrages me that I have to talk." "We're either together or we don't exist. I can't stand that there might be something missing here. I refuse to think that way." "I'm here alone and I want to be there. I don't want to talk to there." "There is no place except where I am."

"Outraged" by the necessity of speech, L senses his own wrath as absolutely disorganizing. He calls it a "whiteness," "pure heat." He imagines no possibility of its discriminate spending.

Difference and singularity were the provocative terms. For L, difference signals a primal treachery, a loss of self-sufficiency. For L, both sexuality and speech are reminders that "copulation" is insufficient compensation for the loss of a unity whose loss he feels was gratuitous. So outraged, L is plagued by envy. (Klein's sense of envy is apt for L: "Envy not only seeks to rob . . . but also to put badness . . . bad parts of the self, into [her] . . . in order to spoil and destroy her" (Klein 1957: 181).)

In his one experience of intercourse before the treatment started, L concluded that his companion, who had presented herself as a shy virgin, must really have been a "slut," because she enjoyed L and her pleasure came so easily. Convinced that she had misled him, he asked her whether he might call up some friends so that they too could share in the pleasure of her company. She left in tears, but L's righteous indignation allowed him no remorse.

The erotics of envy, like the erotics of Freud's "fort/da" from "Beyond the pleasure principle" (1920a), has as its aim the elimination of the traumatic source. For L, wanting itself is traumatic, whether that wanting is sensed as emanating from the other or from himself. For L, the source of wanting is a matter of indifference. Wanting itself—always excessive—is his target. Eliminate wanting and what remains is, by definition, satisfactory. The problem is not that something is missing. The problem is that something is wanted.

On a subway ride home from a session, L was asked directions by an obviously timid woman whom he found attractive, that is, someone whose obvious wanting allowed him a momentary—contrasting—sensation of sufficiency. While on the train, though, they agreed to a coffee. With this agreement, L's sense of balance began to break down. The woman who had been the demeaned—wanting—other was, with the agreement, now the traumatic cause of wanting in L. L explained: "I began to hate her. I had to get rid of her. I could see what she was, just a cheap, easy score."

At the agreed-upon stop, the woman got off the train, but L stayed behind, laughing at her through the closed door. Her lack was again evidence of his sufficiency. Balance was restored. He now wanted nothing and had it all; she had nothing and wanted it all.

But this too was precarious. L wanted her back. He panicked. He searched the neighborhood near her station; he hired a private detective. Reflecting on the incident, he spoke of his "stupidity," but also evoked her with a kind of nostalgia: "She seemed to like me." That is, she wanted what he had. This is the only configuration through which L can enduringly bear the consciousness of wanting: being wanted by an absent other. He often says to me, "The only moment in the session that actually counts is when you open the door and ask me to come in. It's a sign that you want me, that you've been thinking about me. Once I'm inside, it doesn't matter what happens."

This configuration continually reappeared, most brutally, perhaps, in an incident between L and his father. The father, badly remarried after L's mother's death, wanted to talk with L in confidence, a signal that matters were grim. L was excited. The invitation offered him the chance to refuse it capriciously. Only days after the refusal, L's father committed suicide. L telephoned to inform me of the death and that he would be missing some sessions. "I'm sorry," I said over the phone. Over the subsequent months, L often spoke scornfully of my response: how weak it had made me sound, a sucker.

The configuration had entered the transference: I the desiring one, L the sated, self-sufficient monad, the one who places himself ontologically prior to the onset of wishing: no loss, no re-finding necessary. L's aim, the "aim," one can say of psychosis, is to re-establish that moment, prior to the beginning of experience itself.

L's response to his father's death was a manic one: identifying himself with the now available insignia of patriarchy, L felt he was finally getting his due. He reported moments of pleasure in the way he carried his body; he spoke of enjoying adopting the postures he felt signified the properly mourning son: head tilted, shoulders slumped. At family gatherings, he tried to preside tastefully over dinner from the vacated paternal chair. He wanted to dazzle; he sensed an "aura" about himself.

The consequences of this apparently frictionless incorporation were dear. L's own words began to seem to him "quotations." "How do I know that it is me who is speaking?" The entire triumph quickly turned false, a plagiarism. To counter the accompanying sense of self-eclipse, L quit his job in his father's business. Seeking signs of his own singularity, he memorialized his mother's name with a large gift to a cancer research center. (Even here, though, *his* gift, *her* name; his sufficiency, her desire.) He entered school in order to work at something, to "struggle." But he soon found himself certain that struggle was for others; that for him, will alone would lead to prize-winning books on world hunger. Nothing seemed to stand in his way. He was approaching a state in which he could "have what I want just because I say I have it." Frightened, he hoped to find a kind of ballast in the treatment. He wanted to show himself that in spite of the "cascade" of sudden wealth and limitless prospects, he remained an earnest and pained young man. The sessions themselves, he reflected, must be testimony to his suffering. The logic he employed was syllogistic: Patients suffer, I am in the place of a patient, I must suffer.

In effect, trying to father himself, L only grew more frenetic. Towards me he was consistently haughty and disdainful. He noticed the flaws in my physical appearance, the effort necessary for me to find my words. Such efforts seemed a sign of a lack of "integrity." "Only perfect things interest me," he frequently said.

During this period, whenever I said something he could imagine "using," his despair would only heighten. "I don't want your words or ideas. I want your experience. I want to jump into you. That's the only thing which can work here." Noting my effort, L sensed I wanted something, and since, for him, all wanting was a wanting to incorporate, he was frightened: "How can I listen to you? Who says you won't say one thing now, and another thing later. Who says you won't destroy me by driving me crazy?" Thought and experience in the midst of eclipse, L was continuously uncertain of whether or not he was lying, even hallucinating. He could not bear the possibility of "mistakes." "I can't stand to have to tell what happened. What if I get it wrong? Everyone should just know. Why is it up to me to tell?"

The demands of narrative meant labor; labor meant lack; lack meant catastrophe. "I want there to be no passage of time. The moment it comes into my head I want it in yours. I can't stand to remember what I'm about to say. It's too much work. No one else has to do it. It's an outrage."

Regarding the intrinsically melancholy element of sexuality, Freud writes, "'Tis pity I can't kiss myself." For L, that pity has escalated into an unbearable trauma.

Therefore, for L, all potential erotic objects are cause for alarm, since, for him, all drive derivatives aim to obliterate those objects and to transform the insufficiencies and contingencies of object love into the plenitude and certainty of identification. But this movement toward identification led directly to his delusional moment in the mountains, "the only time I have ever felt alive." The object so loved is destroyed and the "lover" survives in a world populated only by himself: L's delusional moment.

L is traumatized by any approach toward end-pleasure, via either identification or object-love. His erotic solution is to temporize, his major mode of delay: plots of revenge. Such plots bind him to an object in complementary union, the couple, for the moment, sufficient. In the treatment, this scenario of revenge takes the form of a wish to drive me crazy. The scheme, like any mirror-grounded one, is simple in its symmetry. We will reverse positions; I will turn into what he most fears to become. Whenever he senses that what I am saying matters to me, he will "kill it"—render it meaningless. I will slowly come to see that the more I want my words to have meaning, the less they will mean. Finally I will give up, and in that giving up, I will finally know what his life has been like. But like the prisoner's in Kafka's (1948 [1919]) "In the penal colony," the price for my illumination will be dear. I, too weak, will collapse under the weight of what L has been able to bear for his entire life. L will then monitor that collapse. I will be admitted to a psychiatric hospital, incurable. He will take over my practice and my "private" life, driving my patients and loved ones into insanity and suicide, each of them getting what he/she deserved, by virtue of a connection to me. He will then visit me in the hospital, kindly, while I stare at him in mute and impotent fury.

This fantasy is undeniably erotic. That is, its aim is union: the two of us joined in a self-contained sado-masochistic sufficiency, each the other's adequate complement. Potency is linked to impotency, sufficiency to want. The other is stripped of its power to provoke desire. Union becomes synonymous with obliteration.

But, as that fantasy became articulated, it too was a source of trauma, a reminder of L's own limitless wanting. "It comes over me like an infection," he says. It seems incontrovertible evidence that it is he, not I, who should be got rid of. And so the fantasy turns, away from the object, and back toward the mirror. So stricken, L thinks of suicide. But suicide too demands intention, demands a narrative. Stripping those plans of their signifying weight, L is left with only a series of unwritten, elegant suicide notes, and images of weeping relatives and a tormented, contrite analyst. He brings Plath, Berryman and Sexton to his sessions. He speaks of their style, their "admirable maliciousness," their "dash." But all L can do is mimic; there is no place in him for the incorporated object. Denied the weight of triangularity, he can only mime. He can't even stand to want to be like his suicided heroes: "I will never want things. You have to have two sets of ideas in your mind at once: what is and what you want. The moment that happens, I get so furious, I turn white. Everything is the same as everything else—that's the only soothing idea. I've already committed suicide."

For L the represented object, because it is necessarily mediated and thus deficient, is merely a provocative tease. He wants what he calls "the real thing, or nothing at all." This wish echoes Freud:

> It turns out that the cathexis of the word-presentation is not part of the act of repression, but represents the first of the attempts at recovery or cure which so conspicuously dominate the clinical picture of schizophrenia. These endeavours are directed towards regaining the lost object, and it may well be that to achieve this purpose they set off on a path that leads to the object via the verbal part of it, but then find themselves obliged to be content with words instead of things.
>
> (Freud 1915a: 203–204)

But L is not at all "content" with the available word-representations. As he puts it regarding a women he momentarily admired: "I want to take over her body. I want her life to be mine."

R. D. Laing writes of a patient who sends a Mother's Day card to her mother that reads: "Dear Mother, You've been just like a mother to me." A person's search for objects is precisely a search for that "just-likeness." The new object—the one desired—is linked to its repressed predecessors by way of condensations and displacement, metaphor and metonymy. But, in a man like L, just-likeness means not-the-one, means less-than-identical. L pursues not the representation of the thing but the thing itself. As L says, in an unintentionally ironic comment on delusional passions, "I want the *real* thing." The "real thing" that L wants is, of course, in fact, an unreal thing, the first thing, long gone now. The pursuit of that *real thing* is his hallmark. Useful experience and productive thought depend upon the melancholic acceptance of substitutions, on representatives.

Being and becoming a man are ironically founded upon an enduring experience of deficiency. "I am not a man" provides foundational legitimacy to the subjective experience of being and becoming one. L cannot bear the experience of deficiency that alone can propel him to seek its antidote. On the one hand, L contends with absence as "an outrage. I want God to explain why I have to talk." On the other, he finds the momentary sufficiency of identificatory fullness "pure terror." Outrage on one side, pure terror on the other, L has not been able to fashion a middle zone in which to work—to want, to look for, and to find. Without this middle zone, L can make no legitimate claim to being or becoming a man. He walks into a butcher shop and stands next to a customer who is ordering steaks for dinner. L stares at him, aware of an unbridgeable gap: "He has what I want. He is what I want." Then he walks out: "A minute later I was calm."

I think of the following excerpts as "flashes"—moments that illuminate L's consciousness and what seems to me to be appropriately called his "project." This "project" aims at neither being nor becoming a man. For L, a "man" is a limited category, only one part of all that he can imagine. L experiences limit—any limit— as unbearable. As such, he must invent an alternative project, one that subsumes "man" and aims at what he calls "all of it."

1   I could have cut my meal short and been here on time. I feel panicked. What should I do about that panic? Bear it? Examine it closely? What a joke. It

was fun thinking about missing the session. Were you wondering whether I committed suicide? That's the only thing that interests me: which one of us will live through this thing. Loving is inconceivable. I don't care about it. That woman and I have made love. It's nice to sleep with someone. I could just as well say it's not nice. It wouldn't matter to me. First time with a woman in seven years and it's no big deal.

I didn't hear you.

Who cares if you heard me? Very diligent of you to ask, though. There's supposed to be a difference, I guess, between whether you hear me or not. I don't listen. I can't see why you should. Stealing is a lot easier than waiting to get something. Why listen? Just take whatever words you want.

I can do anything I want except be in a room with another person. My life is weightless . . . It's hard to sleep with someone. You get your arm crushed.

2   I am strong, a leader. My father's dead. My mother's dead. I've lost everything and it has no impact. It's the little things that derail me: parking tickets, words.

You're not bitter, are you? Do you get that way from an act of will?

I hate feeling there's so little that is me and so much that is not. The woman calls me sweet names but it doesn't make me feel I've gotten anything. Don't you have something better inside of you than I have? If so, I want it. If not, I can't use you.

L aims here at a display of his own sufficiency. He speaks not of his capacity to satisfy desire, but rather of his capacity to eliminate it. L's speech aims to create a permanent silence. As he says elsewhere, "There is a history to erase here."

3   Maybe I should pull out my wallet and put all the stuff inside in order. Showing that to you would make as much sense as any speaking might do. You could watch. When it was over, if you gave up and told me you had done the best you could, I would agree. I would get up and walk over to the flowers there. No reason for it, just doing whatever I wanted. I wouldn't . analyze a fucking thing.

If you are content without me, then this entire enterprise is impossible. You do the wanting here; I'll do the rest.

L bluntly states his program: "You do the wanting here; I'll do the rest." Such a scheme would transform the other into pure wanting subjectivity, and L into the integral, sufficient object of that wanting. The moment is grounded in the primitive dichotomies of Freud's purified pleasure ego, or of Lacan's Imaginary register: "The other lacks all, I lack nothing." Taking this step even further, moving toward the hypothetically pure case of psychosis, the position of the wanting other is delusionally guaranteed, the contingencies of any particular other superseded. An exemplary case is Schreber, whose inner life is entirely determined by the desires of God Himself. God, lacking, wanted; Schreber, powerless, merely gives in. L approaches this Schreber-like position of "pure" psychosis in the following session.

4 I want you all to go crazy. I'll be the savior. I'll be the arbiter of what is real and what is not. I'll say things like: "There's always hope; don't despair."

When you show me a sign of your weakness, I get strong. I'll put on the white gown and cure you. I'll provide you with insight; I'll be the source of your enthusiasm for life. Everything you know will be just a small piece of what I know.

I'll decide when and if I talk. I'll hire a writing instructor to be here with me. He'll produce perfect syntax and have clear ideas. He would be what you want to be. And he would be mine.

L constructs here a phenomenological moment of near-perfect complementarity between subject and object, each the mirrored inverse of the other. This imaginary yoking of subject to object creates a pair that functions as a totality, with neither surplus nor deficit. The "object" in this case, then, as it approximates an entirely internal construction, hallucination-like, cannot be said to be either absent or present. The categories exert no determining influence. No absence, an "ego" sufficient unto itself—this makes the pursuit of "manhood" both gratuitous and redundant.

5 Your smile yesterday. You did something then. It was you, no doubt. Qualitatively different from anything I could have done. I feel completely nasty. I want to throw a glass, kick a chair. It wouldn't stop there, though. Next step is a knife, my fists. I could stab and shoot easily. Not just once either. I'd cut everything off. It would be an entire project. At first, I'd just stab you to death. Then cut off all the limbs. Then eat the limbs, have the victims eat their own limbs. I'd stop only when I was exhausted and when it was over, it would all be the same as when it started. It would have done nothing to reduce the hate in me.

The solution: self-sufficiency; no object can gain significance enough to qualify as an object, a limiting term, that "thing in regard to which or through which the instinct is able to achieve its aim" (Freud 1915a: 122). L's destructive cascade here is inverse and complementary to the one he experienced on the mountainside; only the valence has changed. In both, drive is limitless. This limitless "demand made upon the mind for work" (Freud 1915a: 122) turns all wishing, all erogeneity, into trauma. Signifying representation, establishing the object as object, blunts demand, and shields the subject from a wish whose persistence would constitute an "extensive breach in the protective shield against stimuli" (Freud 1920a: 31).

L's oscillations—creator one moment, destroyer the next—come over him without any of the attenuating power of representation. He can only become that which he intermittently yearns for and wants to destroy. This movement-toward-becoming replaces representation as the only medium through which L can wish. But to no avail: "It would have done nothing to reduce the hate in me." He becomes both source and target of incorporative wishes. And thus wishing itself exacerbates the very trauma which, at its origin, it aims to erase.

6   I'd like to begin all over. There's a history to erase.
    The fascinating part is dwelling on possibility. Not having to worry about whether or not it's real. The alternative is boring. I couldn't do it. I leave the work for you.
    If I paid attention to your words, I'd have to pay attention to mine. They are too strange. They are too awful to say. I want yours; anybody's will do.
    All I want is to drive you crazy. To do something to my parents even if they're both dead. I know there's a way of possessing the past. Somehow, you've done it. The only way I have to possess the past, though, is to kill it.

The trap for L is that he knows the cannibalistic root of all identification; he lives the wish to identify as a wish to murder. In that sense, he embodies the subjectivity of the brothers in "Totem and taboo" (1913). The resulting dialectic of filial violence and retreat is vivid in the following two sessions.

7   I'm a person with no mind and flailing appendages. You could drive me crazy. You're too careless with reality: one sentence now, and something different later. If I ever believe you, I'm a sucker. Reality is yours. The best I get is you letting me in as a second-class citizen. Someone should pay for this with his life. My father being dead is insufficient. I want someone else dead, every minute someone new.
    Anything I believe is always under attack from the inside. Why not just give in to the attack?

8   Once you hate, you hate. It doesn't mellow.
    I can't stand having to fill the pauses with words. Something is due me. First you pay off that debt, then I'll talk. No compensations will be enough. I'll never talk.
    I want to be the mirror in which you see yourself as ugly. My mother hated to clean me. I disgusted her. How can you stand this?

As Freud (1923) outlines in "The ego and the id," before the father can be internalized—represented as Father—he must first assume the position of erotic object and rival. The consequent endless dialectic of triumph and defeat gives origin to and defines the superego. But L cannot tolerate the excessive—traumatic—erotic consequences that follow from the representation of either that triumph or of that defeat.

L demands certainty, "the real thing." He wants experience reduced to orderable law. All deviation is excessive and traumatic. The incapacity to represent that excess is the primary marker of a pre-Oedipal configuration.

9   So, you know about things, do you? Mr Reality knows all about it. If you don't mind, I'll stay just a few inches off from what you know. My staying that way turns you into an idiot. The next step, with all that you know, is that I become a tragic figure, a bum in Grand Central, say. It's bound to happen. It's a matter of getting even. There's nothing you can do to stop it. Mr Reality can't stop me. You will despair because you can't reverse any of this.

    That despair links us. My role is to sabotage; yours is to suffer.

    It's my turn now. My parents had me so I could love them. That's why I have you. So you can love me.

    I filled a hole. I was an illusion.

The motif here is revenge, vendetta. A debt is owed. L senses that debt as limitless. He has "a hole" and never received his due. Freud: "The child borrowed strength to do this [repress the Oedipus complex], so to speak, from the father, and this loan was an extraordinarily momentous act" (Freud 1923: 32). That loan essentially never consummated, L is located outside the circle of civilization: a complex organization of debtors. L remains the singular, pre-Oedipal outsider, living his own erotic life as a "hole," a phallic absence, and burdened by the Sisyphean project of filling that hole himself.

10 Maybe I shouldn't have a friend. Maybe I shouldn't have anything which could be called mine. If I were to say something was mine, you might understand what I meant, but I wouldn't. You would have the road map, not me. I have to constantly grab for the truth or else it floats away. Who wants to work so hard just to know something? I should be able to know what "mine" means like I know what colors are.

    I lose something if I work here. I speak about myself and my words dangle loosely. I don't want you to take it from me. "The patient came in and I cured him with brilliant technique."

    In fact, I don't think you'd do that. I can see you at a conference and others might be doing it, not you. Still, I can't afford to give you anything which you might want. No, no, no. If you are satisfied, I'm left without. Saying that reduces some tension in me. Don't write that down, though; I'm not really sure it's true.

The "dangling" word, lost at the very moment it takes on value, this is the fantasy that drives L away from the masculine masquerade of "having" the phallus and towards the ostensibly more protective feminine one of "being" it. By phallus, what is meant here is a mediating term—an amalgam of idea and represented part of the body—through which the object of desire is imagined as attainable. When L says: "I lose something if I work here," that work is, in this sense, phallic. It intends contact with an object.

To paraphrase, L seems to say: "My effort at copulation endangers me." For L, signifying speech carries this phallic, copulatory function in a raw way. The word here *is* phallic. In Freud's terms, it functions less as "word" than as "thing." L senses the labor of language itself as proof of an earlier moment of castration. Identification and silence are, then, signs of a sufficiency which is independent of copulation.

> 11 After my grandfather died, I had emotions. It was the same as being crazy, though. It comes and then goes away. I feel bitter, like someone has robbed me of what I once had.
>
> When he died and I walked into the living room, I was really there. Now I walk in and there's no change in me. It's as though there were a 360-degree screen and the first scene has been peeled off. All I can do is watch it disappear. If I think about it, it disappears even faster. How come everything dies out?
>
> Being crazy is the same thing: one minute you think you've discovered the patterns of the universe and the next you can't add $2 + 2$. All I know is that something very bad happened to me and killed a lot of good things.
>
> I may not need to see you feel exactly what I feel. That would be a false test anyway. The real test is whether I can feel hopeless alone.

L speaks here of what he knows and, more importantly, of the limits on that knowing, and his consequent *wish* to know more. As such, he speaks of desire, a desire whose trajectory loops through an other—it is in speaking to me that he may come to know more. The corollary of this object-anchored wish is an attenuation of the necessity for identification: "I may not need to see you feel exactly what I feel." Of his grandfather's death, L speaks of the effects of absence: "I had emotions." And one can again sense the malignant presence of identification when L's own thoughts seem to die and vanish as the grandfather has. "All I can do is watch it disappear . . . How come everything dies out?"

In these reflections, L wants. The pure excessive quantity of wishing has now taken on quality: trauma has become "emotion," sadness.

Paul Ricoeur, in his monumental *Freud and Philosophy*, writes:

> *Would I be interested in the object, could I stress concern for the object, through the consideration of cause, genesis, or function, if I did not expect, from within understanding, this something to "address" itself to me? Is not the expectation of being spoken to what motivates the concern for the object? Implied in this expectation is a confidence in language:* the belief that language, which bears symbols, is not so much spoken by men as spoken to

men, that men are born into language. It is this expectation, this confidence, this belief, that confers on the study of symbols its particular seriousness.

(Ricoeur 1970: 29–30, emphasis added)

L has no such confidence in language, and thus no confidence in "being and becoming." He retreats from language's "symbols," its polyvocality, and aims to find the univocal word, the word with only one meaning, his meaning, the "real thing." This search for univocity has supplanted the search for objects. L is a "man" immobilized. Unable to experience anything missing in himself—unable, therefore, to want—he cannot go after potential objects. As such, he cannot feel himself a "man." For, a man, whatever it might be, is one who wants, who, in fact, is able to transform wanting an object into having a desire. The missing object gives the man the desire that makes him a man. For L, the missing object simply gives him evidence of what he's missing.

Chapter 4

Two ways of looking back[1]

Writing authoritatively—even axiomatically—on the relation between body and mind, Freud locates the elemental force of drives primarily in the form of the demands they make on the mind for work. First and foremost, he suggests that mind serves body; only secondarily, only as a process of ongoing back-channel (conscious and unconscious) negotiations, might this hierarchy be challenged, might the tilt be reduced, might mind take charge and begin to exert demands of its own. The attachment of mind and body, though, is so thorough, so primal, that, in fact, the very notion of either term—body or mind—transmitting demands "on its own" is a supreme fiction. This fiction, in myriad forms, commands a ubiquitous presence: mind over matter, matter over mind—the entire range of human activities shaped by the ethos of discipline and mastery.

Masculinity, of course, like femininity, invariably knows itself as a doctrine of command over sequences of excitement, control and release. The particular objects, rhythms, modes, organs, sources and aims employed in this doctrine are forever contestable, of course. But no version of masculinity includes incontinence and helplessness in its list of required particulars.

Freud precisely locates the site where masculinity confronts itself: the "frontier" through which drives connect body and mind. Here, in this frontier zone, masculinity emerges, here it is formed, here it is continuously challenged. It may be fixed and ossified; it may be flexible and polymorphous. In this zone, mind and body are in a relation of reciprocal infiltration. Each demands compliance from the other, each exacts submission. And here, uneasily, we become boys and men. Reconciled, accepting, triumphant; the range of associated moods is vast and volatile.

The dynamic interplay of reciprocal demands, the ongoing work they actually provoke when, finally, they achieve relative stability—this constitutes the material footing for what we can call a "somatic identity," a sense of one's place in one's body, a sense of one's obligations and responsibilities to both body and mind, to the possibilities of play and leisure, of discipline and competence.

---

1 This chapter includes material that first appeared as Moss, D. (2010a) "All I wish to say," *Cousin Corinne's Reminder,* No. 1.

What happens, then, when this interface is interrupted, when no messages get through, no demands at all, when mind is loosed from its attachment to body, when body loses its capacity to send effective signals, when mind is left on its own, stripped of the orienting fact of having to work?

I ask because: when I was 5 years old, I had polio.

For a brief period, my mind lost its attachment to my body and, in fact, to the outside world as well, since the treatment demanded isolation.

Suddenly, I was paralyzed. I couldn't walk; I could barely breathe. I was alone in a hospital room for about a week—I had no sense of cause, no sense of duration, no sense of what was being done, what would happen. And then, just as suddenly, the connection was restored. I could move again; I could breathe. I was let out of the hospital. I came home, did some moderate rehab exercises, and suffered no physical after-effects. I was fine.

This transient period of paralysis constitutes a kind of natural experiment. It allows me to think about the mind-body connection as something other than essential and permanent. More precisely, it allows me to think about the challenges to my sense of being a sane and surviving boy when suddenly I lost access to my body. One residue of the experiment, it seems to me, is my certainty that the connection can be interrupted and, therefore, a particularly vivid appreciation of the variety of ways that we—in this case boys—manage and maintain it.

Masculinity straddles time; it finds both its supports and its weaknesses in the past, the present and the future. One of its tasks, then, is to construct its own history, to generate some form of narrative that refers to its origins, its development, its influences—how it has come to be. When it is challenged, as mine was with polio, it is burdened with the work of making sense of the challenge—of inserting it, as Freud says, into the personal story whose title, in effect, is "I was, am, and will be a Man." The possible points of insertion are many. The resultant histories owe nothing to each other but share a common debt to the remembered challenge.

Here, then, are two such stories of mine.

The first complies with traditional narrative structure. We can call it "sincere"— I seem to be reflecting directly, honestly, and introspectively. I try to see "what happened" and then tell myself what I see. I look at the event in the same way I might look at a horizon: I make out a tree there, a hill here, a hint of movement, a guess at distance.

The traditional structuring of memory allows me to position the events constituting "what happened" in simple relation to all that has happened to me before and since. That is, once my memory takes on this structure, no matter how extreme the remembered events might have been, I can easily place them next to— link them with—other memories. I can insert my experience with polio into sane, adult categories of memory. I see on the horizon the kinds of things one always sees on horizons—trees, hills, and distance.

This way of structuring memory allows for describing extreme states of mind as variants of common states of mind. Whatever happened, and the associated states of mind in which it happened, can here be thought of as some recognizable version, some variant, of the events and states of mind that happen now.

The second version of my memory of being ill is non-traditionally structured; as such, it qualifies as "fiction." It violates memory's narrative structure. We cannot fairly ask this narrative if it is "real," if it tells what really happened. We cannot ask that it do that, but in fact, for me, it does. It offers a second version of "what happened."

Each of these versions owes a substantial debt to the "fact" of polio. This fact makes an undeniable claim on both versions. By undeniable claim I mean simply that—in fact— there were signs, symptoms, diagnosis, recovery. These facts are comparable in structure to the facts that, for example, allow us to say of a given person that he is a man. The fact of polio, like the fact of "man," is of a special and limited kind—a kernel.

The kernel seems to erupt, though, when we place it under the heat of the question: "What is it like?"—to be a man, to have polio. Ask that and the empirical kernel turns into a generative memory. The kernel now generates possibility/possibilities, two of which I've just narrated. That is, as long as we take the kernel, polio in this case, into account, our subsequent obligations precipitously diminish, approaching zero.

The kernel's demands are insistent. They must be met. We are aware of when they are met and when evaded. Fail to meet them and you are lying. Only when the demands of such facts are met can we reasonably ask "What was it like for you to have polio?" "What is it like for you to be a man?" Though in some sense both limited and limiting, in another sense the fact of polio—like the fact of "being" a "man"—provides a deep and fungible reservoir that can be repeatedly spent without ever being diminished. The original kernel has now taken on the aspect of a mythological goddess, a source spawning endless possibilities.

Story #1

We all knew about polio then, like we all knew about cleft palates and blind people and retards. These things could happen to you, but only if you deserved them.

For instance, a blind guy used to come around to sell pencils. What we all knew, without anyone ever asking how we knew it, was that the guy was blind because he had once tried to kidnap someone. He was caught and punished. They poured acid on his eyes. Now that that was taken care of, he couldn't see and, therefore, he couldn't kidnap. But he still could try, so that's why we stayed away from him and never opened our doors if he knocked.

And there was Bobby, just down the street. He was my best friend for a while and he talked strangely. I was the only kid who could understand what he was saying. We did everything together, the best of which was catching grasshoppers in a glass jar with holes punched into its tin cover. The grasshoppers would get excited and squirt tobacco and then we'd gather the tobacco on sheets of paper, spreading it thinly and watching it crust. But that all ended when I found out he needed surgery on his mouth and lip and that he couldn't go to regular school. That was the first I realized that he had a condition, a cleft palate.

With that information, I knew that I could get whatever he had. His mouth had gotten that way for a reason. I didn't know the reason and didn't want to hang around long enough to find out.

The best, and only, thing to do was to never see him again, so I didn't.

I got polio when I stopped seeing Bobby. There had to have been a reason.

I remember the spinal tap, the position you're put in: curled up, very still, holding someone's hand. Things then blur until I'm being rolled down a long hallway in the hospital. At the near end of the hallway, there's a large, loud room filled with kids. We pass that quickly. Then, as we keep going, the rooms get smaller: fours, then twos. None of those are for me. At the end of the corridor, though, is a single room with a closed door. This one, the last, will be mine. The door to this room always stays closed. There is a small window in the door. Beyond this room lurks a cliff. Beyond this room you die.

I am in an oxygen tent. The air is cold. I cannot move. Each day a nurse comes in and does something to me. Each day my mom visits. Sometimes she stays at the window where I can see her face. Other times she comes in. She never touches me, though. She's not supposed to. Later she tells me she was afraid she could hurt me. I spend a lot of time by myself. I do not feel frightened. I pay attention to numbers. I add, multiply, divide them; I build rows, columns, and triangles of them. The numbers do my bidding, exactly. My dad is not in the picture at all. I have no memory of him visiting and never asked him where he had been.

The most vivid presence of my time in the hospital was the doctor. Each day in the late afternoon he came in. He would look at me and say things in a soft voice. I knew that as long as he was around nothing bad would happen to me. He always wore a suit and tie, a grey suit. After about a week, he asked me if I would like to be moved out of this room, up the hall, to the room with five other kids. I knew then that I would live, that I would get better, that the trial had ended, and that I had been found innocent. I also knew then that I wanted to become a doctor.

I got polio so that I could become a doctor—could wear a grey suit and could find Bobby, have a chance to apologize to him.

Here's the second version of my illness.

Story #2

I was standing on the sidewalk looking at license plates, adding up the numbers on a green 1949 Buick: HN 4876 – 25. Five fives, the best there is.

Two men came running around the corner. The one in front couldn't see me. He was staying low to keep his turn narrow. He ran into me hard and I was thrown into the air. I saw the roofs of houses and I came down far from where I went up. I landed on the back of my head. Vertebrae were broken and the skull caved in.

The doctor said: "You have lost control of your bodily functions. Your mental capacities have not been affected. You are here in the hospital. If you do not get better, you will never leave."

My mother said: "This is your X-ray. Your bones are pudding. The back of your brain has been squashed. The front of your brain is like it always was. The front is who you are. The back is only how you work."

My mother said: "Do not ask questions. Do not cry."

On the X-ray, my spine rises. A blurring begins at the base of the brain. The base is dense and compacted. The ventricles are asymmetrical. Fluid presses against brain tissue. Toward the front of the brain, the tissue turns less compacted. The frontal lobes are intact. The division between the ventricles and the gray matter is clear and distinct.

The information I was given was not helpful. The explanations were too abstract. The speakers spoke properly but with insufficient consideration. I was a child. My condition made questions impossible.

Though no harm was intended, I used the information in a harmful manner. There were two parts to my spine, one straight and one deformed. I visualized them parallel to each other. Then I tried to squeeze the two together into a single straight line.

This effort taxed me. When I tried to squeeze them together, I held my breath. I did this in order to focus my attention. I wanted no distractions. I wanted nothing to move. But holding my breath caused damage. Whenever my breath was held, pressures built up in the machine. When I exhaled, those pressures were released in a rush.

The pressures produced an overload in the machine's circuitry. The machine took compensatory action. Forces and rates of movement became rapid and erratic. The machine is designed to stabilize. Its dysfunctioning resulted in new mal-formations in my brain and spinal cord.

Because no one knew what I was doing, the malformations posed insurmount-able problems for my doctor. He was no longer able to understand my condition. He told me he was withdrawing from my case. "Your son is dying," he told my mother.

"There is nothing more to hope for," he told me.

After that, a volunteer was assigned to my case. She sat next to me. She noticed that I often held my breath. She told me to stop. She told me I must never again do it. The volunteer informed me of dreadful consequences.

The volunteer told the doctor what she had seen.

The doctor said to me: "On the machine, everything you do or imagine will only interfere with the treatment. You must do nothing. You must imagine nothing. You must let the encounter between nature and the machine take its course."

I was placed in a closed steel cylinder containing cold oxygen under great pressure. I could not shiver. I could neither talk nor open my eyes. Nothing in me could move.

I could give no signal. I was uncertain whether anyone could tell I was alive. I feared I had been transformed into something that had never been.

The only sensation I had was an intermittent vibration in my skin. This vibration was new to me. Because I had never felt it before and had never thought of it as a possibility, I believed I was not making it up.

The vibration passed through me and left behind a sensation of thickness beneath my skin. The source of the vibration could be located. First it was in one place and then in another. This movement provided me with a sense of time.

I thought the machine was a second life. If it stopped, life would stop. There will be 11 lives in all, I thought. Each life will include at least one element from an earlier one. Each life will last less than seven years. I will live a maximum of 77 years. Seven sevens, I thought, the best there is.

It is a test, I thought. They want me to obey. Someone is watching, I thought. Everything is deserved.

I could hear the oxygen moving. I could feel the weight coming down on my chest, lifting up, coming down. The oxygen simultaneously filled the cylinder and filled my chest. I could not tell where my skin left off and the oxygen began.

The only thing my body retained was a sense of heaviness. The heaviness was great. I was afraid my body would fall through whatever was underneath me.

I dreamt.

In the dream I am moving rapidly through the air. I cannot tell what is propelling me and why I am not falling. I can swivel my head 360 degrees. I look for what is supporting me but I see nothing.

I start to fall.

The earth is covered with shards of steel. The fall is silent. I hit the shards of steel. My skin bursts in many places and I bleed in spurts.

I have since been informed that this dream is typical.

My grandmother reminded me of my obligations as a Jew. She said I was twice indebted: to her for the blood she had once given me and to Abraham for everything else. She said these debts must be honored. Until they are honored, she said, dying was not within my rights. She said: "You are our only revenge. You are our Hitler. Promises have been made. The dead are watching and must not be disappointed."

She said the machine will work forever. In America, every part can be replaced. Every vital fluid can be found, everything kept clean. What has been done once can be done again. What has been achieved can be repeated.

She said: "You will die only by an act of will. As long as you are alive, Hitler has lost."

All of these things were encouraging.

On the body there are several ethically important sites: two legs, asymmetrical; two arms, asymmetrical; mouth, penis, balls, asshole; fingers, asymmetrical; eyebrows, neck, ears, knees, thighs, wrists.

Before I went on the machine, I was in control of these sites. It was possible to achieve goodness.

On the machine, the body is without possibilities. The body is sand. The skin is sand and the sheet it rests on is sand.

On the machine, the body is purified of its biological dimension.

I wanted my mind a sphere. I wanted the elimination of quality. I wanted to throw a dog against a garage door. I wanted to become the machine.

I was never alone. I was kept in a large room with other people on machines. Before I went on the machine, the most private thing I knew was counting. On the machine, I was able to count without causing detectable interference. I could not measure, though. I had to count without counting anything particular. I had to count without expectation or disappointment. These things brought with them an inclination to breathe more quickly. This destabilized the operation of the machine and had to be avoided.

People on machines die in bunches, one then the next. The connections between us are profound. If one of us interferes with the machine, the entire row is seized in consequence.

Properly maintained, the machine will function forever.

Fear creates interference and destroys the community.

For instance, in the beginning, at night, my skin seemed to harden into scales. It seemed to divide itself into plates. My fingers turned webbed. I was very frightened. My throat clamped closed. This made my oxygen inaccessible. But the moving weight over my chest kept moving. Pressure built up.

I became faint and nauseated.

I vomited.

Vomiting caused a significant interference in the functioning of the machine.

All the people in the room suffered from that interference.

Later I was taught how to ignore frightening sensations. I had to protect the others from disturbance.

It is a terrible thing to cause others to thrash about.

This terror was the ground for our community.

There are two groups of people who want us dead.

One group wants to touch us. They are excited because there is no limit to what they can do. They come in the early morning. They hope they are neither seen nor remembered.

Whatever they can put against our skin will excite them. What they can put inside our skin will excite them.

They breathe into our mouths. They press our chests. They turn off the machine and put themselves in its place. They tell us they love us.

They deposit fluids inside of us and clean us up. They do what they never thought they would be able to do. For that opportunity, they are grateful to us.

When the time of gratitude is over, they want all reminder of their pleasures removed. If we are gone, they are innocent. I have seen them take some of the others away.

Another group wants to kill us on sight. These people are excited by the idea of cutting off the power. I have seen their eyes when they first enter the room. They are astonished by this dream come true. These people have read the Bible. From childhood, they have been tempted with certain ideas.

We are the sinners they have been waiting to find. We are the ones they are destined to wipe from the face of the earth.

They say these things out loud to us. They want us to know what is about to happen.

They are careful. They do not want their opportunity spoiled. They proceed slowly, one at a time, leaving no trace of a pattern.

Each of us was brought here in the back seat of a spectacular vehicle. We have had large numbers of people immediately assigned to us for long periods of time. We have grown accustomed to conditions of extreme regularity. When we leave, we will be in great need. We will suffer from states of confusion. That need and that suffering will be the basis of our future affinity.

Our genetic debts have been canceled. We no longer have the mother we once had.

There is a photo. She is peering in from the periphery. She is reaching over. She is touching her lips to my face. She wants something. She looks afraid of the damage she can do. Thank you, Mother. You have been just like a mother to me.

Whatever has been done to us has followed a well-developed protocol. We have learned what to expect. People on machines are afflicted with a certain shyness. Approach alarms us. Whatever can be done can be fatal.

My doctor informed me of a curative procedure. He came to my bed. He was alone. He said that trouble had developed, that more scar tissue had formed. He spoke of an experimental technique of laser curettage, meticulous openings. Resistance is reduced, he said, a streamlined flow restored.

"I promise you nothing," he said. There is much to lose, more to gain.

"I want your permission," he said.

I gave it to him.

My lesson has been learned. I have learned that nothing is my own. Nothing ever was my own and nothing ever will be my own.

The fetal tissue has settled in. Synapses have developed across all major neuronal structures. The necrotic residue has been flushed out.

Soon will come movement and the capacity to breathe. Then I will be taken off the machine.

I will be given sufficient funds. I will visit many cities before deciding on a residence. I will have a driver.

My skull will be covered by a temporary occipital patch.

In the season following this one, the others like me will all be brought together. We will stand next to each other and touch our hands together. We will speak without others listening. We will answer questions and allow examinations. Each year we will be brought together. Each year we will touch hands and speak together and allow examinations.

These are the only plans.

There is nothing more I wish to say.

Chapter 5

Psychoanalysis and male homosexuality/the ideal of neutrality[1]

I divide this chapter into two parts. The first part is essentially an appreciation of Kenneth Lewes's groundbreaking book, *Psychoanalysis and Male Homosexuality*. The appreciation is focused on the book's remarkable realization of an ethos of neutrality. Lewes thinks. He positions himself as a kind of psychoanalytic journalist, imbedded at the point of contact between, on one side, psychoanalytic theorizing, ideology and practice and, on the other, homosexual theorizing, ideology and practice. He sends us his report.

The second part of this chapter focuses on my work with two men, one homosexual, one heterosexual. With each man, I continually notice my own prejudices, my own pull away from Lewes's realized ideal of neutrality, and toward a moralizing, normalizing, conservative platform. This "platform," in fact, seems to me to be the resultant of two competing forces. One force emanates from my own personal "identity," a pull toward the sensuous immediate certainty of "feeling." A second force emanates from the pull of "conceptual thought"—its appeal, against the appeal of feeling, lies in its claim of universality. Each force works against the other.

The result, then, while I'm working, is a continuous tension: in one direction toward the universalist appeal of conceptual thought, in the counter-direction the pull towards idiosyncratic "identity." This tension, although reducible, cannot be eliminated. For me, the central requirement of neutrality is that it simultaneously evade and take into account both of these pulls. This leaves a wide swath of possibility, a swath wide enough, that is, to leave one always uncertain and always aiming at self-correction, as one senses oneself pulled away from the middle and toward either of the two dangerous sides: disembodied conceptual thought and idiosyncratic sensuous identity.

1 This chapter includes material that first appeared as the Foreword to Kenneth Lewes's *Psychoanalysis and Male Homosexuality: 20th Anniversary Edition*, 2009, and material that first appeared in *DIVISION/Review* as "Sensuous Personal Identity vs Conceptual Universal Reason: Competing Claims on the Analyst While Listening to Sexually Charged Material," Fall 2011. Used with permission.

By way of two brief clinical vignettes, I reflect upon some of the difficulties posed by this irreducible predicament and the resultant melancholy that follows when, whatever I do, I can neither achieve the neutrality I aim for nor stay true to either the concept that promises to frame the clinical situation or the identity that promises to frame me.

Part I

Much remains disquietingly fraught in the cultural sector marked out by the intersection of psychoanalysis and male homosexuality. The changes in the sector have been both momentous and precipitous. Most obviously, of course, this sector is now ostensibly gay-friendly. At a certain moment, pressures suddenly turned effective; progressive sentiments convincingly won the day. Decades of suspicion were transfigured into signs of welcome. Interdiction turned into affirmation, psychopathology into difference. By any measure, it seemed that all of the closed doors had suddenly opened.

And yet . . .

Despite the groundbreaking restructuring and despite the radical reordering of what can and cannot take place, of what can and cannot be said and thought, despite, that is, a radical reordering of the demands of conscience, there has still not been a thoroughgoing critique, a thoroughgoing re-conceptualization, a redoing of the foundational premises whose homophobic effects have infiltrated this sector for one hundred years.

Instead of a re-conceptualization of the determinants of those effects, instead of a necessarily disruptive examination of how a systematized form of hatred—homophobia—found its way into the very foundations of liberatory psychoanalysis, we have, instead, in effect, a declaration that all expressions of that hatred are null and void.

From this day forward . . . homophobia will be banned and its long-standing targets, once excluded, will be welcomed. The enormity of this implicit declaration must be respected. Almost all of us are grateful for the change of tone, the change of constituency, the enfranchisement, and the transformed ethos that has reconfigured our borders, our interfaces, and the very fabric of our collegial and clinical lives. And yet, questions remain, fundamental ones, psychoanalytic ones.

1   What, after all, are we witnessing when we witness, in effect, the absolute eradication of all signs of homophobia, all markers of it in official psychoanalysis; all published suggestions that male homosexuality might, in any way, pose a problem for psychoanalytic theory and practice; all barriers to candidacy for gay applicants?
2   Was the entire homophobic edifice so brittle, so fragile, so incapable of self-preservation that its vanishing has left behind such little apparent trace?
3   Does what we are witnessing represent a radical change; are we in the midst of a fundamental rearrangement of thinking, feeling, and acting; or, contrarily,

are we in the midst of what, to employ clinical jargon, might be called a "flight into health?"

Kenneth Lewes's book, *Psychoanalysis and Male Homosexuality,* offers an effective medium through which to begin to take up these questions. Published more than twenty years ago, the book's sober reflections certainly contributed to the changes of the past two decades. Those same reflections also can help us now as we try to make sense of what has happened, what is happening, and what might yet be needed to be done. I suggest, then, that we follow his lead, that we postpone the noisy celebration for now.

Psychoanalysis and male homosexuality seem bound no less intensively than, say, the police and black people are bound in every urban American center. We can now wonder about how, and whether, psychoanalysis can "think" male homosexuality without, in fact, "policing" it. Can we construct a psychoanalysis that aims to establish conceptual order without at the same time aiming to establish law and order?

Using our new-found willingness to pathologize homophobia rather than homosexuality, we can, in effect, "police" the psychoanalytic police, in the hope of reforming them, replacing a clinical theory based on dominance and regulation with one based on structure and taxonomy. Instead of simply using psychoanalysis to generate a one-directional practice that orders and regulates the male homosexuality it runs into, we can use both psychoanalysis and male homosexuality to generate a two-directional practice that might order relations between the two. We can use male homosexuality to think about psychoanalysis while simultaneously using psychoanalysis to think about male homosexuality. We have precedent on our side. After all, Freud, instead of simply adding to the regulatory apparatus of medical science, perched himself on the side of sexuality and, from there, one could say, wrote psychoanalysis.

"How could sexuality regulate and generate a new kind of thinking?" he might have wondered. What happens to psychoanalysis when we write it from over there, on the side of one of its long-suffering objects, male homosexuality? The task demands that we turn psychoanalysis into an object and reflect upon it from the point of view of its former object.

Let's take on the task by beginning with Lewes's title, *Psychoanalysis and Male Homosexuality.* The title invites us to imagine this pair of terms, *psychoanalysis* and *male homosexuality,* in some kind of relation to each other, at some point of intersection. The invitation cannot be refused. *Invitation,* then, is the wrong word. Better would be *stimulation.* The title stimulates, provokes, and reminds. That is, we see the title and, necessarily, imagine something; some kind of relation: conflict, resolution, harmony, opposition, synergy, indifference, antipathy. The range of possibilities is wide.

We begin, then, with the chance to catch ourselves in an act of prejudice, of prejudging, of lining up the pair in some particular way. The possibilities are limitless. I, for one, see the title and find a flurry of them. I find the 'and' of Bonnie *and* Clyde; I find cops *and* robbers, black *and* white, doctor *and* patient, high *and* low. This is, of course, my own decidedly nonrandom list. What's important about the list is that I did not think it. I did not, in any commonsensical way, even construct it. The list found me as much as I found it. The list was there, waiting for me. That is the sense I have in mind when I refer to prejudgment: this list of association precedes my thought, tilts my thought, simultaneously launches it and weighs it down. The load is not balanced; it lacks symmetry. The load is ideological: simultaneously private and public. It pulls from the most commonplace cultural shelves while simultaneously pointing to a reservoir of unarticulated private appetites. And what is the load? As I reflect on it, the load includes sexy criminals, law and order, good and bad, sublime and crude, illness and cure. This is just the beginning, of course, just a first flurry prompted by a neutral title. The point is that I cannot even make it through the title clear-headedly. None of us can. The best we can do, I think, is to be in a state of continuous self-reflection, a state in which we continuously try to assess the shifting load we're carrying and the consequent tilt our thinking must bear.

In mediating the construction of this associational list, the 'and' of Lewes's title functions as a neutral connector, not entirely unlike a psychoanalyst: aiming to put commonly separated terms into novel relation to one another. Treating the connector as neutral frees us to treat anything we might sense in the connection as, in fact, coming from us.

The most obvious point of intersection of the title's two terms is *sexuality.*

Psychoanalysis, in both theory and practice, is sexual. In taking sexuality as its primary object, from its inception it has necessarily become sexual itself. Whether interdicting or sanctioning, whether neutral or invested, the discipline is caught up with, and becomes part of, the sexualities on which it has so doggedly focused for more than one hundred years. It not only "discovers" the sexual lurking in the ostensibly driest of symptoms, it actually transports the sexual to those symptoms. Psychoanalysis sexualizes its objects while gazing at them. Psychoanalysis "thinks" sexuality, but, as it itself has consistently demonstrated, there can be no definitive line drawn that would separate sexual thinking from sexuality itself.

In thinking sexuality, psychoanalysis orders sexual ideas, sexual fantasies, sexual possibilities. Ordering itself turns into a sexualized and sexualizing activity. Despite its never-ending efforts to stay clean, to stay neutral, to resist its objects' seductions, psychoanalysis can never find a way to jump back quickly enough from the sexual ground it might wish to merely describe. It has sexual paint on the bottom of its shoes.

Again, as it itself so consistently demonstrated, its banner of "no" must affirm a hidden "yes." Its mood of austerity, its ethos of abstinence, its barriers against all forms of direct sensuous contact have the indirect effect of locating and sanctioning an alternative site—there and then—for what it, psychoanalysis, cannot permit here and now. That alternative site, what Freud called an "other scene," is, in fact, in principle, everywhere and limitless.

Psychoanalytic thinking proceeds as though, for the moment, the sexual can be bracketed out, as though, for the moment, we can think about sexuality, without, in fact, enacting it. But this bracketing out is both temporary and contingent.

Psychoanalysis is seductive. It simultaneously speaks of, and promises, an expanded range of possibilities and a clear-eyed look at consequences. It exposes the costs and benefits of hiding, of disguising, of being open and direct. What do you want? What can you get? How can you get it? What must you pay? These are the kinds of questions that structure psychoanalytic sexuality. Psychoanalysis is, of course, a clinical-theoretical discipline, while less overtly (more sexually) it functions as a disciplinary discipline. It orders, yes, but in doing so, it also gives orders.

Thinking of sexual economies, psychoanalysis is itself a discipline of sexual economy. Psychoanalytic treatment promises optimal sexual efficiency. Within the orienting frames of psychoanalysis, symptoms are symptoms because, in effect, they cost too much. They are not worth it. The sexuality they might permit comes at too dear a price.

Here, at this point of exchange—some kind of satisfaction in exchange for, or even as an equivalent of, some kind of suffering—psychoanalysis does much of its sexual work. Perhaps the terms can be modified. Perhaps a better arrangement can be brokered, a better, more favorable compromise worked out: more satisfaction at less cost, ancient debts eradicated, a little more freedom purchased.

The sexual psychoanalytic labor of putting your dirty thoughts into words is worth it only because it promises to unburden you from having to wash and rewash your already red-raw hands. Psychoanalysis offers a way of sorting out sexuality, housing it differently; freeing those hands to touch something other than themselves, say. It establishes divisions, categories. It offers privacy, secrecy and control, a chance to carry on a sexualized life on terms that you might set yourself, a sexuality that is essentially imperceptible in the public sphere, a sexuality that allows you to assume the tasks of a citizen, that allows you, that is, to "function."

And here, with the notion of "function," and its attendant elements of proper work, of appropriate limits, of good form, of the extrinsic burdens imposed by the necessity to integrate, we begin to sense that however liberatory the sexual economy offered by psychoanalysis, it too, like any economy it might displace, will have its costs.

And here, at this point where cost and "function" converge, we can, I think, locate the most volatile encounter between psychoanalysis and male homosexuality. How do we determine what something costs, what its intrinsic costs are? By costs, here, I mean sacrifice. What must be sacrificed in order to have what you want? How are those sacrifices determined? How are they measured? How essential are they? What are the fundamental structural costs of my desires? How can those costs be modified?

To think about the determinants of male homosexuality is, in effect, to think about the exchanges, the costs, that go into its production and maintenance. What must be sacrificed in order to live life as a male homosexual? Two terms shimmer in that question: *what* and *must*. These are psychoanalytic questions. They are also the questions of "male homosexuality." The two terms approach the questions from points of view that are not necessarily harmonious.

Psychoanalysis aims to separate the contingent from the essential. The aim of any psychoanalytic treatment is to expose desires, to illuminate their costs, to distinguish which of those costs are essential and which contingent, and to make possible a reconfiguration of desire and cost that increases the one and diminishes the other. Psychoanalytic treatment is painful to the extent that it affirms that sacrifice is necessary, that there is an essential gap between what can be imagined and what can be realized. Psychoanalytic theory and practice rest on the premise of that gap.

The particulars of that gap—its size and its contents—are, in effect, under constant surveillance. Clinical theory is the systematized record of that surveillance. But no clinical theory—none—can survive the assumption that the gap can be reduced to zero. That utopian assumption is necessarily in opposition to the working possibilities of psychoanalysis. That gap functions as the very premise of the discipline.

Traditional sexualities, all of them, including male homosexuality, aim to reduce that gap to zero. Psychoanalysis aims to preserve it. Here is a point of direct opposition.

Neither aim receives broad cultural support. Psychoanalysis, insisting on the irreducibly melancholy dimension of sexuality, takes a scornful view of the social/personal project of erotic perfectibility. It treats that view as an illusion, a kind of secular religion. For its trouble, then, psychoanalysis is consistently pushed to the margins, where it struggles to survive.

Male homosexuality, claiming desire's rights, also takes a scornful view of the widespread notion that desire must be sacrificed in the name of the greater good. It, too, like psychoanalysis, is consistently pushed to the margins where it struggles to survive. Each looks for cover; each, perhaps, can look to the other for cover, but both, finding little, and embittered and proud, struggle to survive. The two are more competitors than allies, then, each vigilant, eager to survive, in a cultural setting, a niche, that is fundamentally hostile to both.

This shared burden of trying to survive—and perhaps having to compete—lends a strain of pathos to the ongoing interface between psychoanalysis and male homosexuality. The pathos is a product of necessity, the necessity a product of structure.

We all know the cynical fruits of experience. Theory is for losers. The search for structure, for pattern, for foundations leads nowhere. Go beneath experience, treat the empirical as merely empirical, and you wind up in the now transcended nether zone where thought seeks out imaginary prey while elsewhere predators find real prey. Join the predators. This is the cynical lesson of cynical experience. Practice/action/immediacy: this is where the rewards lie. Does it really matter how things are structured? Isn't the real problem the more concrete one? The one that presents itself today? The one that plays out now?

We now have the opportunity to reconsider our own relations to immediacy and common sense, to what feels right and necessary, to the soft satisfactions of proceeding in accordance with what our times and circumstances will dictate.

What must be true of minds that allow any of us to endure the melancholy, the loneliness, necessary to think on our own, to leave behind life's comforts, life's companions, life's rewards, and to pursue, instead, the dry, sad zone of structure?

Think of Bruno Ganz, playing one of the angels in Wim Wenders's *Wings of Desire*; think of the way he looks on, lovingly, mournfully, at the mess, the frantic mess, of quotidian urban life. Consider the look on his face; that mournful look, that sense that what he sees is such a mess, such a gratuitous, yet essential, mess. The task he sets himself is to think this gratuitous essential mess.

Gratuitous and essential; the terms are incompatible. Thinking this incompatibility, this is a task we might take on: to look, as though with the eyes of a hovering angel, on the melancholy pairings of, first, psychoanalysis and male homosexuality, and then, more generally, of psychoanalysis and male sexuality.

Part 2

Mr A is a 22-year-old university student who sought treatment because of his "addiction" to pornography. He lives with his girlfriend of two years, whom he describes as "beautiful and good." He is very concerned, however, about the volatility of his feelings toward her. His admiration often vanishes. At these moments, he thinks of her as a "nag," dull and oppressive. So many others would be better for him: smarter, sharper, sexier, more adventurous. What he means by "better for him" is that they would have what it takes to make him feel better about himself. Concerns about his own standing preoccupy him: his goodness, his intelligence, his sexual attractiveness, his income, the loyalty of his friends and family. He is an exceptional student. Departments already have begun competing for his future at the university. He is proud of his intellectual accomplishments and feels triumphant when those accomplishments are recognized via awards, scholarships, etc. The triumph is particularly satisfying in relation to his father. The father is also an academic, whose achievements, though substantial, have not won him national recognition. Patient and father agree that the son is on path to far outdo him. They also agree that the son's girlfriend is herself a "better woman than my mom ever was."

From a recent session:

> My girlfriend and I were sitting at an outdoor café. We were barely speaking. There were all these other women I could see, beautiful and talking. They seemed intelligent, full of ideas. My girlfriend said maybe we should find a better café. It wasn't the café, though, it was her. She had nothing to say. I shouldn't be with her. Someone else. She doesn't have the edge, the smarts, the wit I need. It's like not getting enough compensation. I'm worth more.
> [Your girlfriend ought to provide you with what is otherwise missing.]

That's right. Like that girl from a few years ago. She had it. She'd walk down the street and you could see how everyone wanted her. She'd walk into a room and guys would look at each other, each one knowing what the other one meant. What they meant was: "She's the one." That's it. That's what I deserve. That's what I want. A woman that guys look at and say "she's the one."

[The woman and the guys merge into one thing, don't they—the thing you call "that's what I want"?]

Yeah, if everything goes right, I get the woman and I get the guys.

It is impossible to listen to this sequence without being aware of its homosexual component: "I get the guys." Getting the woman, that is, seems here a means of getting the guys. And yet, on listening, I immediately sense this apparently central element of the material as located on its periphery.

The sense of where this homoerotic element belongs comes to me as a kind of perception. I have no awareness of any activity that precedes this "perception." The authority of this "perception" approximates the authority of a "fact," although this is a "fact" of a special—suspect—kind. I know, or think I know, that "facts" like this one cannot be trusted. Nonetheless, given its first appearance to me as a "fact," my first—automatic—thought/impulse is to treat "getting the guys" as a marginal element, that is, as a disguised representation of what immediately seems to me the missing central element—fleeing the woman.

This thought/impulse is not a product of evidence; it certainly lacks the enduring force of conviction. It feels, instead, like a tilt, a reflex, a posture from which I begin to think. This tilt has a sensuous valence, not a cognitive one.

The tilt is undeniable and demanding; the demand it makes is for work. Freud describes a similar demand made by "drives," in general. Drives demand work of the mind. This demand is a direct effect of the mind's attachment to the body. Following Freud, then, I think of my experience of perceptual tilt as drive-related, that is, as a consequence of my mind's attachment to my body. The tilt I feel pulls my mind toward an alignment with demands emanating from my body. The mental work demanded of me is to satisfy this drive-based tilt: to provide it with theoretical cover, to adorn it with thought.

The work of adornment is effortless and instantaneous, which alerts me to the possibility that what I'm doing is more rationalization than rational thinking. In this first moment, though, I cannot clearly distinguish the two. So I get to work. I produce a "thoughtful" image: the girlfriend who doesn't "have" the ideas, the wit, the edge, the smarts—who lacks what the patient wants. I am ready to orient further work around the question of what makes this image of "lack" unbearable.

In classical terms, then, my first thought/impulse is to organize what I am hearing around the notion of "castration anxiety." My patient's flight from his girlfriend, I immediately feel, is a flight from an encounter with a dreaded image of castration. That is, in this initial moment, I feel my patient is in sensuous flight from a figure he "sees" as lacking the sexual essentials he needs.

I sensuously identify with him. I "see" him "seeing" female lack and I then cover my "sighting" with thought. With this, the demand for bodily alignment and conceptual adornment is met.

Of course, "castration anxiety" is not the culprit here. Were the identity-driven demand different, I might use the same concept to ask an entirely different question, to "see" an entirely different patient, that is, what makes the woman a necessary appendage in this patient's aim of "getting the men." Perhaps, I might have thought: without the possession of the woman to signify his own phallic integrity, the encounter with "the men" would bring this patient too close to a dreaded image of himself as lacking the essential he needs. The notion of "flight from men" does not occupy my tilted castration-anxiety oriented center, although the notion of "flight from women" does.

The concept "castration anxiety," like all concepts, seems to tilt me neither in one direction nor another. What then is responsible for the tilt? This question— what tilts the clinical analyst away from neutrality—informs all psychoanalytic work. What are the forces that make achieving neutrality so difficult and preserving it impossible? When this two-part question arises here, in regard to homo- and heterosexual object choice, I presume myself in the midst of a particularly vivid and local example of an often obscured, but always fundamental problem.

Patients, of course, are not neutral. They have no obligation toward neutrality. If anything, they are obliged away from it, obliged, that is, and loyal to their own particularity, their own identity. The essence of identity resides in its deviation from neutrality. In some sense, this is what we mean by "identity": an enduringly non-universal and non-neutral presence that organizes and structures experience, that gives experience "personal" rather than "neutral" meaning. Patients in analysis mean to call the analyst toward them, toward their identities, and, therefore, in effect, to call the analyst away from any pre-existing obligation to neutrality. "I get the woman and I get the guys," for instance, represents such a call, as though the weight of the phrase lies in its unspoken, "You see what I mean, don't you?"

The analyst contends with an identity-fueled impulse similar to the patient's: the analyst feels this impulse in the form of calling the patient towards himself, calling for the patient to see things, experience things, as the analyst does. Like the patient, the analyst feels the desire to have his own identity carry weight; for example, in response to the patient's call, the analyst might, in effect, be inclined to make a complementary one, something like: "It won't work, your aspiration to get the woman and the guys. We both know, don't we, that you will, sooner or later, have to renounce one and (melancholically) settle for the other." Or, to put it more bluntly, to give it the sensuous pull demanded by, in this case, my identity: "You ought to internalize the men you currently desire. Then you will be better able to tolerate the anxiety-provoking otherness of a desired woman."

What distinguishes analyst and patient from each other, however, is that, in addition to the pull of identity, the analyst also feels at least two other pulls: toward conceptual clarity and toward interpretive neutrality. Whatever the analyst ends up doing represents the resultant of these converging forces: the pull of identity—

shared with, but in direct opposition to, the patient's pull toward identity—and the pulls toward conceptual clarity and interpretive neutrality, which are the analyst's alone.

So, then, to return to the issue of my own tilt, it must be me—the analyst with a personal identity—who is responsible for the initial tilt: no concept, no idea, no theory. The first use of theory and concept is to provide cover, to give an account, of the identity-fueled pull that precedes their utilization. In that first impulse, some element of my own identity manifests itself as a force that feels deeper and more reliable than any concept or theory, including the concept of "neutrality." Said another way, my identity—like everyone's, I think—is decidedly non-"neutral."

This non-neutral identity lives in open opposition to my aspirations toward conceptual clarity and interpretive neutrality. Conceptual clarity and interpretive neutrality each demand to be treated as ideals. Yet, my own identity demands that I treat each of them with skepticism—more as sirens than as ideals.

For the analyst, while conceptual clarity and interpretive neutrality position themselves as ideals still to be achieved, identity claims itself as an ideal already accomplished.

Before getting on to some further reflections on what seems to me the irresolvable tension between identity and neutrality, I want to present another pertinent clinical example, this one involving my treatment of a homosexual man.

The patient is a 50-year-old man, married for eight years to another man. Though committed to his spouse, my patient is plagued with doubt as to whether the relationship ought to continue. "Fundamentally," he says, "I do not feel loved." Sessions are peppered with examples of what he means: a lack of tenderness, suspicions of infidelity, sustained periods of indifference, a lack of sexual desire. In spite of all of this, however, the patient remains uncertain. "Perhaps it's me," he repeatedly says. "Perhaps I'm making it up. Who knows? He thinks the relationship is great, just as it is. He says I'm crazy."

From a recent session:

I spent the weekend with Joan, one of my oldest closest friends. It was wonderful. The main thing about it was how delighted she seemed to be with me. She wanted to talk and talk. She was so happy for me when I told her about the deals I was putting together for work. She heard me out. She wanted to hear me out. I could tell by her face that nothing I said was causing her to feel burdened. And then it went the other way too. Once I knew she wanted to be with me, I wanted to be with her. Listening, whatever she wanted. She doesn't have an easy life. Kids aren't doing well. Husband is no gift. This is what I want. This kind of being together. It's possible. I know it is. I used to get it at school. They loved me. Kids who graduated after me remembered me in their graduation speeches.

Why do I put up with all of this? I know it's not necessary. But I can't state my case. I can't really draw a line.

[You're appealing to me to judge the soundness of your sense of things, of what you deserve, and of what you have.]

I don't trust myself. It could all be wrong.

Unlike in the first case, here, listening to this man, I do not wonder about the patient's flight from intimacy and connectedness to his spouse. Unlike the patient himself, I do indeed trust him. I do not think he is "wrong." Here, just as in the first case, my initial thought/impulse tilts me toward orienting the material around a flight from women, and not around a flight from a man. My hunch—another word, I think, for a thought grounded in sensuousness and identity ("gut")—is that the patient is "right," that his husband in fact denies him access to love and that the patient's pursuit of it, in this marriage, and perhaps even with men in general, is a doomed one. I do not immediately wonder what might be dangerous about homosexual intimacy, but rather what might be dangerous about heterosexual intimacy.

And, as with the first case, "flight" here refers to castration anxiety: flight from an encounter with a category of person, in this case, "woman," who too closely coincides with a dreaded image of irreparable deficiency.

I think the notion of "flight" qualifies as "neutral." It may be wrong, but if so, I consider it "neutrally" wrong. Orienting myself around an axis of flight simply means giving anxiety a central place in the determination of sexual object choice. The operative force of anxiety is flight. The impulse to flee is the central identifying marker of anxiety. I think that any impulse toward an object includes a contribution from an impulse to flee that object's negative complement.

As in the first case, what is decidedly non-neutral here is the presumptive tilt I give regarding flight's direction. This presumptive tilt precedes and informs my thinking. Of course, I hold myself back from voicing the tilted thought directly or even, I hope, indirectly. And it is precisely this "holding myself back" that warrants further scrutiny.

My ideal of neutral listening is in direct conflict with the actual non-neutrality that precedes and informs my listening. Non-neutrality—here, and, I think, more generally—infiltrates my mind as a kind of sensuous experience, pressing its own implicit claim to be interpreted as authentic, reliable, and self-evident. Neutrality, in contrast, lacks sensuousness. Its appeal is more abstract, conceptual, and counter-intuitive. It demands renunciation; more precisely, it demands the renunciation of the authority of sensuousness. Neutrality, in order to be realized, not only demands that I achieve a neutral posture in relation to my patient, but also that I achieve the same posture in relation to my own sensuousness. By "sensuousness" here, I refer to the entire set of meaningful experiences, grounded in my body, through which I position myself in relation to issues of reality and of pleasure. Neutrality demands that I foreswear allegiance to sensuousness, to the use of my own body as a moral/conceptual compass. It is a demand I cannot meet. The claims of sensuousness persist; I trust them no less than I trust the claims of neutral reason. In fact, I spot an important parallel here.

Listening to my two patients, I cannot achieve an actually neutral position as I contend with the problematic of flights-from vs movements-toward. A similar predicament holds between the claims of sensuousness and the claims of neutral reason: no matter which direction I move, I cannot confidently distinguish between flight-from and movement-toward.

After all, sensuousness may represent a regressive retreat—a flight from—the ruthless and disorienting demands of reason. Sensuousness also may represent a deep clear contact with a most basic stratum of human life, and movement toward it. Reason may represent a beacon of possibility, the only way forward, the only way to counteract the primitivity of sensuous givens. It also may represent flight— an anxious movement away from essential structure, a kind of denial of sensuous authority, an authority that, in fact, ironically may function as the ground for the neutral reason it seems, in the moment, to oppose.

Here, contending with the flight-from/pull-toward problem as it shows itself in the tension between sensuousness and reason, I feel capable of what seems a more neutral position than the one I'm in with my patients. I am uncertain of which of the two, sensuousness or reason, to actually trust, and my uncertainty seems to extend all the way down. I can think of no third term, no potentially reliable adjudicating referent. That is, I can maintain neutrality as long as I can refrain from action. Action itself, especially interpretive action, demands a momentary break from neutrality, a kind of lunging, toward or away from the pull of identity, toward or away from the pull of reason. One takes a stab at it and gets ready for the uncertainties to show up again immediately in the form of apparent consequences. This, then, is the clinical labor of pursuing neutrality, as best I know it: a state characterized by full engagement, too much information, insufficient confidence, and the intermittent necessity to act. The result, as with these two patients, is a continuous series of "looks," each made up of perceptually grounded flashes, of sensuous pulls, of conceptual correctives—a sequence of images cinematically strung together into a story whose sense simultaneously provides a balm, a relief, and a lure.

So, then, I return to the two patients and the ongoing problem of maintaining neutrality. From the point of view of "identity," heterosexuality makes immediate "sense" to me. That is, it rings sensuously true. It is more than a temptation; it is, and has been, a source. And although it carries a clear element of flight, a turn away from men, that turn, made perhaps long ago, feels "sensible." Confronting hetero-sexuality, then, in order to approach neutrality, I must work against the identifi-catory tilt demanded of me by way of my body's connection to my mind.

Homosexuality, however, makes less immediate "sense" to me. It feels like a temptation, a possibility best left abandoned, a risk too costly to take. I can imagine it, but, like imagining diving from cliffs, the images I find come to me in the form of warnings more than of enticements. That is, from the point of view of "identity," I must work to give homosexuality sensuous sense. And here I must work against my own disidentifying "identity" in order to achieve a "neutral" position.

In both cases, the pursuit of neutrality demands ongoing work against the sensuous demands of identity. And simultaneously, the necessity to speak from a position of sensuous identity demands ongoing work against the universalist claims of conceptual thought.

The analyst navigates in a zone bracketed on one side by the idiosyncratic demands of sensuous identity and on the other by the universalistic claims of conceptual thought. His/her direct, and complex, navigational aim is to optimally utilize both sides while running into neither. Avoiding crashes—this is the analyst's direct aim. The indirect aim is an always-elusive neutrality.

Chapter 6

Internalized homophobia in men

Wanting in the first-person singular, hating in the first-person plural[1]

In this chapter, I mean to address some of the vexing conceptual, clinical, and sociopolitical difficulties attached to the term *internalized homophobia*. For reasons not yet adequately theorized and too complex to be taken up here, internalized homophobia presents itself much differently in men than in women. Limiting my focus to men reflects the fact that it is mostly in men that internalized homophobia generates the extreme and unbearable states of mind—the suicidal and homicidal despair, the private and public emergencies—that I want to address.

I will use the term *internalized homophobia* as potentially applicable to anyone. In doing so, I am working against its conventional usage, where its application is limited to people whose primary object choice is homosexual. Conventionally used, internalized homophobia aims to describe, and to partially account for, a sexual identity characterized by persistent, structured negative feelings, particularly shame and self-loathing. Implicit in this use of the phrase is the idea that such feelings represent the dynamic outcome of an internalization of the dominant culture's attitude toward homosexuality.

The conventional restriction on the term's usage has at least two major determinants. First, it intends to give recognition to the fact that gay and lesbian people bear the brunt of the pain engendered by internalized homophobia. For heterosexuals, the internal interdiction against homosexual aims and objects will matter less, or at least less directly, as long as the availability of other aims and objects provides acceptable levels of erotic stability and pleasure. Second, since the homophobia internalized is conceptualized as an integral element of hetero-sexist prejudice and privilege, restricted usage of the term gives explicit recognition to the manifest and crucial dichotomy between victims and perpetrators.

1 Material from this chapter first appeared in Moss, D. (2002) "Internalized homophobia in men: Wanting in the first person singular, hating in the first person plural," *Psychoanalytic Quarterly*, 71: 21–50. Used with permission.

Brief clinical examples

The following two contrasting clinical situations may serve to illustrate the rationale for the conventional restriction of the term *internalized homophobia*, as well as illustrating, I think, some limits to the reach of that rationale.

Mr D

"I hate myself because I'm gay" was Mr D's chief complaint in seeking analytic treatment. That self-directed hatred, organized around and against his sexuality, pervaded Mr D's entire erotic, professional, and personal life. He was emotionally isolated, unable to work, hopeless, and "at my wit's end." His recent "coming out," which he had thought might have a cathartic, clarifying effect, had instead led to an increasing sense of personal disquiet and to a nearly intolerable intensification of long-standing tensions between himself and his parents. What he had hoped might be an affirmation had instead been experienced as a confession, an admission of something pathological inside of him. "They believe I'm sick," he said of his parents and others, "and maybe they're right."

Mr E

Mr E, a heterosexual man who was a promising opera singer, entered analytic treatment after a sudden loss of interest in his career. He was now working as a low-level clerk, had severed his musical connections, and spent most of his free waking hours daydreaming about various "important" pursuits in which he might indulge: pilot, doctor, mountain climber, explorer. Years into his treatment, he said of his decision to quit that "singing had somehow turned over on me." Associating to the sexual overtones of this phrase, he added, "The opera world is dominated by gay men. I could never tell whether they thought I was a good singer or I was cute. You are always putting on tights and makeup, girlie things. Everyone is scoping out everyone else. What was I doing there? Maybe I was there because I was meant to be. Maybe I was gay without knowing it. I had to get out."

Discussion

Although both Mr D and Mr E might be thought of as suffering from internalized fear and hatred of homosexual yearnings, the conventional restriction on the use of the term *internalized homophobia* would, of course, make it applicable only to Mr D. This restriction acknowledges that because Mr D was gay, his suffering from internalized homophobia was more acute, more generalized, and more fundamental—more an element of his very identity than the suffering of Mr E. It is indeed essential that that acknowledgment of difference be made.

Yet along with this manifest difference, the internally generated homophobic interdictions experienced by both Mr D and Mr E turned out to share common dynamic determinants. Both men fiercely identified with their fathers. For both, these identifications were, in part, ways of defending against an intolerable mix of sexual and murderous impulses associated with separating from their fathers. Mr D's fear that his erotic longings were "sick," as well as Mr E's urgent sense that he needed to "get out" from proximity to gay men, expressed a faint awareness in each of them of the threatening intensity with which they loved as an object, their fathers. That intensity was the danger. Both Mr D and Mr E wanted the father eliminated because the intensity with which they desired their fathers felt as though it were jeopardizing any chance for them to establish discreet identities of their own.

For each man, homosexuality, then, provided a means of satisfying a fantasy of erotic union with the father, while internalized homophobia provided a means by which to obliterate any sign of this fantasy. For each, the father exerted an unbearable erotic attraction, and each wanted the source of that attraction eradicated. Analytic work with both Mr D and Mr E, therefore, would hinge not on direct consideration of the different consequences each bore as a result of internalized homophobia; rather, it would revolve around consideration of the underlying envy of the father with which each man contended, in part by employing the internalization of homophobia to both express and obscure access to that envy.

A broader definition of internalized homophobia

To promote theoretical and clinical access to such shared underlying psycho-dynamics, I will not limit my considerations of internalized homophobia to people whose conscious object choice is homosexual. This broader application might leave unnamed the particular anguish experienced by gay and lesbian people when they find themselves harboring the very same prejudices against homosexuality that they encounter in the dominant culture. I recognize that both the processes by which those dominant culturally situated prejudices are internalized and the pain that follows such internalization are, indeed, particular, warranting categories of their own. I think, however, that we need not suppose that such categories will corres-pond and overlap with pertinent clinical ones.

By employing a broader, clinically oriented sense of the term, I intend to conceptualize internalized homophobia as a symptom. At a minimum, to think of it in this way is to think of internalized homophobia as the outcome of a trans-formation, the product of an unconscious process of substitution, a representa-tive of, or replacement for, something else. In any given person, the complex determinants of this process of substitution bear no directly discernible relationship to that person's conscious erotic aims and object choices. It is because we cannot read internalized homophobia's unconscious determinants by a direct reading of conscious aims and objects that we must theorize those determinants. The status of internalized homophobia is, in this regard, parallel to that of what might be called *internalized misogyny*. Certainly, in considering internalized misogyny, it would be absurd to compare the degree of conscious suffering of women with that of men. Nonetheless, were we to treat this stark and transparent material difference as a fundamental one in principle, we might indirectly inhibit access to a consideration of the generalized, fundamental fear of the feminine that afflicts both men and women. This in turn would leave us unable to pursue its nontransparent, even more fundamental, determinants.

I proceed with the clear understanding that substantial arguments exist against my proposed broadening of the conventional reach of the term *internalized homophobia*. Much of that understanding derives from an ongoing dialogue with Ralph Roughton, whose multifaceted work over many years has played a key role within American psychoanalysis in heightening our understanding of homophobia and our capacities to work against its malign influence. His clearly stated, deeply conceptualized point of view on the use of the phrase *internalized homophobia* warrants citation here:

> When one has grown up with a profound but vague sense of being defective, it helps to have a name for it. Appropriating that same name for the very "perpetrators" of the abuse seemed to trivialize the real experience of gay people. . . . Doesn't it make a difference whether one has in fact been abused or only had the fantasy of being potentially abused? . . . At a conceptual level, I agree that there is some unconscious dynamic similarity, but I think it is a mistake to use the same term for such different experience.
>
> (R. Roughton, personal communication, 2000)

I don't see internalized homophobia in gay people as a symptom substituting for something else. Yes, many homosexual people react symptomatically to their sexuality, but I think that comes long after the damage has begun. My concept of internalized homophobia is that it is not just about sex, but about self-concept. It starts before awareness of sexuality. It begins much earlier with a feeling that you are different, and that this difference is bad and must be kept a secret. This is also a way that internalized homophobia is different from racial, ethnic, or gender stigma. In each of those, you are at least like your family. The typical gay child does not fit the expectations of his family, realizes that he doesn't have the right kind of feelings and interests, and feels the ill-defined shame of inadequacy in his very being, without understanding why or what he has done wrong.

> My main point is that I do not agree that the same term is adequate to describe both conceptual formations. It may be a symptom in a heterosexual person, but in the homosexual person, it shapes the formation of identity and self-concept in a very significant way that I think is profoundly different. What is needed therapeutically is not to discover what the "symptom" substitutes for, but to alter one's basic concept of oneself.
>
> (R. Roughton, personal communication, 2000)

Whether it is most appropriate and most effective to employ the narrow or broad reach of the term *internalized homophobia* will depend, then, as Roughton so clearly articulated, on the level of presentation that one means to address. I think that in clinical work aimed at the presenting surface—at the conscious, identity-oriented dimension of internalized homophobia—the narrower use of the term is essential. Anything else would risk diluting the focus and drifting toward a distractingly abstract universalism. But if and when such clinical work runs into limits, that is, if, under the influence of analysis, the internalized homophobia loses its apparently integral, determining character and appears to have arisen as the result of a defensive transformation, then perhaps the broader usage might better apply. This kind of clinical development would be marked, at the minimum, by what might appear to be the symptom's apparently asocial tenacity, its persistence in spite of a thoroughgoing examination of its socially adaptive functions.

In this regard, I think of a gay man who, long after coming out, was plagued by the feeling that his sexuality, no matter how pleasurable, was fundamentally "sick." Being sick, as was revealed only after extensive analytic work, was the necessary ingredient for a sadomasochistic enactment with his otherwise indifferent doctor father. For this man, homosexuality had to be sick in order to make his filial homoeroticism effective. His sickness covertly mediated his wishes for both erotic and identificatory connections to his father. It also provided ample punishment for the hate-tinged sexuality through which he imagined such connections. Although—as with this man—such tenacity may indicate the profound effects of enduringly malignant, discreet, socially mediated determinants, it also marks the influence of ongoing, intrapsychic, collateral determinants of various sorts: defensive, wishful, and self-punitive ones. In the presence of such tenacity, then, internalized homophobia must be approached as deeply nested and thickly determined.

Internalized homophobia as a symptom

Homophobia is a symptom; internalized homophobia is also a symptom. Each, then, is "a sign of, and a substitute for, an instinctual satisfaction which has remained in abeyance" (Freud 1926: 91). Both homophobia and internalized homophobia take form as overt renunciations of something sexual. In both of these symptoms, the sexual drive is the immediate—proximate—presenting problem.

I am conceptualizing *drive* here as did Freud (1915b), as "the demand made upon the mind for work as a result of its connection to the body" (p. 122). Often, that demand is experienced as same-sex desire, which, for a multitude of interdicting factors, cannot be met. In such cases, homophobia and internalized homophobia are likely symptomatic outcomes. The interdicting factors include private fantasy, dyadic dynamics, and prevalent cultural norms. The sources of interdiction converge to target each of the component parts of the drive's demand. Homophobia explicitly targets the drive's object, while internalized homophobia targets the drive's aim and source.

Internalized homophobia is conceptually unstable. It can be used to describe relatively accessible dimensions of experience, and also to infer profoundly inaccessible unconscious dynamics. The various uses of this single term can easily contradict each other. What follows is an effort to conceptualize the predominantly unconscious determinants of internalized homophobia.

In homophobia, regardless of the external or internal target, the original source of anxiety is the *idea* that a particular homoerotic impulse is dangerous. In the construction of *externalized* homophobia (a conceptual redundancy), that idea is projected and reconfigured into a perception. One *sees* a version of what was, moments before, merely a thought. The sense that one is perceiving a danger is accompanied by an idea that, in principle, others can see that danger also. One *thinks* danger alone, but one *sees* it in company. The plural voice *sees* danger and hates its carrier. The idiosyncratic singular voice *thinks* danger and aims, alone, to avert it. The difference between the plural and singular voices is the difference between what seems like *knowledge* and what seems like *feeling*.

In the most benign development, with or without clinical intervention, the influence of this plural voice would vanish. What would be left would, at first, be anxiety-ridden impulse, felt as a private problem, subjectively structured in the voice of the idiosyncratic first-person singular. This kind of dynamic movement— away from a publicly grounded subjectivity, toward a privately grounded one— might be both the evidence for and the test of increased internal capacities. The externally located, neurotically derived, frightening object would have undergone a retransformation back toward its original condition as a frightening impulse.

More malignantly, thought itself is fixedly transformed into an object of perception. One then sees danger in one's own thoughts, and this danger, since it is perceived, can no longer endure as an object of thought. Parts of one's own mind thus lose their status as "words," and now—perhaps again—become objects of perception, "things." The domain of the phobia is expanding. Danger has been externalized into the phobic object, but the phobic object is insufficient to its task of containment. *Idea* now loses its crucial status of *trial action*; it turns into an object of certainty, a perception. Dangerous impulse has again been displaced, but only from one part of the mind to another: one sees danger signs, yes, but the signs, even though experienced as percepts, are still inside and cannot be fled.

Under the influence of internalized homophobia, gay and lesbian people live out a paradoxical relation to their desired objects. This paradox can be outlined as follows: since their erotic equilibrium depends upon both a vigilant avoidance of the object and a vigilant renunciation of the aim, success in object finding leads to subjective impoverishment, rather than to subjective enrichment, to disorganization rather than to synthesis. The conclusion of one's erotic work—object finding— annuls, rather than fulfills, the promise of its beginning—object seeking. When the object is found and the aim achieved, the subject is defiled. The affirmative, hopeful dimension of object choice is eclipsed by the certainty that finding the object will only make things worse. One hates oneself for wanting what one wants, and, therefore, for being what one is. The founding opposition between desire and repulsion collapses, and the result is a fundamental stasis. Instead of being the site of possibility and redemption, the object merely taunts. The yield of both wishing and identifying, of pursuing what one wants and who one wants to be, is a vicious narrative of repeated promise and repeated disappointment. Love damns rather than redeems.

When the pain associated with such apparently irresolvable conflicts becomes itself intolerable—when internalized homophobia as a symptom can no longer bind and contain its own determinants—the result can lead to murder and suicide. The killer intends to finally obliterate the homosexual subject and/or object. This most extreme measure might seem to be a necessity when the symptomatic transformations that have established the object as repressed, displaced, feared, and hated have all failed. A sense of this malignant sequence of transformations is vividly conveyed in a documentary entitled *Licensed to Kill* (1998). This film shows excerpts of interviews with men who have killed homosexual men. Each man refers to an experience of rage prior to the killings. Without exception, the rage is accounted for as a reaction to someone's assumption that the killer might be open to homosexual activity. One man is particularly articulate, and he tells of his long hatred of whatever inside him drove him to seek homosexual contact. In addition to this source of pain, he spoke of the egregious insult associated with frequently being rejected in such encounters. He found it especially terrible to be rejected while doing what he "hated having to do in the first place."

"Hating having to do [it] in the first place"—this man's description of his own relation to homoerotic impulses—is the exemplary subjective marker of an erotic life substantially shaped by symptomatic internalized homophobia. For this individual, the manifest costs of the symptom were dear, yet they still did not purchase stability. His solution to this two-pronged insult of high costs and no return was to effect a further transformation. Unable by means of internalized homophobia to rid himself of his own homosexual aims, he did his best to rid the world of his homosexual objects.

A literary example of internalized homophobia

A paragraph of Hubert Selby's novel *Last Exit to Brooklyn* (1957), which I have discussed elsewhere from a different perspective (Moss 2001), provides another example of this marker—"hating having to do [it] in the first place" (although psychodynamically, the complaint might be more precisely registered as "loving it in the first place; but in the second place, hating both it and anything in myself that once loved it"). The novel describes the reactions of Harry, the main character, as he watches his infant son:

> Harry looked at his son as he lay on the table playing with a diaper. He covered his head with it and giggled. Harry watched him wave the diaper for a few seconds. He looked at his son's penis. He stared at it, then touched it. He wondered if an eight-month-old kid could feel anything different there. Maybe

it felt the same no matter where you touched him. It got hard sometimes when he had to piss, but he didn't think that meant anything. His hand was still on his son's penis when he heard his wife walking into the room. He pulled his hand away. He stood back. Mary took the clean diaper from the baby's hand and kissed his stomach. Harry watched her rub the baby's stomach with her cheek, her neck brushing his penis occasionally. It looked as if she were going to put it in her mouth. He turned away. His stomach knotted, a slight nausea starting.

(Selby 1957: 117)

Harry's lush and idiosyncratic, homoerotic daydream is instantaneously trans-formed into a stock, prototypical tale of a woman's insatiable heterosexual appetite: *she* was going to put it in her mouth. We see the internal origin of Harry's desire—his aroused curiosity regarding his son's penis. He is safe in this condition of aroused desire only when alone with his object. Arousal turns dangerous with the arrival of his wife; she is the bearer of interdiction. For Harry, the interdiction seems to arise simultaneously from both within and without. What puts Harry into danger is his own sexual aim, and what signals that danger is the appearance of his wife. Harry attacks the signal and represses the aim. After this two-pronged attack, the danger persists, but has been transformed; it is now located entirely in his wife, who is both erotically transgressive and erotically interdicting. As with the classically described construction of a phobia, danger has been condensed, displaced, and externalized.

"It looked as if she were going to put it in her mouth." Harry, safely nauseous, and thus no longer caught up in his own sexual and identificatory appetites, is now the one who would interdict his wife's unregulated sexual appetite. The internal world safe again, Harry can try to flee danger located externally. Selby catches that effort well when he describes how, minutes later, their child asleep, Harry and his wife take to their own bed:

Mary rolled over onto her back when Harry came into the room. She said nothing, but watched him undress—Harry turning his back toward her and piling his clothes on the chair by the bed—Mary looking at the hair on the base of his spine, thinking of the dirt ingrained in the calluses on his hands and under his fingernails. Harry sat on the edge of the bed for a moment, but it was inevitable; he would have to lie down next to her. He lowered his head to the pillow, then lifted his legs onto the bed, Mary holding the covers up so he could slide his legs under. She pulled the covers up to his chest and leaned on her side facing him . . . He could control nothing. The fuckin' bitch. Why can't she just leave me alone. Why don't she go away somewhere with that fuckin' kid.

(Selby 1957: 118–119)

The sequence Selby depicts is clear and exemplary. In his erotic reverie with his son, Harry is wanting in the first-person singular; he is alone with his object; his aims are hazy and tentative. Then, with the appearance of a third party, his wanting is discovered. The threatening external world has made itself known. The world, in the form of his wife, now wants Harry to want only what it wants him to want, nothing other and nothing more. Harry's singular desire collapses under the weight of his sense of the world's demands. He cannot resist it, cannot simultaneously endure those demands and his own desires. His collapse is fleeting, however. He recovers access to passion via the transformation of first-person singular wanting, now proven fragile. This transformation ends with Harry's occupation of what seems like a much less fragile position. Hating both his wife and son, he abandons his dangerous individual voice and identifies with the men of a beleaguered masculinity. Via this identification, Harry's voice takes on the plural valence of a homogeneous crowd.

Harry's singular wanting begins with his contact with his son and with his son's penis. Harry "watches," "looks," "stares," "touches," and "wonders." He seems to be simultaneously desiring and identifying with his son, engaging in a kind of reverie about the sexual links between the two of them. This reverie is private and singular. Harry is alone and is tentatively relating to a newly emerging object. When his wife enters the room, Harry's psychic economy undergoes a sudden transformation: "He pulled his hand away. He stood back." Harry is suddenly exposed to the presence of a potentially condemning third party. Alone with his object, Harry seemed outside the reach of danger, but now, suddenly exposed to this third-party presence, Harry is stricken with anxiety. His reverie ends, and with it his erotized identification with his son. He is still alone, but his first-person singular sensation of erotic excitement has been replaced by nausea and a "knotted" stomach, both of which are also first-person singular experiences.

But this aloneness begins to erode as Harry envisions his wife "about to put it in her mouth." Unlike the emerging and unfinished picture of his son that the singular-voiced Harry was constructing, the terrifying specter of his wife comes to him fully formed. Whereas the relation to his son was earlier mediated by fantasy and idea, the relation to his wife is here mediated by what seems like direct perception. Harry no longer "wonders"; instead, he sees: "It looked as if she were going to put it in her mouth." Unlike the son, then, the wife is not experienced as *his* psychically constructed object, but rather as an empirical object, a figure in the world, embodying uncontrolled sexual appetite, a figure with which Harry, and men like him, must contend. Harry is now in the presence of a nearly mythic figure, the insatiable woman. This emergent figure comes into stark relief for him when he and his wife are in bed: "He could control nothing. The fuckin' bitch. Why can't she just leave me alone. Why don't she just go away somewhere with that fuckin' kid."

With this image of being left alone, left safe from insatiable feminine wanting, Harry implicitly links himself to a world of frightened, self-righteous, and self-regulated men, acting in self-defense, and joined together against the erotic contagion borne by women and children. He begins the sequence aroused and wanting; he ends the sequence aroused and wanting. The cardinal difference between the beginning and the end is that in the beginning, his wanting is expressed in the first-person singular voice: his wishes are tentative; his object is opaque. In the end, however, he is no longer alone; his wishes are certain, his object transparent. Now he is, in his own mind, a man amongst men. Like them and with them, his wanting is organized around the experience of hating. His wife has replaced his son as the primary object. Harry's blunt new aim is simply that she vanish.

Freud (1915b) captured well the endpoint of this volatile dynamic by which love, when dangerous, is transfigured into hate: "The ego hates, abhors, and pursues with intent to destroy all objects which are a source of unpleasurable feeling for it, without taking into account whether they mean a frustration of sexual satisfaction" (p. 138). What I mean to designate here as internalized homophobia is the conceptual midpoint in this transformation of object love into object hate: the moment when wanting, located internally, is treated as a threat. The subject has retreated from the dangerous object, but is still possessed by the wish that put him or her into danger in the first place. This wish now becomes the target of defense. En route to finally hating the external object, one will also "hate, abhor, and pursue with intent to destroy" anything internal whose influence might have contributed to the subject's reckless proximity to the dangerous object. When the object in question is dangerous because it is same-sexed, this attack against anything that has brought the subject near that object attack warrants the label *internalized homophobia*.

The plural voice we sense in Harry's "Why don't she go away somewhere with that fuckin' kid" is a combined, synthetic voice, one that yokes nature and culture. It corresponds to the conventional sense of internalized homophobia. In that moment of exasperated resignation, Harry does indeed appear to have taken in the culture's aggressive prohibitions against homoerotic desire. He also seems to have taken in its (probably related) inclination to read women as transgressive provocateurs.

But this taking in of cultural norms, including the homophobic one, is not simply a passive process. While the culture does indeed write itself on Harry's available sexual slate, Harry is also furiously at work, writing himself on the culture's slate, borrowing all he can from it in order to solve the terrible problem posed by a sexuality for which he cannot find adequate words, a sexuality that puts his identity at too great a risk and thus remains too private to be affirmatively spoken of. We sense Harry's actively seeking out, and easily finding, culturally located fantasies through which he can reconfigure his entire relationship to his own disruptive sexuality. Once these cultural fantasies are identified, his dangerous ideas can be transformed into dangerous perceptions. In the moment of resolution, when he finds himself hating his wife and son and wishing them gone, subjectivity and objectivity have converged. Harry is no longer a single individual who wonders what meanings should be attached to the fragments of desire available to him. Instead, he has become a kind of icon, a man like any man, who simply wants the bad things to vanish. In stark contrast to his tentative encounter with his son, for

Harry at this point, there is nothing idiosyncratic, nothing merely his, in the elemental wish to be left alone.

A blending of nature and culture

We can hear the same effort to synthesize nature and culture, to turn idea into perception, whenever we hear the accusation "faggot," to give a common example. The word attacks both the externally located object and any internal aim that might lead to proximity with that object. The word defines its hated objects, internal and external, and calls out for their exile, elimination, and disappearance.

This was brutally exemplified in the trial testimony that led to Private Calvin Glover's conviction for premeditated murder in the killing of a gay colleague. One witness reported that his drill sergeant unapologetically bellowed a homophobic cadence in leading the platoon on a five-mile run: "Faggot, faggot down the street/Shoot him, shoot till he retreats" (SLDN 2000). The cadence here marks homosexuality as a perceptible violation of the order of things, and identifies the first-person plural chorus—with danger extirpated internally and clearly located externally—as the voice of both law and order.

The synthetic "we," exposed so vividly in this cadence, is present, though usually in more muted form, even when the accusatory label of "faggot" (or any of its semantic kin) is self-directed, as is often the case in internalized homophobia. Material obtained from the analysis of a heterosexual man in his forties, Mr F, might serve to illustrate this. What follows is taken from the beginning of a Monday session, just after a weekend during which Mr F learned that his wife might never be able to get pregnant, and that a cardiac arrhythmia had been discovered in his younger brother. (The patient's father had died of a heart attack while in his fifties.)

Mr F: I'm thinking of both of them [his brother and his wife]. I'm afraid of caring too much. Afraid it means I'm a fruit. Too much expression. I feel such a loss—never being able to have a child. It's fruity how intense I feel. It's being a coward and weak; it's not a man. I'm too sensitive. I'm afraid of being gay. It's a matter of not being oriented properly, the way the world wants you to be. Everything I say now sounds cowardly. Even if I'm gay, I know I'm also straight. I'm sure of that, but still there's this—being a fruit. I want to be expressive, that's the problem. Maybe I'm overly affected, then I don't express enough.

Analyst: You're afraid, but unsure of what, and also aren't sure of what it might feel like to be so afraid in front of me.

Mr F: I know what I'm afraid of. I'm afraid my brother and I are both going to die.

This kind of accusation—"fruit," with its direct appeal to the external world, its implicit endorsement of and identification with a packaged version of unambiguous masculinity—catches both the active and passive dimensions of internalized homophobia. While struggling against the internalized and unwanted cultural norm that equates masculinity with constricted expression, the patient is also putting that norm to defensive use. He strives to identify with a masculinity whose strength he hopes will protect him and whose equation of affectivity and "fruitiness" he hopes will supplement his own taxed powers of inhibition. This employment of a cultural supplement, this identificatory appeal to plurality, makes such a form of self-reproach distinct. The plural voice seems to be asking something like: "Who are you, a mere individual, a fruit, to defy us?" This contrasts with the idiosyncratic singular voice of the condemning, imperious superego, whose presence is so familiar to us in daily clinical work.

Sociocultural condemnation versus superego condemnation

At least since the time of "The ego and the id" (Freud 1923), we have been theoretically equipped to hear, conceptualize, and interpret the superego's singular voice of condemnation as a monument to parental authority:

> The superego arises, as we know, from an identification with the father taken as a model. Every such identification is in the nature of a desexualization or even of a sublimation. It now seems as though when a transformation of this kind takes place, an instinctual defusion occurs at the same time. After sublimation, the erotic component no longer has the power to bind the whole of the destructiveness that was combined with it, and this is released in the form of an inclination to aggression and destruction. This defusion would be the source of the general character of harshness and cruelty exhibited by the ideal—its dictatorial "Thou shalt."
>
> (Freud 1923: 54–55)

Another brief clinical example may be illustrative here. Mr G, also a man in his forties, while speaking of an ongoing problem with inhibited ambition, remarked, "Wanting or trying to do something, anything, just brings on the damning voice. 'Who are you,' it says, 'to want that?'" What is most notable here, I think, is that, although Mr G was inhibited by a feeling of "Who are you to want that?" the "you" is not categorized; it is neither "faggot" nor "fruit." The accusation carries no name, no explicit signifier, and thus lacks a public dimension, lacks reach or projection into the external world. Therefore, the accusation is experienced by the patient as a private matter, a problem, as it were, between his superego and ego. It is this absence of an identifiable external dimension, and, therefore, the lack of any immediate sign of internalization of a specific, culturally mediated sanction, that I think is representative of the condemning first-person singular voice that Freud was describing in the quotation above. There is no immediate sign of an external dimension in the accusation. Rather, we must theorize the history of the external world's presence in it, to infer, via traces, the influence of now abandoned object relations.

In the case of Mr G, even though the source of this voice's prohibitive authority was inaccessible, the patient knew that source to be in *his* contemporary interior, and, therefore, to have its origins in his historical involvement with the objects of his world. That knowledge structured his treatment. No matter how difficult our analytic work was, Mr G and I both enjoyed the confidence stemming from our shared sense that that which constricted him was, at base, something other than the world—a subjectivity laden with worldly history, but nonetheless a discreet entity whose every particular was, in principle, within our therapeutic reach. No such confidence is available when condemnation takes on the voice of a much wider plurality—anonymous, unanimous, and extraparental. At such times, the patient's identity bearings, as well as our therapeutic ones, become considerably less stable.

At its most fundamental levels of operation, homophobia's first-person plural voice is the voice of taboo. Since a thorough examination of homophobia's status as taboo is beyond the scope of this chapter, a descriptive sketch will have to suffice. For that sketch, I rely heavily on Gayle Rubin's highly influential essay "The traffic in women: Notes on the 'political economy' of sex" (1975). According to Rubin:

> The incest taboo presupposes a prior, less articulate taboo on homosexuality. A prohibition against some heterosexual unions assumes a taboo against non-heterosexual unions. Gender is not only an identification with one sex; it also entails that sexual desire be directed toward the other sex. The sexual division of labor is implicated in both aspects of gender—male and female it creates them, and it creates them heterosexual. The suppression of the homosexual component of human sexuality, and by corollary, the oppression of homosexuals, is therefore a product of the same system whose rules and relations oppress women.
>
> (Rubin 1975: 180)

> Some basic generalities about the organization of human sexuality can be derived from an exegesis of Lévi-Strauss's theories of kinship. These are the incest taboo, obligatory heterosexuality, and an asymmetric division of the sexes.
>
> (Rubin 1975: 183)

As with the plural voice of any taboo, internalized homophobia's plural voice regulates appetites—in this case, sexual ones. Homosexual aims and objects are meant to feel unrealizable, just as insects or dogs are meant to feel inedible, for example. When such regulations are firmly in place, we do not sense them as having either an internal or an external origin. We are not meant to feel merely that *I* do not like to eat dogs or insects; instead, we must believe that using dogs or insects as food is transgressive per se. The regulatory force of internalized homophobia governs whom it is possible to be by stipulating whom it is possible to have. Families and cultures do the internalizing work of civilization. That work is most successful when it is least apparent, when it is in fact undetectable. And it is least apparent when people sense that the conditions placed on their achievement of satisfaction and a sense of personal identity are immutable.

Such restrictions then seem, like oneself, an integral part of the way things are, have been, and always will be. The limits on what one can do, want, and have—on one's aims and objects—seem not like limits at all. Rather, they seem an integral part of reality; what they prohibit seems to be a violation of reality. Under such conditions, transgressive impulses, such as, for example, homosexual ones, will appear to violate not only internal and external prohibitions, which in principle might be sensed as contingent; more important, they will appear to violate the permanent order of things. Within that permanent order—in fact, at the very heart of that order—is the interdiction of transgressive impulses. Clinically, we sense the presence of internalized homophobia only when its operations are not completely successful, when, in spite of all the force mustered against it, transgressive impulse makes its presence known.

Descriptive clinical vignettes

Mr C

The following vignette from Mr C's treatment typifies some of the dynamics and consequences of what I think is usually meant by *internalized homophobia*. In its typicality, the situation can and must be read transparently, as the operation of straightforward oppressive power.

One day, Mr C and his male lover were walking together in public. A car stopped to let them cross. Mr C was surprised and pleased: New York City, gracious driver, safe place. As they passed the car, however, the driver screamed out the window: "C'mon, girls, get moving!" Upon hearing this, the first thing Mr C was aware of was a wish to smash the car and kill the driver. He inhibited himself and kept walking. Within minutes, he had a rush of feeling that stayed with him for some time: how helplessly transparent he and his lover were, how visible their "queerness" was, and how disgusting they were. He suddenly found himself allied with the driver in a shared contempt for himself, his lover, and for the very notion of coupled men.

This is a brutal example, as well as a representative one, of the combined effects of power and sexuality. A symptomatic expression of sexuality—in this case, the driver's sadistic homophobia—may originate externally. The driver's taunting provoked a chain of reactions in the patient that ended with his joining with the driver—internalizing him—and taunting himself. This internalization was defensive. To have resisted the driver's sadistic taunt, to have kept it external, would have meant that Mr C had to endure not only the driver's hatred, but also his own reactive and transparently dangerous wish to kill the driver. For Mr C, this impulse to kill was itself a conscious marker of his effort to preserve the integrity of both his homosexual identity in general, and his erotic relation to his lover in particular.

Less consciously, the murderous impulse resonated with Mr C's abundant and bitter memories of a self-involved father, bizarrely out of touch and chronically unable to recognize his own son. The association between the contemporary taunt and these childhood memories, now laced with vengeful patricidal fantasy, made the impulse to kill unbearable. Mr C could not tolerate the disorganizing threat posed by the possibility of its generalization, nor his sense that the driver was merely giving voice to a widespread feeling, one the patient originally located in his father, that "people want me to disappear from the face of the earth." It was safer for Mr C to contend with the self-limiting and self-directed violence of internalized homophobia than to face the potentially limitless violence associated with fantasies of retribution. Its limitlessness was a product not of the immediate provocation, but of the relation between that provocation and Mr C's history. The murderous impulse against which he had to defend would have as its target not only today's driver, but also a pyramid of associated objects, the base of which was formed by the patient's earliest recollections of his father's wish "to have me disappear from the face of the earth."

For Mr C, this process took place with such immediacy and such force that its discreet, particular elements blurred, and they were unavailable as objects of thought or working through. His vengeful, homicidal wish put the patient in danger. The internalized homophobia that followed turned on the repression of that wish. The safer resolution of "we hate me" displaced its more dangerous predecessor, "I want to kill him."

In the session following this incident, Mr C spoke of how hard it was to be in my presence. Our similarities now seemed meager compared to our differences. In the past, the patient had affectionately and slowly "queered" me, by which he meant that he had found in me sufficient evidence of both an affinity for and identification with outsiders, so that my presumed heterosexuality lost much of its importance as a marker of my essentially alien identity. But now the best we could muster would be an icy standoff, he believed, with neither of us harming the other. The incident on the street had had the effect of reinstalling sexual preference as an essential marker of identity, and homophobia as an insurmountable, bedrock condition. Mr C noted that "you're either on one side or the other."

I commented that keeping us elementally separate like this seemed a safe way for him to manage an otherwise destabilizing mix of affectionate, violent and vengeful impulses, all simultaneously aimed at me. The mix would surface only were he to feel that we were back in our usual degree of contact and intimacy, with me in my usual position as "queer." His transiently internalized homophobia attacked both his analyst and his lover; that is, he now renounced analysis as impossible, just as he had recently renounced his homosexuality as impossible. Each renunciation was the direct result of an encounter with sadistic homophobia. The internalization of that homophobia provided a kind of terrible safety, since an identity infused with a continuous and containable, endurable, internal violence was preferable to an identity lost via the limitless consequences of externally directed violence.

It should be remembered that a gay person takes in from the surrounding object world—internalizes—ideas, judgments, and sentiments that directly oppose and attack his or her own sexual impulses toward that object world. The taking in, however painful its consequences, can be transparently seen, and thus interpreted, as an act of adaptation. It is more or less rationally designed to preserve one's precarious place in that object world. The internalization of homophobia here transforms an unstable and unbearable situation of danger into a more stable, more bearable, situation of pain and renunciation.

Mr C's situation exemplifies the conventional use of the term *internalized homophobia* discussed at the beginning of this chapter. We can see in this patient what Roughton (personal communication, 2000) might have been referring to when he noted that internalized homophobia "shapes in a very significant way the formation of identity and self-concept." But Mr C's case also seems to me to exemplify the symptomatic status of internalized homophobia, its status as a relatively stable transformation of a prior unstable condition. In addition to suffering the effects of what seemed like a direct assault on his identity, Mr C also appeared to have symptomatically and defensively identified with the aggressor— here, the driver of the car, and earlier, his father—thus transforming a raw, murderous impulse into a sadistically tinged, self-directed one.

Mr A

The following account is derived from the first year of Mr A's analysis, and is intended to highlight some of the operations of internalized homophobia in a heterosexual man.

Mr A was the youngest of four children and the only boy. When he was 5 years old, his parents divorced. He was left alone "in a house full of girls." He remembered frequently seeing his mother naked through her partially open bedroom door. He was "disgusted" by her "big black bush": "It was the ugliest thing I had ever seen." She often took his temperature rectally and "pinched me on the butt." He also remembered hearing her "moaning" at night, and associated the sound to something sexual that he was unable to figure out.

Mr A welcomed his father's visits during childhood, since "he could take me away from that." But his father's visits were also painful because his father was openly competitive with Mr A, becoming furious and rejecting when outperformed. The patient came to realize that "I had to do it alone." He further resolved his problems by asserting that "I was going to want nothing. My parents had nothing I wanted. Girls were ridiculous, and no boy could compete with me. People were disgusting to me. I was the best at everything; I had it all."

Regarding his erotic/aggressive attachments to both his parents—a mother sensed as excessively sexual, and a father perceived as both too absent and too competitive—Mr A's primary defensive operation was the transformation of dangerous wishes for attachment and union into dangerous objects to be kept at bay. He was transfixed by his mother, caught by his fascination with her body. He would excitedly rummage through her drawers and peek into her room, hoping to get a glimpse of what, when found, would only frighten him.

Mr A further recalled that when he was six years old, he decided that he would no longer spend time at home. After school, he would go downtown, shopping, wandering around, anything. "I was the only 6-year-old around who could take care of himself like that," he recalled proudly. "I wanted nothing more to do with my mother. She was crazy! She couldn't keep her hands off me." He found safety in this narrative of abusive seduction. His mother was the only danger.

Mr A employed a similar defensive tactic in regard to his father. "I have never loved anyone like I loved him," he recalled. But this yearning entailed an excessive risk of abandonment and retaliation. Mr A once had a running race with his father, and realized that he, the boy, was faster than the man. "That was the end of it," Mr A related. "I was finished with him. He was weak and helpless." Both parents had now been dealt with. And by the time Mr A was 8 years old, he was spending almost all of his time alone. "I was fine—I was already a man. The less I had to do with any of them, the better."

The patient's feeling that he was "already a man" lasted until puberty, when he began to feel overwhelmed by sexual urgency. But girls frightened him: "I couldn't get the image of that black bush out of my mind." He was a star athlete and an honor student. He sought the company of "the cool kids," but "I never fit in. They always knew what to do with each other, and I didn't get it."

At around this time, Mr A first became aware of the category *homosexual*. "I didn't get that either; how could a boy like a boy? It was sick. They were like girls. No way could I ever be like that! Me and my friends had nothing to do with them. They were weird, like from another planet." Mr A's predicament in adolescence resonated with his predicament from childhood. His own desires again drew him into danger. If directed toward girls, he was reminded of the "black bush" and its excesses. If toward boys, as he had desired his father, his masculinity seemed jeopardized. And as had been the case in childhood, his solution was again to externalize the dangers.

In childhood, it was the crazy mother, as well as the weak and useless father, from whom Mr A designed means of flight, whereas in adulthood, it was *the homosexual* who housed danger and from whom he could flee. Both the "black bush" and the weak and useless father were condensed into the figure of the promiscuous sissy: "All they want is to get fucked in the ass. It's dirty; there's no end to it. Go that way and it's all over." This externalizing resolution, like that of Selby's character Harry, originated in Mr A's desire to preserve object ties with his mother and father.

Links to both the patient's parents were excessively erotized. Here, for example, is a representative recollection from Mr A about his mother: "She always used to pinch my ass as a way of saying hello. 'How cute your body is,' she would say. I never knew what to do. There was something I wanted from her, but not that, and I couldn't figure out what it was." And, also representative, here is a typical memory of his father's remarks to him: "Don't try to hide that little thing. I've seen it, and that's just the way it is. Boys' are little; their dads' are big." It is evident from these accounts that Mr A's task was to figure out ways to protect object relations with both parents, and for this he had to dilute the excessive sexuality and aggression that permeated them.

The patient's "discovery" of the category of homosexuality in adolescence proved useful. Homosexuality became the dangerous category whose negation, both internally and externally, was the precondition for Mr A to affirm the safety of his own interiority. Heterosexuality, for Mr A, was what remained once sexual excesses had been purged. This solution, the barren product of a massive retreat, brought him scant sexual fulfillment—he remained abstinent throughout adolescence. But it did bring him a sense of safety. His most pronounced, covertly sexual, and symptomatic activity in high school consisted of locating and renouncing male homosexual classmates. By late adolescence, then, for Mr A, the most threatening sexual dangers were firmly located in the external homosexual object.

But this solution was not stable. Trying his hand at heterosexual relations, Mr A found himself intermittently impotent. He accounted for this by viewing it as a result of his early exposure to his mother, but this thought failed to comfort him. And for the first time, he began to be afraid that other people, particularly homosexual men, would look at him and see something in his manner—his clothing, eyes, or gestures—that would give them the idea that he, too, was homosexual. He assiduously costumed himself as masculine, but that, too, failed. He wondered whether his exaggerated manner of dressing would be noticed. He grew increasingly anxious, self-conscious about where he placed his hands and legs, and worried about the rhythm of his speech. He then became concerned that his pursuit of the perfect heterosexual posture produced, in fact, exactly the kind of constant preening that had long been for him a marker of male homosexuality. He could then be neither spontaneous nor careful, since each tactic threatened him with exposure. He turned to prostitutes and massage parlors, but could not rid himself of the awareness that he was "trying to prove something." All that had once been effective now seemed to boomerang.

Mr A's previous equilibrium had depended on the externalization and objectification of dangerous "homosexual" objects. As long as they could be kept external, his interior would, by a kind of never-to-be-tested inference, remain safe. This indirect affirmation proved insufficient in the face of heterosexual impotence. Overwhelmed—as he had once been in childhood—by the convergence of affectionate yearnings and the female genital, Mr A found that his externalization collapsed. Around women whom he liked, he felt completely unsure of himself. "I wish I had their power," he remarked wistfully. But this yearning to identify with what he most wanted was unbearable. Now the dangerous object—a layered construction of the feminine and the homosexual—could no longer be kept outside.

Finally, Mr A sought analysis. His first statements to me about himself were: "I can't get a woman," "I constantly worry about whether I'm gay," and "I can never tell what I think or feel."

The patient's ongoing effort to secure a sense of masculine identity posed a quandary typical for many men. Masculinity felt like an attribute he was missing. It, therefore, had to be found in other men, then cultivated, and finally internalized. Mr A thus yearned to be with the kind of men who could provide him with the masculinity he craved. Joined with them, feeling himself at one with them, he could almost identify with them, thus partaking in a masculinity that he sensed was originally theirs.

A hallmark of the masculinity sought by Mr A was a complete absence of any sign of homoerotic desire. The man Mr A wanted to be in fantasy was a man who desired only to be with women. For Mr A, any sign of a desire for what a man already had was a sign that one was not already a man, and, therefore, an indication of potential femininity. The intense desire to become a man through being with men, even when satisfied, thus invalidated the very masculinity that it might achieve. Mr A could not tolerate being a man because this experience was inevitably infiltrated with a simultaneous experience of *wanting* to be a man. In the first-person singular voice, such wanting was too close to wanting to be with a man. That voice was transformed, then, into its plural form: "Men like us, who desire nothing from each other, hate men like them, who desire everything from each other."

But this transformation was also ineffective. It offered Mr A nothing in his relations with women, and its tactic of masquerade, of successfully "passing" as the man the patient wanted to be, became the paradigmatic sign of masculine failure. Now, everywhere he looked—inside and outside—Mr A confronted an infiltrating homoerotic desire from which he could no longer manage even temporary escape. Only upon reaching such desperation could he finally, via analysis, turn to a man—this time perhaps not for immediate reconfiguration, but for enduring help.

Conclusion

Internalized homophobia is a symptomatic structure. Conceptually, it is best thought of as a multilevel phenomenon. At a minimum, it refers both to the widespread internalization of the dominant culture's interdiction against homosexuality and to a particular individual's defensive, and possibly idiosyncratic, employment of that interdiction. Because it is in part the product of an individual's shaping of him- or herself in accord with normative pressures, internalized homophobia is experienced in the first-person plural voice. The force of internalized homophobia's first-person plural voice stems from its promise of safety and power. The normatively freighted plurality *we* identifies the individual as a member of a strong, masculine collective. The first-person plural voice in men thus simultaneously satisfies homoerotic yearning and protects against it; it forbids union between men while promising solidarity amongst men.

In internalized homophobia, *we* yokes the threatened to the strong. In unanimous voice, individuals banding together can then identify, segregate, and attack what is outside/dangerous/deficient. Those who are unable to find sufficient private resources with which to deal with transgressive, sexually-driven sources of anxiety can thus bind with their "betters" in common assault against an external, despised, common enemy. This binding together of vulnerable men provides the identificatory exoskeleton for the homophobic first-person plural narrative. In the homophobic male imagination, homosexuality circulates via the violence of unbidden penetration, while male heterosexuality, forever threatened, circulates via peaceful and reciprocal exchange.

Lest we forget the stakes involved, I conclude this chapter with two quotations, each representing the destination toward which the logic of homophobia points:

> It's because we're men like them that the SS will finally prove powerless before us. It's because they shall have sought to call the unity of this human race into question that they'll finally be crushed. Yet their behavior, and our situation, are only a magnification, an extreme caricature—in which nobody wants or is perhaps able to recognize himself—of forms of behavior and of situations that exist in the world, that even make up the existence of that older "real world" we dream about. For in fact everything happens in that world as though there were a number of human species, or, rather, as though belonging to a single human species wasn't certain, as though you could join the species or leave it, could be halfway in it or belong to it fully, or never belong to it, try though you might for generations, division into races or classes being the canon of the species and sustaining the axiom we're always prepared to use, the ultimate line of defense: "They aren't people like us."
>
> (Antelme 1957: 219)

> Being a very drunk homofobick I flipped out and began to pistol whip the fag with my gun. [From a letter written in jail by Aaron McKinney, one of the convicted murderers of Matthew Shepard.]
>
> (Loffreda 2000: 114)

Chapter 7

On situating homophobia[1]

Given the apparently profound advances in gay and lesbian civil rights over the past two decades, this chapter, with its focus on AIDS and the homophobia it both illuminated and spawned, may seem anachronistic. If it does, indeed, prove to be anachronistic, the anachronism will be social and historical. That is, virulent passions will have been quieted. We will have moved on to a new period. Regulatory forces will have undergone adjustment. There can be no doubt that such historical movement represents benign change. I think, though, that no matter how benign the change, and how far-reaching its effects, prudence is called for if we attempt a psychoanalytic judgment regarding what, in fact, has happened. By, "in fact" here, I mean "structurally." Psychoanalytic inquiry regarding this matter seems to me, then, to necessarily be organized around two related questions: 1) What happened during the AIDS crisis that so enraged a relatively latent homophobia and so permitted its once suppressed expression? and 2) What has happened since? Has the passing of AIDS as a catastrophic and untreatable American plague influenced the subsequent burst of liberalizing legislation and sentiment? If it has, what can we say about underlying structural change? Has malignant homophobia undergone structural modification? Or, on the contrary, has it simply receded, deprived, in this historic period, of the inflammatory energy it once found in a plague-related panic?

These kinds of questions, of course, are historically familiar. They are often asked of other malignant, and perhaps similar, structures like fascism or racism. Are these social structures best thought of as static cultural susceptibilities, chronic and periodically erupting—opportunistic—forces? Or are they best thought of as non-static, non-chronic forces, forces that can be bound, tamed, forces that might finally be amenable, in fact, to radical historical transformation, to fundamental repair?

Such questions resemble typical psychoanalytic clinical questions: to what extent can apparently malignant forces in a patient be permanently tamed, bound, by

1 Material from this chapter first appeared in Moss, D. (1997) "On situating homophobia," *Journal of the American Psychoanalytic Association*, 45: 201–215. Used with permission.

thought and word, by interpretation; to what extent, on the other hand, might those forces lie beyond the reach of interpretation and, as such, always poised for opportunistic eruption?

So, then, I consider this chapter enduringly permanent in its relevance. It represents, in my view, an effort to think about a malignant eruption of a symptomatic social structure that borrowed energy and meaning from momentarily aroused and enormously profound sexually-tinged anxieties. Those anxieties seem, for the moment, relatively quelled. Examining what happened when they were stoked might turn out to be simply a look backward at a regressive historical moment. It might also prove instructive were they to ever be similarly stoked again. It seems to me too early to tell.

***

The Authoritarian Personality (Adorno, Frenkel-Brunswik, Levinson and Sanford 1950) is perhaps the greatest achievement of a now receding tradition of politically engaged, psychoanalytically informed social science. Written in the United States immediately in the wake of the Holocaust, its "major concern was with the potentially fascistic individual" and with the psychosocial-historical conditions under which that latent potential had been and might again be realized. Perhaps the work's most well-known legacy is its F-scale, a linear measure of fascist or antidemocratic potential. The F-scale consists of a series of statements with which subjects either agree or disagree. The statements are designed to "serve as rationalizations for irrational tendencies." High scorers affirmed their affinities not only with the irrational, but also with antidemocratic thought.

Two statements included in the scale are the following: (a) "Nowadays with so many different kinds of people moving around so much and mixing together so freely, one has to be especially careful to protect himself against infection and disease," and (b) "Homosexuality is an especially rotten form of delinquency and ought to be severely punished."

Though ostensibly referring to two quite separate ideational sectors—contagion and homosexuality—the two statements are in fact systematically yoked to each other. People who agree with one tend to agree with the other, and people who agree with both tend to be particularly high scorers.

Such affinities presented the project a twofold problem. The first was basically clinical. The authors, in order to conceptualize the underlying psychodynamic and structural determinants that bind such statements to each other, sought out the covert unities of which such ostensibly independent statements are a part. The second aspect of the problem was extra-clinical: to conceptualize the mediations through which these underlying individual dynamics seem both to be fed by and to tap into a deep wellspring of demographically widespread antidemocratic propensities. The authors proceeded on the premise that antidemocratic authoritarianism is both destructive and irrational, a symptom with multiple functions to which large numbers of people are vulnerable.

The statements regarding contagion and homosexuality, like all the others clustering in the F-scale, were treated by Adorno and his colleagues from an essentially formal point of view: as mere markers, pegs around which to infer authoritarianism's covert determinants. The face value of such statements was overshadowed by their value as pointers. Today, however, these two statements' face value hits us with force. Especially when we read them as linked, we notice not their abstract function as markers, but rather the appearance they give of a terrible and eerie concreteness: "homosexuality, rotten, disease, punish, careful."

Fifty years ago this cluster could be treated as a merely formal entity, but today, because of the emergent presence of a virus, this formal character has for many been transformed. Suddenly, there can now seem to be an empirical grounding for a once unquestionably irrational affinity. In the presence of the virus, the cluster can give the appearance of being structured by reason.

To find "affinities structured by reason"—this is what thought aims at. Nature, then, via the virus, seems to have presented certain thinkers sufficient evidence to affirm, among themselves, that it is now reason—even if, fifty years ago it was passion—that binds the two statements together.

Such thought legitimates itself by leaning on nature. Comparable socially malignant narratives have been built around, say, the Jew's nose and the "Negro's" hair. For psychoanalysis, the paradigm of this narrative category is the female genital and its configuration in fantasized narratives as an absent or diminutive male genital. In each case—Jew's nose, "Negro's" hair, female genital, the HIV virus—a manifestation of nature is put to retroactive use to offer narrative support for a cause-and-effect tale in which punishment and inferiority are each warranted by way of an after-the-fact accounting of phenomena that themselves originate both before the fact and besides the fact.

The HIV virus, by serving as a kind of historically mediated day residue, offers fantasy a convenient site on which to join the two statements from the F-scale into a linear narrative linking the idea of delinquent homosexual sex to the most severe punishment: in the case of AIDS, death. This narrative artificially binds nature to a punitive morality: nature does both the judging and the punishing. Once morality is thus "naturalized," it takes on the valence of absolute law, beyond civilization and beyond discourse. Extreme conclusions follow with all the force and momentum of any uncontestable logic.

This absolute law's circular premises are invariable: nature will punish delinquent bodies, and its punishments will be necessarily just, precisely because they will be natural. Morality is thus grounded in nature and outside of culture. Such is the category of narrative that moralistically finds a causal bond linking homosexuality to the HIV virus. This narrative has led to a reconfiguration of many of the ways in which antihomosexual fantasy presents itself. Such fantasy is, of course, overdetermined, with substantial contributions coming from both sides of the cultural/psychical interface. Given the pervasive availability of this narrative and its many derivatives, long-standing aversive constructions, relatively benign, whose moralistic conclusions have led to rigid and thickly justified avoidance of the frightening homosexual object can now easily be transformed into far more malignant constructions whose conclusions, again thickly justified, lead to the death of the frightening homosexual object.

All such narratives warrant the appellation *homophobia.* I will use the term first in a broad and nontechnical sense, in the hope of catching the full range of meanings conveyed in both its commonplace and its academic usage; I will then try to place the term, so understood, in clinical context. In what follows, *homophobia* will refer to the entire spectrum of conscious and unconscious fantasy-feeling-idea-sentiment through which persons structure and are structured by an avoidant/aversive relation to all things sensed as homosexual. By employing the suffix -*phobia,* I do not mean to imply that this spectrum ought to be placed among the traditional psychoanalytic categories of phobia. Though some of the homophobic phenomena I have in mind may indeed be structured like clinical phobias— organized around a primary, unconscious defense of displacement—I mean the category *homophobia* as something broader than that, something best thought of as a conceptual analog to *racism* or *misogyny.* Each of these three analogous modes of organization—homophobia, racism, and misogyny—refers to a historically dense phenomenon that is insufficiently grasped if understood solely in terms of psychodynamics. All these phenomena are determined in part by processes of displacement, but their historical and social determinants make them both conceptually thicker and more variable in presentation than the traditional psychoanalytic categories of phobia.

With the devastating emergence of AIDS over the past decade came a burst of overt homophobic sentiment and activity in the United States. The latter development is itself accompanied by an increasingly visible, insurgent, and self-consciously articulated gay and lesbian presence. These phenomena are clearly yoked. On the one hand, the mortal threat posed by HIV provokes highly vulnerable groups into intensified group identifications and adaptive strategies of self-defense; on the other, the same threat of HIV provokes widespread and urgent disidentifications that fuel reactive aggression. The convergence of these increasingly visible homophilic and homophobic sentiments generates what Paula Treichler (1988) felicitously calls the "epidemic of signification" surrounding the HIV epidemic.

By way of this mix of the viral epidemic and the associated epidemic of signification, a high pitch of anxiety has come to saturate much contemporary sexual discourse. For many, the reality-based reconvergence of erotics and fatal illness has led to a conscious and pervasive sense of alarm. Realistic dangers resonate with fantasized ones. The danger of sexually transmitted illness and death stirs up anxieties originating in infantile sexuality. Such anxieties now seem to reappear, this time occasioned by the "facts." (I have put quotation marks around the word to indicate not that the facts are untrue but rather that they have passed through the grid of fantasy and have thus been transformed into psychic rather than material "facts.") This apparent reappearance makes such "facts" seem the realization of unconscious dangers associated with any penetration of the body—loss of the object, of the object's love, of castration anxiety, superego anxiety.

The result is a number of powerful, and powerfully believed, erotic fictions linking homosexuality and danger. For many in the academic/AIDS activist community, psychoanalytic theory has provided a useful grid by which to understand and counter some of the destructive dimensions of these fictions (see, in particular, Crimp 1988; Lewes 1988, 1992). One such fiction posits the disease as the warranted punishment for the enacted desire, and thereby intensifies homophobia in both the homosexual and non-homosexual population. Psychoanalytic theory, by offering methods of analysis that help sustain the crucial differences between correlation and cause, fantasy and thought, has proven consistently useful in helping to articulate the archaic fantasies underlying this fiction. Thought, of course, will question the relation between act and infection, while fantasy will moralize the desire. The title of Bersani's very influential essay, "Is the rectum a grave?" (1988), aptly catches the paradigmatic punitive underlying homophobic fantasy in an extreme, and thus extremely revealing, version. The influence of the same fantasy equation—rectum as grave—is evident also, however attenuated, in the ostensibly more benign (and certainly more socially sanctioned) inquiries premised on the notion of an intrinsic, natural relation linking homosexuality to danger and premature mortality. Nunokawa (1992) addresses the fantastic/erotic underpinnings of this link.

In the domain defined by the intersection of HIV transmission and certain homosexual acts, bodily penetration is the central concern, for both thought and fantasy. Thought insists that the virus is transmitted via essentially meaningless modalities. For fantasy, however, there exists no such thing as meaninglessness; here the idea of viral transmission via blood and semen turns pertinent bodily surfaces and orifices into erotically signifying objects, sites of pleasure and pain, danger and retribution.

Driven with either thought or fantasy in the lead, this focus on bodily penetrations and surfaces takes the HIV/homosexuality inquiry into the realm of clinical psychoanalysis, particularly into the realm charted by Freud's still audacious notion that "the ego is first and foremost a bodily ego; it is not merely a surface entity, but is itself the projection of a surface" (Freud 1923: 16).

New versions of old narratives have emerged: homosexual bodies as sites of contagion, as naturally doomed, as arenas of punishment, as theaters for moral retribution—all these fantastic constructions have become objects for interpretive work. The aim of such work is to expose the determinants and mitigate the consequences of such malignant elaborations. It is important to note that most of this work has taken place outside the clinical psychoanalytic sphere.

As with *The Authoritarian Personality,* much of this work appropriates psychoanalytic theory in an explicitly interested, nonclinical, way. The theory is put to the service of an urgent, historically specific task. Though addressing clinically pertinent entities—anti-Semitism in *The Authoritarian Personality,* homophobia now—such work takes on a noticeably first-person tone—if not necessarily a first-person voice. We encounter author as engaged theoretician; the work is not mediated by any pretense of clinical disinterest.

By contrast, the psychoanalytic clinical literature, in addressing this upsurge in both the realistic and the fantasized dangers surrounding homoerotics, has maintained a steady, disinterested course, keeping its clinical focus via a number of reports on the treatment of HIV-positive patients and tangentially sustaining its long-standing concern with the psychodynamics of homophilias (see, for example, Hildebrand 1992). Unlike the engaged literature cited above, our recent literature on the points of convergence of HIV and homosexuality has remained essentially silent on the homophobias per se. (By "our" I mean the English-language literature appearing in the *International Journal of Psycho-Analysis,* the *International Review of Psycho-Analysis,* the *Psychoanalytic Quarterly,* and the *Journal of the American Psychoanalytic Association.*)

There is nothing overtly willed about such clinical silences. Clinical theory is, in fact, written willy-nilly. It is reactive, responding to presenting clinical problems. We write about what we see and hear. This is what determines our overall clinical agenda. When presented with female patients, we tend to see problems associated with female sexuality; when presented with homosexual patients, we tend to see problems associated with homosexuality. These are the problems most of us have been taught to see, what for most of us our theory has theorized. We do not see what theory has not paved the path for us to see. For the most part, our clinical educations, our received theories, have left us much less prepared, with either homosexual patients or with women, to see, to theorize, to work and write clinically, on what may well seem to us the marginal problems of misogyny and homophobia.

We, like Freud before us—recall Dora's neglected "gynecophilia"—can see only what we are prepared to see. Like him, we still ask the cardinal clinical questions: What do women want? What is the meaning of homosexuality?

But we do not yet ask spontaneously a set of companion questions that one could imagine as clinical—such questions as: 1) What is wished for via structured misogynies and homophobias? and 2) What gives them their characteristic forms, their virulence, and their still astonishing prevalence?

Such questions, off the theoretical center, will necessarily seem off the clinical center. Whatever inclination we might have to ask them is easily inhibited by a sense that we lack the theoretical support for a clinical follow-through.

For many, our not asking is a kind of silence, and, like any silence not explicitly accounted for, this one regarding homophobias can, has, and will continue to be read suspiciously.

The most obvious suspicious reading would treat the silence as a marker of a not-quite-avowed indifference, a kind of profession-wide disidentification with the targets of these hatreds. (This apparent disidentification is selective. For fifty years, by contrast, the literature has seriously, and identificatorily, addressed the determinants and consequences of anti-Semitism.)

Of indifference, Freud (1915b: 136) writes, it "fall[s] into place as a special case of hate or dislike." Silence as a marker of indifference; indifference as a special case of "hate or dislike"—the case can be made, and has been, for both homophobia and misogyny.

For a century, our highly theorized clinical silences have been extraordinary in their generative power and utility. Regarding both misogynies and homophobias, however, our inclinations toward, not a theorized silence, but rather a passively arrived-at muteness, have served us far less well.

"A symptom," Freud (1926: 91) writes, "is a sign of, and a substitute for, an instinctual satisfaction which has remained in abeyance; it is a consequence of the process of repression." Homophobia, then, is indeed a symptom: a sign and a substitute for a renounced satisfaction, a consequence of repression. It is an explicitly sexual response to a danger that itself is sensed as explicitly sexual. Since any or all of the constitutive elements of the sexual drive—source, aim, and object—might have mediated that danger, any or all of them might qualify as homophobia's target.

Like any symptom, homophobia aims to restore the status quo ante—the safe time before the danger's emergence. The first step in this labor of restoration is flight—the systematic repudiation of all the bodies and parts of bodies, inside or outside, all the fantasies, actions, and persons, inside and out, through which the danger might have made itself present.

Aiming to restore the status quo ante, the homophobic impulse is, therefore, nostalgic. It orients itself around a fantasy of the good old days, parrying danger and reconstructing a lost world. The homophobe (like the formally congruent racist or misogynist) knows himself as a participant in a heroic tradition. This sense of tradition is crucial to homophobia. It gives the symptom a characteristic mark. Homophobes, unlike agoraphobes, say, are always, at least implicitly, members of a movement. The homophobic person is hooked in to like-minded fellows, and they are all hooked in to the ancients.

The homophobe makes no pretense of originality. It is not his fear he speaks to you about. Rather, he has tapped in to something both natural and mythic. That contact with nature and myth lends homophobic knowledge its aura of revelation. Homophobic awareness is not learned; rather, it crystallizes. One *knows*: what to hate, what to fear, what to do. The endless vein of this legacy is well captured by the poet John Ashbery (1992: 46): "The midgets stand on giants who stand on midgets in Palookaville."

Case example 1

A 30-year-old man entered analysis frightened of intermittent impotence and a fear of his own "latent homosexuality." He was particularly disturbed by recurrent conscious images of penises forcibly penetrating his mouth and anus. He wanted to "get married, live in the suburbs, have some kids." But his sexual relationships, always with women, had all been brief. "The moment you're vulnerable, you're dead."

The clustered epithets he used to characterize such vulnerable states deserve mention; they reveal, in their total lack of originality, his hooked-in state of mind. Wet, he called vulnerability; faggy, pussyish, like a woman, pink, punk, weak, needy, fucked, unmanned. His antidotes also bespoke his traditionalism: his hero was the Charles Bronson of *Death Wish,* the righteous vigilante, hard, cold, selfless. One hears in this standard cluster of misogyny and homophobia a systematic effort to repudiate threat and to affirm purity. Heteroerotic identifications interweave with homoerotic disidentifications. But there is nothing idiosyncratic in this interweaving. His language, passions, and tactics are all entirely standard.

Two years into the analysis he reported the following incident. He had been awakened the night before by an anonymous telephone call. The caller somehow knew his name. This intrigued my patient. The caller's intentions were blatantly sexual. My patient grew excited and he and the caller "spoke dirty" to each other, "intimately." Each was masturbating. "I have never in my life felt closer to another person," said my patient the next morning. As the phone conversation continued, my patient realized that his caller was a man, which did not interfere with his excitement. He brought himself to orgasm while knowing he was speaking with a man. He quickly ended the conversation.

He felt transiently disturbed at the "homosexuality" of what had occurred. "But then I relaxed. I thought, what a pity that a nice guy like that has to resort to homosexuality and telephone sex. I thought he should go into therapy." Things then returned to place, and by the morning, my patient's feelings of "manhood, masculinity, and potency" had been restored.

Although affectively attenuated by pity, the border constituted between subject and object is clear. The border is constructed by an act of repudiation. The subjective schema is also clear, if convoluted: "While I too might have once—even, in jest, a moment ago—been like that, now I, *we,* who, really, have always been otherwise, can afford to pity them, whom we repudiate."

Case example 2

D is a gay man, who hates being gay and gay people. Here is a representative outburst from an analytic session:

> I fucking hate this. Dressing for someone else, all these social niceties, all this shit. I'm so hostile to all this stuff. I don't know why. I don't want there to be any expectations on me. I feel bitter and angry. I expected that to come much later, when I'm older. I don't get it now. I'm so angry about something. I don't know what I'm angry about. I hate things—a lot of stuff. But I don't know what to do about it. I don't think I like people. I'm tired of feeling pushed around. I'm having conversations with people and I think, "This is boring, this is so boring." That happens a lot. My attention wanders. Wherever I am, I hate

it. And then I look back at things and I think, oh that was great, but when it's happening, I hate it. I was fucking miserable. I don't have patience. What is it? Why am I so pissed off all the time? I don't like where I am in life. Is it really just that? Or is it something permanent?

In short, D seems to hate being conscious. Consciousness is his medium of perception and he seems to hate all that he perceives. He lives as though in a sphere of thorny desires, surrounded by them. These desires—persistent, implacable, ornery and dangerous—lurk everywhere, inside and out. D can locate no zone of safety, no source of relief.

D especially seems to hate the people he desires and himself for desiring them; in fact, so it seems, he hates desire itself; hates, it seems, all feeling and all bodies, his, yours, ours, no matter whose. He seems to hate everything that brings him into contact with any form of thorny desire. As such, he seems to hate it all.

D seems to hate—he claims to hate—"I fucking hate this"—he says. But, in my view, more than hating it all, D seems angered by it all. I think the difference between hatred and anger is particularly important. Hatred aims only at the destruction of the hated object. Anger, on the other hand, indicates a lurking fantasy of a just alternative to the unjust/unfair object. Hatred aims at obliteration, anger at replacement. Just as depression marks the gap between the ideal and the real, so anger marks the gap between what is and what ought to be.

D's is an indignant, outraged anger. That is, D lives as though the way things are is not the way they ought to be, as though there is something elementally wrong, unjust, about who he is, how he is, about the people who surround him, and about the tasks demanded of him by everyday life.

In effect, D, angry and indignant, stares out from an enclosed psychic sphere. Staring out, he comes into emotional contact with a second—imaginary—sphere. He is excluded from this one. It is the inverse of his: here, desires are properly ordered and just. The contact between D and this second sphere is an intimate one. Each indignity in the one sphere co-exists with its soothing inverse in the other.

In this second, inverted sphere, he, and we—all of us—are, or would be, all that we ought to be, want what we ought to want. If we are to take into account D's psychic reality, we must, I think, include both spheres. We also must be certain to refrain from judging either to be more real than the other. It is only when we see the two as paired that we can begin to appreciate D's clinical presentation. By way of his continuous, and unjust, suffering, he comes into emotional contact with continuous blissful possibility.

D seems to proceed with the idea that an elemental mistake has been made, that, in some sense, really, he's innocent, burdened, even punished, for something he didn't do. That is, he seems to feel that there is something egregious and excessive about his personal condition. Throughout most of the sessions, of course, he stresses that being gay is the prime example of just such an egregious and excessive something. He never asked for it and doesn't deserve it.

A sexuality he never asked for and doesn't deserve: that is, a misplaced sexuality, one that doesn't belong wherever D finds it, either in himself or in others. This, I think, is a common marker of homophobia, internalized or not. This marker is certainly present in D, that is, a sense of outraged anger at a sexuality that belongs elsewhere, and whose presence here, wherever it is—in him, in others—represents an affront to the proper order of things.

D's homophobia, then, marks a particularly charged point of contact between the two spheres: the disordered sphere here, the proper one there—disordered sexuality here, the proper one there—on just the other side. For D, of course, this nearly continuous strand of homophobia is complicated by his sense that what he feels about his sexuality he also feels about his entire mind—out of order, wrong— and about the entire world, one that exacts much and returns almost nothing.

Desire and demand, both disordered. Put another way, D lives in a world of disordered unwanted appetites, his and ours. Appetites, of course, are elemental, without cause. Whenever and whatever D wants, whatever and whenever others want from him, D seems to hate the appetites that surround him, inside and out. That is, it's not so much the people he hates, but rather their—and his—appetites, whether in the form of desires or in the form of demands.

I want to take a closer look at this psychic state.

In clinical work, we rarely hear, in any serious sense, people saying I hate myself and love my body; or I hate my body and love myself. The elemental tilt at the frontier of mind and body is toward equilibration. D's indignant anger targets both his body and his ego in more or less equal measure.

The same equilibration holds true at a second frontier, this one between ego and object—between D and the external world. A similar equilibration seems to have taken place. He targets the misplaced sexuality of his sphere wherever he locates it, inside or outside. Satisfaction and pleasure might be linked and, therefore, might be possible, but only in the other sphere, the sphere in which minds and bodies are arranged in accordance with the proper order of things.

What is going on?

Let's take this 360-degree sphere of thorny appetites—unbidden and unjust— and turn to Freud for a way of conceptualizing it. Drives, he writes, exert their influence "as . . . the demand made upon the mind for work in consequence of its connection with the body" (Freud 1915b: 122). Either emanating directly from the interior of the body or indirectly from the objects of the external world, drives impinge on mind via a demand for work. Drives demand the work that leads to their satisfaction.

D is surrounded by a continuous demand for work. That is, from a Freudian point of view, he is surrounded by the continuous impact of drives. His body demands work; his objects demand work; his mind demands work. All of these demands for work might, of course, be experienced as a necessary means of satisfaction. One does not feel indignant toward demands for work per se. All that is required is that the demands be just, that ample satisfaction follows. For D, though, this is the situation in the other sphere, but not in his. For him, the work of drive is a source of indignant anger because its promise of satisfaction seems either non-existent or hollow.

D's indignant anger, then, can be conceptualized as a reaction to a slew of sources that each demand work while delivering little or no satisfaction. For D, all such sources demand uninterrupted work, but deliver pain instead of satisfaction. In some sense, then, we can think of D as feeling himself a slave to drive.

Consistent with this idea, it's valuable to remember that for D the only moment in which bitterness temporarily abates comes in a sexual encounter with someone whom he can order about, someone who himself does all the work, whom D can, in effect, enslave. I take this sequence as the only one in the clinical material in which D seems content. For a blessed moment, he is unburdened of the unjust demand for insufficiently compensated work.

For now, D, unlike *The Threepenny Opera*'s Pirate Jenny, is unable to consciously imagine, and delightfully relish, the vision of his beheaded adversaries. In order to achieve the liberation Jenny imagines for herself, D would, of course, have to behead himself. And I think this, although a temptation, simply adds to the pile of demands with which D is burdened. For D, only there, in the other sphere, can people imagine the violence that might lead to their permanent liberation. D, in his, must settle for angry indignation. The clinical task, then, is to foster the possibilities for a violent imagination, a slave revolt, a bursting out of one sphere and an appropriation of the rights and privileges now residing in his.

Case discussion

In both patients, homophobia affirms one identity by repudiating another. An erotic structure grounded in a mythic version of nature and formed by a direct act of repudiation and a derivative act of identification—when we reach this far in our consideration of homophobia, we find ourselves on a path that intersects the one Freud (1937) found himself on in "Analysis terminable and interminable." That text concludes with the idea that sexuality itself is grounded on a "natural" act of repudiation:

> We often have the impression that with the wish for a penis and the masculine protest we have penetrated through all the psychological strata and have reached bedrock, and that thus our activities are at an end. This is probably true, since, for the psychical field, the biological field does in fact play the part of the underlying bedrock. The repudiation of femininity can be *nothing else than a biological fact,* a part of the great riddle of sex.
>
> (Freud 1937: 252, emphasis added)

We do not have to agree with Freud that this ground is biological; nor must we concur when he refers to what is necessarily repudiated as "feminine." But when, in a footnote, he conceptualizes this elemental repudiation as a symptomatic expression of castration anxiety, there seems ample reason to listen.

His argument is simple. Castration anxiety is intrinsic to sexuality. The first response to anxiety is to repudiate the source of danger. Freud's move is to then equate this first danger with the "feminine." He buttresses his argument by putting nature on his side, citing "biological fact."

For Freud, anxiety is an intrinsic feature of sexuality. Also intrinsic, therefore, is a reactive repudiation whose aim is to externalize the danger and thereby make it possible to flee. We are driven to conclude, then, that for Freud sexuality is structured like a phobia. As with any phobia, sexuality implies a dichotomous erotic world: on one side safety, on the other danger.

Homophobia is a phobia, a symptomatic division of the erotic world into safe and dangerous sectors. Whatever its social-historical-familial-psychic particularities, its structure is probably a local variant on the more fundamental, more radical phobic theme that since Freud we see haunting sexuality itself.

One of the impossible tasks left us by Freud has been the conceptualization of bedrock. We know bedrock only inferentially, as the limit point of any possible interpretive labor. The distance between bedrock—essence—and phenomenon defines the conceptual space for interpretation. Bedrock defies interpretation, while phenomena insist upon it.

The task for us, then, is to see whether homophobia warrants a place in the bedrock, or belongs instead among the many interpretable forms of structured phobias—the prejudices. Freud's reference to a biological "repudiation of femininity" seems to imply near-bedrock status for both male homophobia and its formal companion, misogyny. But the form of Freud's argument, his use of nature as a conceptual guarantor, itself repeats the form of homophobic argument, in which the distance between culture and nature is collapsed, and the true converges with the natural.

Systematized prejudices brook no argument. Their truths are held to be self-evident. This self-evident aura marks an indirect appeal to bedrock, an apparently confident reading of an apparently transparent nature. Such confidence may not be warranted. If the repudiation of femininity is not natural—bedrock—then two of its prominent and destructive derivatives, misogyny and homophobia, like the other systematized prejudices, would be amenable to mutative interpretation.

Regarding those other prejudices, Brian Bird (1957), writing on anti-Black racism, coins the term *incorprojection* to catch the same complicated generative dynamic of repudiation and affirmation that seems to operate in homophobias. Of this dynamic he writes:

> The new mechanism possesses a special quality best described as the power to pass a conflict right on through the ego; or to pass an object, or at least a relationship to an object, right on through. Or it can be said that the mechanism does its work by simultaneously dropping one object relationship and acquiring another, or by simultaneously taking one object in and extruding another."

(p. 504)

Bird gives a clinical example. A hears his friend B speak prejudicially about Jews and Blacks. He gets extremely angry. This anger puzzles him, however, since he usually is indifferent to racial slurs. Upon analysis, it is revealed that a recent success of A's has prompted envy in B. B, not wanting to jeopardize the friendship with A by revealing his envy, has *incorporated* A's criticism of envying people and simultaneously *projected* his own envy onto Jews and Blacks. Thus, in one move he preserves his identification with A and intensifies his disidentification with Jews and Blacks. A potential envy-ridden conflict, grounded in his love for A, has "passed through" him and become reinscribed as a set of racist remarks about dangerous, envying Jews and Blacks.

For Bird, the sequence begins with B believing both that he is missing something and that A has it; thus the hierarchy. B envies A this item, that is, wishes to harm A and appropriate the item. But because of the retaliatory dangers involved in this, B repudiates the wish and looks for and finds C. C is one who, like B, does not have the envied item. B then identifies with A and accuses C of enviously coveting what A and B both have. A and B are now united; C is the means of their union.

The sequence is clear: 1) not having it; 2) envying the one who seems to possess it; 3) seeking and finding another who seems without it; 4) identifying with the one who has it; and 5) fearing the greedy attacks of the one without it. Bird's "incor-projective" sequence as described here is exactly like the sequence enacted by my patient in his anonymous sexual phone call: in that sequence I occupy the position of A, the patient B, and the caller C. Rather than envy me, the patient homoerotically unites with me by way of the presumably shared pity we each feel toward the desperately homosexual caller.

For Freud, it is femininity that is repudiated; for Bird, envy. If we assume that each theorist is simply giving a different name to the same repudiated item, then we would have taken a roundabout path to nowhere. We would be left with the tedious stereotypical equation: feminine = envious.

But a closer look reveals that the two repudiated items are not at all identical. The feminine in Freud's bedrock repudiation is dangerous because of the danger of castration; what is repudiated is a passive wish toward a male. For Bird, however, the bedrock repudiation of envy aims to alleviate not castration anxiety mediated by passive wishes, but retaliatory dangers brought on by aggressive, hostile, appropriative wishes.

Via Freud, our focus is directed toward the once inside, now outside object that has been repudiated for its passive wishes. Freud, perhaps symptomatically, calls this object "the feminine." Only by way of this repudiation can Freud's subject maintain his own erotic competence.

But with Bird we pay little attention to the repudiated object; our focus remains fixed on the repudiating subject. We watch as he continually finds objects into whom he can repudiate his envious aggression so as to bolster his always fragile claims to have now benignly identified with his once envied object.

For Freud, what is repudiated are passive wishes; for Bird, destructive envious ones.

If we then couple the two formulations, treating each as partial, the resultant allows us to see that for B the very possibility of sexuality seems to depend on a double repudiation: the passive, so-called feminine, repudiated "down" onto C, and the aggressive-envious—can we call it "masculine"?—also repudiated down onto C. This double repudiation is a precondition of B's ability to identify with A. For B, the hated C is an erotic necessity.

In *The Authoritarian Personality*, Adorno seems to catch both of these repudiated elements, writing first that the anti-Semite falls negatively in love with the Jew, and second, that all race hatred is envy. A single object toward which one simultaneously has passive yearnings and envious destructive ones—this is the unstable conundrum from which homophobia and other structured prejudices offer an exit. After the repudiations, C alone carries the burden of what were once B's intolerably contradictory wishes. C, then, whether woman, homosexual, or person of color, is then hated for the insatiety of his/her appetites. This hatred betrays B's ongoing envy, displaced now from the potentially retaliating A to the definitionally weak C.

In ignoring upward-directed envy and condensing all that is repudiated onto the single term *feminine*, the theory here seems to enact Bird's mechanism of incorprojection. The result is a point of view which, as Bird describes it, identifies itself upward, so to speak. In this case the result seems to bind the theory identificatorily to the upwardly located "masculine" object.

Now, Bird's notion of incorprojection was originally intended to be limited to such phobic structures as racism. But we can expand the reach of this B figure and essentially use it to conceptualize any person in whom sexuality is emerging. That is, the emergence of sexuality per se places one in an unstable middle position like B's. The instability is consequent to two sets of wishes—passive ones and envious ones—toward a single object of desire. Each is dangerous, and each provokes repudiation downward and identification upward.

The figure Freud describes, who "biologically" repudiates femininity, is simply and symptomatically aiming to establish a safe and stable sexuality. The structure is phobic: masculine means safe and inside; feminine means dangerous and outside.

Freud's formulation offers us little interpretive purchase on the ostensibly bedrock repudiation of the feminine. (The same problem haunts Freud's interpretation of the Schreber case, where, while the dynamics of homosexuality are brilliantly theorized, the narcissistically organized dynamics binding homophobia, feminine repudiation and castration anxiety are treated as conceptual givens—bedrock.) My patient's homophobic and misogynist epithets, for instance, would, given Freud's restricted vision, reflect only the patient's close encounter with this anxiety-generating feminine bedrock. But when we add Bird's considerations, our interpretive field springs wide open. We no longer need join the patient in looking downward and interpreting his now other-than-bedrock fear of the feminine; rather we look upward, against the grain of his averted gaze.

We are then able to see him anxiously repudiate his own dangerous masculinity only in order to then be able to fantastically and safely identify with it. It is this finally doomed and indirect, self-canceling, path toward masculinity that is the most interpretively accessible dimension of both homophobia and misogyny. B's relations to A are necessarily characterized by both envy and passive yearning.

Bird's theoretical contribution serves as a clinical safeguard against joining patient B, and a theoretical safeguard against joining Freud, in transiently forgetting that initial repudiation of what should only ironically be called "the masculine."

Sexuality's always at least marginally present phobic object is constructed out of this double act of repudiation. Therefore, the central characteristic of that object is a malignant appetite. Its wants are excessive; it is at once simultaneously too passive and too greedy. We can sense here the core character of the homophobe's homosexual, the misogynist's woman, the anti-Semite's Jew. Their passivities mark them as sly and insidious, their envy as insatiable.

Bird's patient's category of whiteness, Freud's of the masculine, the homo-phobe's of the heterosexual, are all constructed as fantastic sites on which erotic appetites are properly managed—what is wanted is what can be had, and had in proper, natural measure.

Chapter 8

Freud's "female homosexual"

One way of looking at a woman[1]

Given the elemental status of sexual difference, our ways of looking at a woman will necessarily provide an inverted mirror of our ways of looking at a man. If we bracket out the commonalities we might find between the sexes, the contrasting remainders will constitute whatever we mean by "sexual difference." "Difference," then, inversely binds the terms "man" and "woman" no less than sameness directly does.

In this chapter, I look at the way Freud looked at one woman, in this case, a homosexual woman. Freud aims to conceptualize the determinants and meanings of her sexual object choice. He considers that choice to have been the result of a series of transformations, a sequence driven not merely by a movement toward what she wants but also—and for Freud most importantly—a movement away from what she cannot tolerate. He conveys confidence in his capacities to sense the latent flight hidden in her manifest desire.

I mean here to focus on that confidence, a confidence grounded, finally, in the dual premises of heterosexual primacy: that women, if only they can bear the narcissistic insult of it, will turn toward men to provide them with the phallus they lack; and that men, if only they can bear the anxiety of it, will turn toward women to provide them with the interiority that their penises cannot. These premises, if active, precede and inform all looking at all men and all women. Disturb the premises and the resulting looks will necessarily be disrupted, not so much in the dimension of what one is seeing but rather in the level of confidence and belief in what one sees.

Let us strip these premises of their axiomatic status and thereby take issue with Freud's confidence. We may then, of course, employ the premises any way we see fit, only not as axioms. Once we take away their axiomatic status, we will necessarily become aware that we are, in fact, employing them; we are putting them to use, that is, we want them. If we recognize that we want them, then the

1 Material from this chapter first appeared in Moss, D. and Zeavin, L. (1999) "The female homosexual: c'est nous," in R. Lester and E. Schoenberg (eds) *That Obscure Subject of Desire: Freud's Female Homosexual Revisited*, London: Routledge. Used with permission.

premises themselves take on the same complex valence as the sexual object choices they otherwise mean to organize. The premises lose their status as axioms and instead become objects of desire; "if only I had an axiom" might be one analyst's wish; "if only my words were themselves axiomatic" might be another's. We can hear in these imagined wishes the echo of their explicitly sexual counterparts: "if only I had a phallus"; "if only I were the phallus."

Axiomatic certainty defines and constricts our conceptual range. Recognizing the absence of reliable axioms, then, we will simultaneously lose definitional precision and increase conceptual range. We can ask of these lost, but still desired, conceptual premises the same kinds of questions Freud, and future analysts, have long asked of once lost, but still desired, sexual objects.

Here are two such questions: 1) Might we be turning to these objects of desire for relief from the anxiety engendered by their absence? and 2) Might their axiomatic status offer us conceptual cover in addition to conceptual power?

Ask questions such as these and we immediately lose contact with the firm ground that once might have satisfied our wished-for sense of confidence.

Confidence needs axioms. Lacking axioms, then, all that we will confidently find when thinking of sexual object choice will be simply, finally, and irreducibly the fact of our wishing for them. We will realize, then, that our listening, like our patients' speaking, is necessarily infiltrated with desire. Of that alone can we be confident.

By inserting the analyst's desire into the conceptual slot vacated by axiomatic heterosexuality, we then have the power to illuminate the radical uncertainties attached to any effort to clarify and categorize the determinants and meanings of female—and male—sexual desire.

What follows is an extended improvisation provoked by a reading of a classical Freudian text, "The psychogenesis of a case of homosexuality in a woman" (Freud 1920b). By "classical," I mean two things: first, that the text has achieved canonical status, and second, that it contains and gives voice to ideological tensions that characterize Freud's entire oeuvre and that continue to enrich and bedevil psychoanalytic theory and practice today.

This improvisation means to illuminate and utilize those tensions. Contemporary texts establish their legitimacy by explicit or implicit reference to predecessors. Classical texts form the foundation on which all pertinent successors rest. They are an enduring presence. Whether sensed as resource, debt, or hindrance, the classical—no matter how thickly mediated or disguised—provides form and structure to the new. One speaks into, against, or around the classical but never independently of it. The classical exerts force.

In Freud's (1920b) text on the female homosexual, one manifestation of this force is the text's pedestrian employment of misogynist and homophobic sentiments. Planted elsewhere in history, we have no trouble spotting these sentiments, and our ability to see through homophobic and misogynist rhetoric tempts us to think ourselves free of the forces that engendered those offensive sentiments.

But this presumption ironically exemplifies the force of the classical in action. As modern as we are, we have become habitually alert to the deforming power of the classical—its misogynist and/or homophobic premises, say. We defend ourselves against that power, and in the process we grow less alert to our defenses than to the ostensible threats that they so effectively ward off. Thus protected from our "classical" past, we grow confident in our contemporary habits of thought.

I want to attend not so much to the loud and openly deforming influences of the classical but rather to its more quiet and often less noticeable legacy of confidence. This legacy of confidence underwrites a belief in our own texts' freedom from deformation. It is only by a mixture of direct and indirect appeals to our classical predecessors that we distinguish texts produced by thought and experience from those produced by fantasy and prejudice. Validity depends upon continuity. The classical, thus, grants legitimacy to the contemporary.

Freud's text is an occasion for this project. As psychoanalysts, we are in continuous relation to our discipline's ongoing output and distant history. That history originates with Freud. No psychoanalytic output can avert the original Freudian theme. And through that theme, we remain tethered, no matter how loosely, to the classical traditions from which it was produced.

In what follows, I purposely avoid referencing potential intersections with contemporary arguments and discussions. I suppress intervening contexts in order to intensify my sense of contact with Freud's text. The potential costs of this tactic include a possible narrowing or pinching of perspective; the potential gain is a heightening of focus.

Besides the obvious debt to Freud, I sense an explicit theoretical obligation only to Laplanche and Pontalis's (1968) improvisational text, "Fantasy and the origins of sexuality."

In "The psychogenesis of a case of homosexuality in a woman," Freud (1920b) interprets a clinical situation whose main feature is the emergence of homosexual feeling and action in a young woman. At the crux of his interpretation is the notion of disappointment. Freud posits the woman of his study as doubly disappointed: no phallus and no heterosexual object. He then interprets her homosexual object-choice as an embittering and vengeful compensation for these disappointments. Her revenge is prompted by a sense of unjust deprivation, while her bitterness derives from the fundamental ineffectiveness of her fantasized solution. Freud then argues, in effect, that this ineffectiveness is categorical, that fantasized solutions like hers do not, and can never, compensate for real disappointments.

Freud's "double disappointment" interpretation of this paradigm case of homosexuality in a woman does not originate solely from a consideration of the case's sexual particulars. It necessarily emerges instead from the application of a pre-existing and more general theory of sexuality. By *necessarily,* I mean simply that, explicitly or implicitly, a general theory supports and determines any particular clinical interpretation. Therefore, although I will take Freud to task for his use of the "double disappointment" interpretation in this case, the object of my argument will be that aspect of his general sexual theory on which this particular interpretation seems to lean.

The aspect of the theory I will look at most critically is Freud's classical notion that phallic disappointment is fundamentally a female problem. I will argue that this interpretation represents a constricted use of Freud's own theory of sexuality and that a consistent reading of that theory posits phallic disappointment as an intrinsic element of genital sexuality regardless of gender and regardless of heterosexual or homosexual object-choice. After explicitly addressing the pertinent theoretical issues, I offer two exemplary clinical vignettes.

Because I aim to counter Freud's sexual theorizing with Freudian sexual theorizing, I begin with a consideration of the status of sexual theory itself, particularly of the conditions that make sexual theorizing a continuing necessity for psychoanalysis.

The necessity of sexual theory in psychoanalysis derives from our conviction— our knowledge even —that regarding the origins, raw ingredients, and meanings of its own sexuality, the first-person singular voice labors under severe epistemological constraints. Whether via introspection or interview, the yield from first-person direct inquiry is radically fragmentary— inevitably, and on its face, insufficient. At its most comprehensive, regarding sexual origins, the first-person voice chronicles an apparently coherent sequence of influences. But the starting point for these narratives of influence is either overtly inaccessible or is obscured by the clarity provided by interpretable myths of origin.

We think of the sexual narrative directly available to the reflective first-person voice as referring to manifest sexuality, a sexuality whose relation to its own underlying generative sexual thoughts resembles the relation between the manifest dream and its underlying generative dream thoughts. Just as the dream's formative thoughts are opaque to the dreamer, so sexuality's formative impulses remain opaque to the sexualized person. And with sexuality, as with dreams, where the first-person voice does not know, it constructs. The story it tells itself, or tells us, about its own sexual origins is a product of secondary elaboration.

Therefore, although the first-person voice may speak with precision about the clusters of sexual sensations and erotized persons it currently pursues and avoids, that voice, no matter how meticulous, is structurally unreliable when it comes to the infantile history and original precursors of those sensations and persons.

The most convincing feature of the honest and straightforward first-person voice is its sincerity. Sincerity is epistemologically self-enclosed; it functions as its own validation. It appeals to an experience of direct access and is, therefore, radically anti-theoretical. There is a kind of hallucinatory conviction to sincerity's claims. What it knows, the first-person sincere voice knows via experiences that have been mediated so as to feel immediate and vivid.

The resultant sense of perceptual contact generates the idea that one has encountered the real thing. Knowledge so gained is particularly hard to forswear. Even when conscious of both the cost and the insufficiency of relying on this kind of knowledge—as in the presence of symptoms—the sincere first-person voice will aim to preserve its confidence in its own privileged position; it will believe that to it alone do sexuality's mysteries become clear. Insufficiency and cost—pain, in the Freudian sense—are not enough to displace the first-person voice from its own sincere ground. It seems a constituent element of "I" that it must "know" more about its own sexuality than might any "You" or "He" or "She."

Regarding sexual origins, it is only because we reject both the validity and reliability of truth claims grounded in sincerity that sexual theorizing becomes a necessity. Via sexual theorizing, we place ourselves in direct argument with the foundational premises of first-person erotic sincerity.

Sincerity is sexuality's voice of urgency: "I *really* want this," or "I *really* am this." To theorize thoroughly the formation, and, therefore, the meaning, of sexuality is, then, to theorize simultaneously the formation, and meaning, of the sincere first-person voice. An adequate psychoanalytic theory of sexuality would have three intertwined objects: 1) sexuality itself: the fantasies and deeds through which the erotized body seeks satisfaction; 2) the voice through which that seeking is given expression; and 3) the relation between the voice and the erotized body.

None of the three objects can be read directly; none is transparent. When the object appears transparent and directly legible to its interpreter, we can assume that, in that moment of transparency, the interpreter has abandoned theory in favor of sincerity.

Regarding both infantile and female sexuality, Freud writes as a theoretician. That is, his ideas are derived. The theorized objects of his inquiry are posited as out of the reach of direct observation. From the wide array of adult sexual manifestations, Freud infers the particulars of both infantile and female sexuality. At the heart of his inference, for both infant and female, is a body inadequate to the task of wish-fulfillment. Lacking the phallus, infant and woman must make do with renunciations (i.e. clitoral masturbation for the girl) and fantasy.

Freud's voice turns sincere and non-theoretical, though, when he writes about male sexuality. For Freud, the male body—in contrast to both the female's and the infant's—is transparent. He reads penis = phallus directly, as though here reality is suddenly transparent, shorn of mediations. And it is this reading that reads the realized male subject as one freed from the specter of phallic disappointment. For Freud here, the male genital is beyond the reach of meaning; it simply *is*: propping up all sexuality, male and female, and sufficient unto itself. For its bearer, the main danger becomes castration—a reduction to the insufficiency of woman or child. For Freud, man has what infant and female want.

This picture of male sufficiency is constructed sincerely, with the confidence of someone who already knows. Here lurks the influence of classical thought, not only in this particular confidence surrounding the essentially metaphysical status of the male genital but also in the more general confidence in metaphysics itself. Freud does not ask what seems an obvious, though nonetheless theoretical, question: "What is it that *men* lack, such that, lacking this, they so urgently want?"

For Freud, male sexuality is disappointed only once, in relation to attaining its object, while female sexuality is disappointed twice, in relation to both its body and to its object. The clinically pertinent disappointments associated with "female sexuality" are arrived at indirectly, via theory, while the contrasting, clinically employed notion of the adequacy of male sexuality is arrived at directly, via sincerity.

The sexualized body, as such, does not speak. Rather, it provokes speech. What speaks in its stead is a thickly mediated, and thickly mediating, "I." A theory of sexuality is, therefore, also a theory of voice. In clinical psychoanalysis, we understand voice by its theorized relation to body; we understand sexuality by its theorized relation to voice. At the heart of our clinical practice, we aim to interpret the ways in which voice and body simultaneously construct and destabilize each other.

The dynamics binding voice and body are not fixed. They are under perpetual negotiation. The priority of the body is immediacy of discharge, while the priority of voice is organization. Infancy is the original and quintessential site for these negotiations. In principle, given bodily pain, the infant's cry (like the adult's) is an argument by direct appeal. It is an alloy of the voice and the body. It, therefore, aims for both the immediate and organized repetition of a satisfaction already known. And also in principle, given pain, caretakers' responses blend a capitulation to immediacy with an argument for a new organization. The caretaker aspires to oversee a more or less precipitous, more or less gradual, series of renunciations and replacements. To the infant, the caretaker "says" change your aim from the direct repetition of that earlier mode of pleasurable organization to this newer one, which is, after all, bound to the first either by similarity or by metaphoric and associational propinquity.

In the negotiations of infancy, voice encounters voice. The theme of this encounter is repetition versus renunciation. And of course, the ground of this ongoing argument (the "civilizing" argument) is fundamentally unsteady because it is fundamentally determined via dialogical dynamics of power and persuasion. The stakes of the dialogue are high, and neither of the participants—infant nor caregiver—is in full control of himself or herself.

Both "speak" sincerely. For both parties, unconsciously originating desires are felt as conscious necessities. The civilizing process entails sustained, forced contact between incompatible necessities. The process takes place as demand encounters demand; flesh alternately presses against and withdraws from flesh. In these contacts of the flesh, bodies are being put to rhetorical use; rhetoric is being put to the bodily use. For the infant, the cry and its vicissitudes are in the service of a body becoming sexual, whereas on the caregiver's side, the vicissitudes of touch and word are in the service of a body already saturated with sexual habit, a voice accustomed to having its say.

The infant's impulse to immediacy directly collides with the caregiver's impulse to pause and consider. The caretaker aims at negotiation, finding the right way to proceed, the proper response. What is right for the caretaker is never entirely self-determined. The voice of the caregiver is not singular; it includes the voice of tradition, the influence of the classical.

Infant and caregiver both mesh and collide. The caretaker looks for traditional solutions to traditional problems. For the infant, each of these proposed solutions results in a mix of satisfaction and disappointment. These mixed experiences both stock memory and seed anticipation. As such, they serve to put the formal, temporally organized structures of subjectivity into place.

In these encounters, caregiver and infant both undergo enormous strain. For the infant, the strain is obvious; needs and desires are overwhelming and satisfaction is far from guaranteed. For the caregiver, the strain resides most pointedly in the reopening of a discourse long ago thought closed—contending with a body-in-formation, giving structure to that body's cries and silences. Each voice in the encounter is vying to define optimally a field of mutually engendered pains and pleasures. *Optimal* here means keeping pleasure inside and pain outside. "Inside" and "outside" are themselves objects of negotiation, since the emerging subjective borders are blurred by unstable identifications—projective and introjective.

The caregiver's ministrations necessarily include an erotic dimension. Voice encounters voice in an immediate asymmetry—the infant needs, the caregiver wants. The organizational imperatives of need are different from those of want. Want allows for substitution whereas need demands the thing itself

It is this rhetorical asymmetry that gives child care its necessarily "seductive" dimension. The caregiver gives what is wanted to someone else. This giving necessarily resonates with significance. To give or to refuse what is wanted, to satisfy or not to satisfy—such activities cannot take place without an erotic dimension. A theory of sexuality will have to account for the infant's interiorization of this erotic dimension—the moment when the infant meets the caregiver's long-standing sexualized voice with a newly sexualized voice of his or her own. This is the moment when both parties seem intently engaged in putting the infant's mouth, say, to uses that suddenly have taken on only a coincidental relation to purposes of nourishment.

At that moment, we can say that two erotized voices are "speaking." Both speak sincerely, and the meanings of each must be found via theory. For each voice, suddenly, there is a surface and a depth. By *surface,* I mean, for example, the skin and mucosa of the mouth, sites on which there is a mutual enactment of wishes. For each voice, these wishes originated earlier and are now mediated by memory. For both voices, the satisfaction of these wishes will depend not only upon the empirical actions taken but also, and more importantly, on the dynamics of representation and resemblance through which those actions are linked to earlier ones. Action will satisfy if, and only if, it can be represented as a repetition of a previous satisfaction.

Each voice aims at repeating a remembered pleasure. Each voice, then, can now be said to have the capacity to argue its own cause, to work the surface so as to have both the surface and the means by which the surface is represented optimally coincide with the representation of what it wants. A sexual argument is taking place, a play of accommodation and opposition between a newly emerging voice (one with a meager repertoire from which to draw resemblances) and a traditional one (one with a vast repertoire).

Infant and caregiver bracket the infant's mouth and together create the possibility of it becoming sexualized. Both participate in sexuality's origin, but neither witnesses it. Suddenly, it is upon them. Regarding sexuality's origin, both are left with only inference, only "theory." With its earliest words, its earliest reports on what it wants and, therefore, wants to do again, the first-person voice reports a knowledge it has gained only after the fact.

To theorize sexuality is to give it a history, a context, to insert it "within the chain of the person's psychic experiences" (Freud, 1900). This act of insertion is problematic. It is often met with resistance, and when it is, the interpretation of sexuality will necessarily expand to include an interpretation of that resistance. Every element of sexuality is open to interpretation and is, therefore, resistable— from the terms by which its explicit acts are described to the concepts by which its beclouded origins are imagined.

In general, the contest is most fierce when the interpretation claims manifest sexual expression as an anxious version of disavowed sexual origin. This is the interpretation that most directly offends sincerity's sensibilities. A sexual theory, then, will receive its most severe test when it interprets ardent desire as covert defense. And indeed, this is the cardinal orienting interpretation of the psycho-analytic theory of sexuality. When we place sexuality's origin within the field set up by the bodily mediated rhetoric surrounding sensual sucking, we are necessarily driven to think of the entire subsequent range of sexual expression as an elaboration of, and a series of transformations performed on, this original oral theme.

The original aim and object of sucking is not easily, nor ever fully, abandoned. Instead of abandonment, then, our sexual theory postulates a series of trans-formations. Each of these transformations takes place via new versions of the conflict-laden civilizing rhetoric, a rhetoric produced by incompatible necessities placed in irreversible sustained contact. These new versions, like the original one, pit impulses toward repetition against impulses toward modification, though with each party now coming to be differentially invested in what ought to be preserved and what ought to be changed. The infant no longer can be identified as solely on the side of repetition, the caretaker no longer solely on the side of modification. The terms of the new sexual argument, though, remain intact: It is a contest, via sexuality, over what is necessary, what is good, and what is real.

At the interface of this argument are two competing sincere voices. Both infant and caregiver give voice to what is necessary, what is good, and what is real. Each knows itself as wishing; neither knows itself as in flight. Thus, both voices are unreliable. The absence of directly articulated anxiety at the civilizing/sexualizing interface engenders the later necessity for sexual theorizing. Because sincerity and sexuality, on both sides of the interface, are each in part a product of anxiety, each side is necessarily disqualified as a reliable historian.

There is nothing contingent about the psychoanalytic reluctance to take at face value the sincere, affirmative claims of first-person sexual histories. That reluctance is axiomatic. Where the first-person voice necessarily speaks only of a series of affirmations in this narrative, we grant an essential place to anxiety. We assume that danger mingles with pleasure in spurring the renunciation of x and y on the way to z.

For the first-person voice, though, to the extent that its sexual expression is sincere, this theorized dimension of anxious aversion cannot be known. Invested in establishing its own sexuality as positive, the first-person voice is, therefore, also invested in effacing any sign of anxiety from what it can deduce of the determinants of its sexual preferences.

In defense of its own sincerity, the first-person voice might, therefore, argue for a theory of sexuality in which only first-person testimony would be admissible. Such theory would be grounded in a methodology of introspection. Its power would be measured by its capacity to produce affect sensed as authentic. Its yield would be a report on *my* sexuality or perhaps, in the presence of a sympathetic witness, on *ours*. This is often the epistemological position of voices explicitly aiming to transfigure the scars left by a history of oppression. For such voices, any theorization of "reality" risks ceding authority to the outside. But to locate epistemological authority outside is to recreate the original oppressive condition. Theory itself takes on an oppressive valence and is, therefore, pushed aside in favor of liberatory "directness"—sincerity.

Contesting the presumed link between liberation and sincerity is a voice that links privileged sincerity not to liberation but to tyranny. This voice would have a direct interest in preserving the contemporary from undue assault. It would counter the epistemological appeals of sincerity with an appeal to epistemological disinterest.

This is the premise of the traditional clinical voice. It refuses the claims of raw introspection, no matter how meticulous, and insists on the balancing presence of a disinterested second-person voice. This second voice is a theorized one. It is constructed out of controlled processes of identification and disidentification and will, in principle, be able to resist the blunt appeal of affect as a measure of truth. Therefore, via the insertion of theory, it will be capable of speaking, with authority, not of its own sexuality and not necessarily of sexuality in general but of *your* sexuality.

Yet another position, the traditionally scientific one—even more cautious— would refuse to grant epistemological authority to either monads or dyads, no matter their methods, and would demand a disengaged third-person voice, one obliged to a mathematically constructed plurality. This voice would then be licensed to speak of a sexuality neither its own nor yours but rather, via the controlled and disinterested observation of many, of *human* sexuality.

Freud's sincerity casts its shadow on his theorizing. I intend to relook at Freud's theorization via a consideration more of the voice in which it was written than of the findings it announces. What it finds, first and foremost, is the determining role of disappointments in the construction of femininity and indeed of female homosexuality. My grounding assumption will be that the disappointments Freud finds as constitutive of the female homosexual—no phallus, no Oedipal object—hardly mark her as a unique subject. Rather than theorizing these disappointments as the determinants of femaleness and/or female homosexuality, I will regard them as the preconditions of sexuality itself. I will look at the female homosexual not as a special case but as a general one. Freud's theorization, then, will come into focus not as inaccurate on its face but as inaccurate in its context. What he saw in the female homosexual can be seen in any "sexual." The corrective I offer is to universalize the disappointments that Freud here symptomatically saw as the single hallmarks of both the "female" and the "homosexual."

What Freud's female homosexual seeks in her erotic life is to restore a state whose very existence is entirely fantastic—the state of erotic sufficiency. This is the promise she hopes to realize via her two-pronged strategy of renunciation and embrace. Freud focuses on this strategy as particular to her and to the category of female homosexuality. I mean to argue that belief in the promise of erotic sufficiency inevitably depends upon just such a two-pronged tactic.

Disappointment presumes expectation, and to expect is to expect *again,* to anticipate the repetition of a satisfaction once had. To be disappointed, then, is to have now lost what one once had.

Sexuality, wanting via one's body, necessarily confesses both to a want in one's body and to the fantasy of that want assuaged. For psychoanalysis, disappointment remains a mundanely ordinary feature of quotidian life as long as the object both lost and wanted can again, literally, be found. The paradigm here is food: the bread once had, now gone, soon to reappear. Though fantasy may accrue to this sequence, it need not accrue for there to be both disappointment and satisfaction. For Freud, those wants that could be satisfied without the mediation of fantasy were called needs. At the same time, disappointment is always layered with fantasy and as such is psychoanalytically meaningful.

Sexuality is sexual, for Freud, to the extent that all three elements in the sequence—the object once had, the object lost, the object again to be found—are fantastic. In contrast to need, sexual desire, for Freud, cannot be satisfied. Whatever is found can only resemble the object represented as lost. Hunger might be temporarily fooled by, but never permanently satisfied by, something like food. This "something like" is the condition of sexuality's object, for Freud.

For Freud, all of sexuality is grounded in double disappointment. Our original genitals are inadequate to their original aims, and our original objects prove finally to be unavailable. But the foundational status of double disappointment is only made explicit in his theorization of female development. For the girl, Freud posits a unique moment of genital disappointment. He writes of her "realizing" its inadequacy "in a flash." This "realization" then incites a turning away from the whole of her previously satisfactory masturbatory activity. It also incites a turning toward the male genital, whose adequacy is "realized" in the self-same "flash." She is certain that what she has lost can only be found again through the self-punishing renunciation of her own active pleasure, which she achieves through turning toward the man who is deemed capable of fulfilling her.

Freud treats the girl's "flash" as inspired. That is, he completely identifies with the girl he is theorizing. Each believes in the *material* reality of her disappointed condition. A theorized psychic reality has been transfigured into an untheorized material reality. With this, Freud and the little girl both see passivity as her only solution.

Freud also identifies with the theorized girl's counterpart, the adequate boy. But unlike the girl, this boy is at no point theorized. His adequacy is simply asserted. Male concern about genital inadequacy is then, by simple inference, construed as concern about feminization.

Here, an untheorized psychic reality—the adequate genital—is now transfigured into an untheorized material reality. Freud confidently uses this figure. It functions like a fetish might. It fills an absence that sincerity reads as material with an object that theory reads as imaginary.

Both theoretically and clinically, the interpretation of defensively driven identifications has long been a Freudian motif. Via Freud, we have been empowered to see and interpret the fiction that these identifications sustain. At the heart of that fiction are the notions that the lost predecessor is present and adequate and that via identification both that presence and that adequacy can be claimed for oneself.

Theory grounded in similar *identifications—sincere theory*—sustains and yields a similar fiction. Such is the case with Freud's representation of male sexuality as grounded in genital adequacy. Via a consideration of the following two cases, I mean to expose some features of the theoretically mediated fictions that follow from such a representation.

Case #1

Ms A entered analysis five years ago, a 35-year-old woman troubled by a sense that she was "not as happy as she might be." At that time, she was single and having a series of unsatisfactory and transient sexual relationships with men. She characterized her desire in terms of her need to have these men want her. Her focus would be on getting them to want to have sex with her, which seemed to quiet her own wanting for a time. Frequently, these liaisons would cease after one encounter, and Ms A would be bewildered and alarmed, feeling "as though I am nothing."

Only after a lengthy period of psychotherapeutic work did Ms A achieve any stable sense of self-regard. Up until then, her conscious desire was entirely organized around getting men; she wanted their total attention. Once her self-esteem was somewhat stabilized, she realized that the men chosen were inevitably "beneath" her—never her intellectual, social, or economic equals. Often they were men she "didn't even like."

She was preoccupied with hope organized around the idea of having the man's penis inside of her. Most encounters, however brief, would have an initial effect of making her feel "better," "fuller," just after sex. Afterward, she experienced terrible defeat if the man did not call; if the man called, it meant that she had something worth wanting. She felt that the man's desire was based on what she did or did not have.

If a man suggested disinterest in her, she experienced "crushing disappointment." She sensed everything meaningful about her was lost. Instantaneously, she could lose her sense of desirability, well-being, and efficacy. She would feel "back to being on my own, alone" and "lacking," "less." These states of deficiency were particularly acute when she would calculate her assets as compared to women who seemed successfully coupled with a man. Via such calculations, she always "came up short."

My theorized sketch of Ms A 's initial presentation

For Ms A, sexual coupling assumes a quantitative dimension. Coupling makes her "more," "bigger," and "extends" her sense of self. Working against the idea that "on her own" she is painfully deficient, she targets a man as the remedy to a persistent sense of insufficiency. On the surface she resembles Freud's classic girl. She imagines herself having once been something she can no longer be unless added onto by a man. The fantasy of sexual having goes only so far. She must concretely have the penis in order to feel completed by it. She then, in fantasy, is restored, her sense of disappointment quieted temporarily as she feels whole again.

Despite great strides and economic success in work (also viewed as making her feel "bigger"), not yet having a relationship with a man continues to be evidence of her inferiority to other women who *have*. With her analyst, Ms A senses herself particularly lacking. The analyst *has*—men, babies, a kind of vital internal substance. She feels herself "full of shit" by comparison.

As Ms A contends with oscillations in her picture of herself, she simultaneously imagines women thinking about her, evaluating her, basing their thoughts and assessments on what she has acquired. If she is with a man, she seeks affirmation in the eyes of a woman—any woman. Such affirmation makes her feel "glorified." Especially if the man in question is unequivocally beautiful, she is reassured of her own sense of goodness through knowing that it is she, not other women, who inspires the man's wanting. Beauty and goodness are linked and reassure her of her special ability to be desired.

A more imperfect man is a mirror to her own failings. "I realize the problem with P is he is small, dark, he is average. There is no problem with that except it is like me—and I do not want to be seen that way, small, dark. It is not the image I wish to have of myself." Emotional vulnerability in a man is another mark of imperfection. A man who is "too open" seems weak to her, distinctly not in possession of "the hard penis I was hoping to have from him." This hard penis has become a central element in the structure of her own desire.

If many women do not want what he has, how important can what he has be? Getting a man wanted by few women only confirms her sense of herself as "damaged goods."

Shadowing Ms A's conscious preoccupying fantasy of getting and having a man is her wish to be at the center of a woman's attention and from there to receive her approbation. Her orienting heterosexual fantasy of getting a man, therefore, is linked to a homosexual fantasy in which she establishes an erotic tie with a woman against whom she can prove herself superior. She must outdo all others, and she must succeed in this outdoing for all time; otherwise, she feels herself to be nothing.

As the youngest of three children, Ms A assumed herself to be an afterthought. The parents' relationship was a source of constant anguish for her. She would peer from the window waiting for their return from evenings together. The mere fact of her parents being together was an ongoing sign of their rejection of her. She still says with conviction that she does not understand why or how they could want to have excluded her.

Her feeling of wanting to be chosen, of needing to outdo all others as a prerequisite for a sense of self-regard, originated in relation to her siblings. She felt that they had already had her mother, and that her mother, "the busiest of women," was too distracted to attend to her. She felt especially jealous of a brother ten years her senior. He had a long period of drug abuse, with extended hospitalizations. Though debilitated, he was also idealized, especially by his younger sister. He fostered this idealization and exploited it, getting her to sell drugs for him. In adolescence, Ms A herself had a history of lying and shoplifting and was once expelled from school for cheating.

But unlike for her older brother, for her these unruly behaviors did not elicit affirmation. Rather, she repeatedly had the sense that even her problems "did not add up," "were not big enough," in comparison to her brother's. When she was expelled from school, her mother slapped her and said, "I cannot have another M!" In other words, there was only room for one.

The analysis has revealed the painful wish to be first: first with her mother and then—that repressed wish's derivative expression—first with a man. Longing for a woman has been replaced in consciousness with longing for a man. And the longing is to be wanted, to be all important, to be so valuable and so superior that no one will ever be able to outdo her.

What Ms A visits and revisits in her recurrent disappointment is the hope that she possesses what it takes to win. What she ultimately wants is her mother's love. She wants to fill the mind of the mother, as her brother once had. Her despair is grounded in the sense that in this instance, once is for all time.

To possess the mother's mind she must be bigger, larger, and more solid. The brother has the mother; she doesn't. The problem of difference is approached via a fantasy of difference. He has what she both wants and needs—needs in order to attract and keep the mother.

The brother's "big" problems and "big" penis are means to enter and fill the mother's mind and body. Having neither her mother's love nor the mind and body to secure it constitutes a brutal attack on her own narcissistic equilibrium. She, therefore, constantly appraises herself, always in relation to other women. Is she as smart as they? Is she as beautiful? If a woman who is fantastically beautiful sits at a table beside her, she is suddenly stricken with the awful sense of being less. She maintains two representations of herself that work to elide each other. In one she is identified with the brother and capable of being "the be all and end all" to those around her. In another she is nothing—if she cannot be the most beautiful, the most intelligent, the most charming, her self-esteem plummets.

At times, she speaks of being the woman wanted above all others. But the slightest evidence that she is not all-important leads to crushing disappointment. She generally characterizes it as a disappointment fundamental to being feminine— a genital disappointment. But this attribution of the disappointment to her anatomical difference obscures a preanatomical and more central disappointment: the failure to have ever attained sufficient proof of her mother's love.

Ms A has tried to account for this formative absence via sexual and narcissistic fantasies. She imagines herself an imperfect person and then lives imperfectly both to prove this and to disprove it by finally winning her mother's attentions.

Ms A envies the brother his capacity to fill their mother's mind and body. Her own inability is construed as the result of being the third child: last in line, a girl, and filled with envy/shit. The interworkings of envy, longing, and narcissistic fragility in this woman might well, to a naïve eye, appear to be the consequence of intractable penis envy. Such an interpretation might be equivalent in this case to Freud's attribution of disappointment in his case of the female homosexual. Disappointment figures largely in Ms A, as it does for Freud's young woman. Both women might be understood to want something from their mothers that is unforthcoming. While each has developed a different manifest solution, the underlying fantasy content seems to be a hybrid of heterosexual desire and homoerotic longing. Each is disappointed—the narcissistic self-accusation of genital deficiency comes as a belated mode of accounting for perceived failures in the mother, the expression of which might further drive the mother away. Without the mother's secure presence, each of these women finds entry into more mutually gratifying sexual relations intensely problematic. The persistence of disappointment is like the persistence of hope. The "female homosexual" and our patient, the female heterosexual, employ the same tactic. Each retreats from both her own body and some of her own objects so as to maintain a fantasy that the mother is still accessible: that *her* love and *her* body will be renunciation's reward.

Case #2

J is a 40-year-old man who initially sought analysis because of inhibitions regarding his career as a singer. Immediately after the analysis began, however, it became clear that he would use the analysis much differently than he had originally proposed. It was to be a prop by which he could completely withdraw from singing, from social life, from commitments in general, so as to descend into full-time clerical work, a life organized around staying occupied and, therefore, distracted from ever having to think about what he might "want."

The analyst was no longer there to help but rather to construct a setting that affirmed the patient's sense of self-sufficiency. Self-sufficiency meant an emotional coolness that was grounded in "wanting nothing." Explaining this, J said, "We have an understanding. What we know is that everything is in its proper place. All is well. Everyone is happy."

His sexual behavior seems to offer him neither satisfaction nor disappointment. He has sex with the woman he lives with, but as he puts it, "not really." "I could never really have sex with her. Not because of her, though. It's anyone. How could I ever have sex with anyone? Then I'd have to explain why I'm not having sex with all the other possible women. My sex has to take place with no possibility of ever having to account for it, for why I wanted it, and for why I did it with the person I did it with. What I have isn't sex, it's the idea of sex. That idea will come true later. For now, I'm still getting ready."

For J, wanting is intolerable. Wanting is pathetic, weak, horrifying. To want is to admit that the world contains what you are missing.

Fundamentally, J lives in a quasi-dream state: a state of continuous, near hallucinatory wish-fulfillment. Primary process rules. There are no substantive contradictions, there is no operative "no," and time is reversible. By conflating idea and perception, he averts what Freud calls "bitter experience" and thus averts the necessity of calling secondary process into play. As J says, "I have what I want because I want it." This omnipotent concatenation— "I have what I want because I want it"—undoes the unbearable idea that "I want what I want because I don't have it."

Each element—the manic sense of omnipotence and the depressive sense of insufficiency—are necessary ingredients of all wishing and thus of all sexuality. J protects against any awareness of insufficiency either in himself or in his object. By psychic definition, disappointment has no place. Conscious life is designed to approximate a state of uninterrupted wish-fulfillment. Instead of "real" sexuality, J experiences what he calls "the idea of sexuality." His conscious sexual life is structured as the obverse of Freud's patient's. She, falling prey to double disappointment, turns depressively away from both her own body and her own original object. J, on the other hand, fends off both disappointments but nonetheless must turn away from both his own body and his object's in order to sustain this victory. "Bitter experience" has been too much for Freud's patient, whereas for J, "bitter experience" is located in an ever-receding future. Each of them, like Ms A, has been unable to reconcile the depressive impact of double disappointment with the omnipotent promises of sexual coupling.

On the way to his early morning analytic appointments J regularly sees a group of schoolgirls on the street. He imagines that they, like he, are excited by the passing encounter. "That's enough for me," he says. The idea of actually doing something, to become a schoolteacher and, therefore, perhaps, a schoolgirl's heartthrob, is a horrible one. "Perhaps" is the problem. J lives in a state of perpetual certainty. There are no contingencies. Of pursuing a teaching career, he says, "I would be despicable and pathetic, some man who wanted something from some girls." If J has a favorite sweater, he never wears it. If he has a good idea, he keeps it to himself. Anything he likes, he hides, keeps pristine. His aspiration for himself is to become an admired "pristine object on the shelf." Fantasy is not only equivalent to deed, it is superior. Deed "dirties" the thing done; fantasy keeps it pure. Deed takes place in the world of bodies and objects. Fantasy takes place anterior to them both. Deed is contiguous with disappointment whereas fantasy trumps it.

To become the "pristine object on the shelf" is, for J, to restore himself to a state of fullness and plenitude, a status once his and then lost catastrophically at the time of what he calls his "breakdown." This breakdown took place as he realized that singing had been, for him, a means to "get it all," "to have it all fall in my lap without ever having to want something," and that this was not going to happen.

What is meant by pristine is virginal—never having been had, never having wanted. J's Bartleby-like descent into the lowest levels of office work offers relief from any moment of wanting. While at work, he actively "thinks" that his firm's highest-ranking executives secretly admire him, see his genius, wish they had the courage to have given it all up like he did, and realize that it is they who have made the big mistake and fallen for all the tricks: the wish for family, pursuit of love, and so forth.

J:　　　　I had a dream. Nothing important. Not really useful to talk about.
Analyst:　You are not sure I will be able to see its relevance to what we're doing.
J:　　　　I was at a party with Mick Jagger. It was very cool. The important thing was to make sure that Mick Jagger did not know how cool I thought it was. If he found out, then he would no longer want to be with me.
Analyst:　You were unsure if you deserved to be with him.
J:　　　　I don't know if I ever told you about the rock and roll band I was in high school. I played guitar. Ever since I stopped and took up singing, not a day has gone by when I don't regret it. By now, I could have been a rock star.

I got my girlfriend to listen to Sheryl Crow. She's a fan now. We were listening last night.

I liked how excited my girlfriend got. I was listening to the backup guitar. I could play like that. I could be her backup. Be on tour with her. Have a relation with her. I would be the guy she'd always been waiting for but never really believed was possible. She would have fucked so many other guys, but the moment it was me, she would know that I was the one. We would be onstage, even fuck onstage. Nothing would be greater, her and me, everyone knowing. The sexiest woman alive, the sexiest man alive, together. It's that or nothing. It's that. It's like it's true. Nothing else is as true as that.

Discussion

The backdrop for J's heterosexual activities is the fantasy that, in effect, they are not taking place. The necessary fiction is that what he is doing is entertaining an idea and not performing an action. J can be sexual as long as he never has a sexual experience. Experience is the problem. And the problematic element integral to experience is the possibility of disappointment.

Freud's patient, like our two, comes to know her own body as a site of insufficiency, a site from which she has to turn away if she is to find any compensatory relief. This initial turning away is, of course, the precondition for any turning toward. Erotic object-seeking is premised on the possibility of finding elsewhere what one has somehow lost, and cannot find, on one's own body. In this sense, one's own necessarily disappoints. Object-choice, the organized turning away from one's own body and toward another's, will depend on the set of fantasies by which one accounts for that disappointment. Those fantasies organize one's wanting, making possible a narrative that tells what one has lost, why one has lost it, where it can be found, the conditions by which it can be obtained, and so forth.

One's body and one's objects are both held to account for one's "bitter experience." Each is turned away from because each is sensed, alternatively, as the primary cause of pain.

In sexuality, the body of one's own that one seeks, like the object that one seeks, is necessarily fantastic. Body and object—if not one, then the other will protect against loss. This is sexuality's orienting wish, the wish to eradicate loss.

Sincerity drives the search; theory, beholden to "bitter experience," accounts for both the endurance and the failure of sincerity's search.

Second aside: Little Richard

I'd close the door and plug in to Little Richard pounding a piano in lipstick and mascara, this wild-looking black man with marcelled hair, pimped-out clothes and bulging eyes. Volume maxed-up, I'd rock around my room, doing the chicken, shaking my head, screaming my lungs out. No one was home. No one could hear me. Little Richard was taking me to where I never thought I'd be. It was a wild place, a black place, a place I'd found by myself. No one was there but me and Little Richard. I knew he was famous and other people listened to these songs. But that didn't matter. It didn't count. What the others were doing on American Bandstand was not the same as what I was doing. I'd see them on TV, looking at each other, dancing with each other, dressed up and shiny. I wasn't on TV. I wasn't dancing with anyone. I wasn't dressed up. And I wasn't shiny. I was in my room, door closed, sweaty and invisible. What I was doing was private. It was just the two of us. For hours each afternoon, me and Little Richard ripped it up, slipped and slid. I was Long Tall Sally, I was Saturday Night, I was Just Got Paid. It wasn't sexual. I wasn't getting ready, wasn't prepping. My moves here stayed here. I'd never dance this way with a girl. I wasn't thinking about any effect this was having on me, of any way to carry what was happening with me and Little Richard outside of my room. I wasn't thinking of change, of ever doing elsewhere what I was doing here. It was always just me and him. Him at the piano, screaming, dressed the way he dressed, wearing his hair as he did, breaking every rule I'd ever heard of. And me right with him, dancing, singing, screaming, getting the words right, even when the words made no sense, when they weren't even words: "Saturday night and I just got paid, bon a lotta money and I pont got daid . . ." It was a private matter. Words, sense, good taste, Ella Fitzgerald, Sarah Vaughan—these were all outside things, public things, things you'd go to school for, you'd tell people about, you'd use to indicate you were on the right track.

My mother was a fan of good music, good singers, good taste. She knew her stuff like a rabbi knows his: good books, good music, orthopedic shoes and wide-wale corduroy, car coats and Hebrew school. Get all that right and you had a chance. Get it wrong and you were dead.

Being a Jew, though, you'd likely get it right. You had a head start, spotters all around—dead spotters, Israeli spotters, uncles and aunts, grandparents who crawled their way across the Atlantic. You had Yom Kippur and solemn prayer. Jews were good. Jews were the best. Being a Jew was like having particularly functional abdominal organs: liver and pancreas and kidneys. These organs were not going to fail you. You were going to die of bullets or poison gas or a heart attack—from outside causes, from some unjustified malevolence. You were not burdened with some internal rot. You were endowed. And all you had to do was to protect your endowment. Good music and good books fed these organs, nurtured them.

And then there was trash. Trash was poison. Trashy clothes, trashy books, trashy music. Douse your organs in trash and they'd wither. Your teeth would go. You'd have no job. You'd be holding a can of beer and get killed in some Asian war. You could see them, the doomed ones, lining up: wiry boys named Wagasy and DeLorenzo, tattoos and Lucky Strikes, white tee shirts and catechism, divorced parents and the Ford Motor Company, older brothers in the service. Girls in skin tights, slouched against their lockers, hips swinging like flags, V-necks and beehives. That was trash. Little Richard was trash.

It wasn't even the wrong track he sang from, but rather a parallel track, one entirely unrelated to what was intended for me. Little Richard's was neither an intersecting nor an alternative track. His was off the grid. Whatever happened on that grid—Little Richard's—whatever it was, I knew I was being cared for. I was safe there, with him, off the grid: let's go, no limit. Little Richard could take it all, could dish it all out. He was pulling me along, always a little further, making me wonder why I'd ever go back.

But, in fact, I never really wondered, not exactly. There was no question of why this was taking place, why it would end, why it would happen again. I always knew I'd have to go back on track, always knew I'd get to come back here whenever I wanted. So 5:30 would come, my dad home from work, time for dinner, time to close this door, shut down the record player and sit at the table with meat loaf, milk and chocolate cake. My dad with his rough hands and dirty nails, nobody talking, ten minutes or so and it was over.

All those afternoons with Little Richard and you can never again believe that reason and rules best map your possibilities. Little Richard's always out there at the edge, screaming his lungs out, screaming at you, saying, why stop, why stop there, come on, come on.

Psychoanalysis at its best does what Little Richard did. Like Little Richard, the analyst, the man, is always out there at the edge, not screaming, but insisting with words and with silence, why stop, why stop there; come on, come on.

Little Richard the man, or, in effect, Dr Little Richard the psychoanalyst, makes you feel that if you stop, it's you that's doing the stopping, it's you that feels exhausted, that this point is good enough, that what's available here will be sustaining, that it's permissible to be too tired to continue, to be afraid even. Stop or go on, it's yours to choose.

This book is also dedicated to Little Richard.

Chapter 9

Looking at a transsexual[1]

In looking at a man, we necessarily look at the manner in which he occupies and lives in his body. Having access only to peripheral signs—his manner, carriage, bearing, presentation, all the words and gestures that constitute the picture we have of him—we then try to infer something of the operative dynamics at work nearer to Freud's "frontier," the point of contact between mind and body. This effort at inference informs and directs our every clinical interpretation. We interpret the manifest periphery—our "picture"—as an expression of work being done closer to the inaccessible center.

When we scan and interpret the available periphery, our attention is organized so that we can think about what this man wants and needs, what he is striving to get, what he is seeking when seeking satisfaction. That is, our attention is organized around the concept of appetite: he is hungry for what, wanting what, missing what, needing what, etc.

In interpreting a man's peripherally accessible appetites, we invariably encounter the organizing presence of our own sense of appropriate appetites. After all, to think of an appetite as excessive or inhibited or deviant—in fact, to think of an appetite at all—we necessarily, even if reluctantly, place it in relation to our personal standards: standard aims, standard objects, standard intensities. These standards derive from our sense of the appropriate and the natural. This is so, I think, even when we—I certainly include myself here—profess no confidence in either "the appropriate" or "the natural" as orienting categories. Entirely unbidden, these categories of the appropriate and natural, harmoniously resonating with our own, only slightly idiosyncratic, versions of "the facts of life," create boundaries and limits on what it is possible for us to think.

Take, for example, tattoos. More present on our patients' bodies today than they once were, tattoos often seem to be making an implicit claim to be read as markers of erotic independence—signifiers of bodily ownership and sexual assertion. For

1 Material from this chapter first appeared in Moss, D. and Zeavin, L. (1999) "The female homosexual: c'est nous," in R. Lester and E. Schoenberg (eds) *That Obscure Subject of Desire: Freud's Female Homosexual Revisited*, London: Routledge. Used with permission.

some of us, "discreetly" placed tattoos might well read exactly like that and, as such, will seem both appropriate and natural in contemporary American culture. But multiply a tattoo's number, change their placement, place them on the neck and face, add images of monsters, say, and they will, at some point, start to seem like markers not of ownership and independence but rather of their contraries. Our tattooed patient will then come to seem owned by the tattoos rather than owning them, possessed by them rather than having them in his possession. At this point, the tattooed man's accounts of his appetite for tattoos will have stopped seeming reliable; we will hear rationale as rationalization, affirmation as denial, etc.

It is here, when, in our minds, tattoos escape the confines of the appropriate, when their owner's voice loses its reliability, that appetite provokes interpretation. No matter his claims, no matter his rationale, no matter the context he evokes, we will, at this point, lose access to disinterested listening as we contend with what now seems like an ugly slathering of tattoos. Try as we might, once this point is reached, we will no longer want to or be able to treat the tattoos as the expression of a natural and appropriate appetite for independence, creativity, and bodily ownership. At this point, whenever it arrives, the tattoos will seem to us to represent an appetite gone awry, turned excessive and foul.

For my purposes, the precise location of this drift into excess is without importance. What is important, though, is that for all of us, I think that such a point exists: the point where appetitive variation seems to cross over into appetitive excess. We do not "think" this point into place. Instead, it pre-exists and limits our capacity to think about tattoos in this case, and about appetites—particularly erotic ones—in general. Our sense of the natural, the commonsensical, the self-protective and the appropriate all limit and set boundaries on our capacities for psychoanalytic thinking about erotic appetites.

Regarding erotic appetites, we think both within and against these unbidden limits and boundaries. Without such boundaries, psychoanalytic thinking—even thinking itself—might not be possible. Each of us works within their confines. They limit and provide structure to both what we can do and what we can think. As Freud famously conceptualized the uninterpretable navel of a dream, so, I think, an uninterpretable center lurks beneath these boundaries. That which frames our thought cannot itself become an object of our thought. Of course, the particular boundaries can be shifted; we might well be able to think more now than we once could. But the fact of limiting boundaries cannot be obliterated. These boundaries define thought's possibilities as well as its impossibilities.

A patient of mine movingly captured some of the pain of this situation of unbidden boundaries. She is anguished by the erotic appetites of her son. After a series of unhappy relationships with women, he had just completed a civil commitment ceremony with a man. My patient said, "I have never seen him as calm and settled as he is now. For the first time in his life he seems happy." She added, though, "It breaks my heart to see him with a man. I hate to say this but I would rather he be unhappy with a woman than happy with a man. I wish it were not true, but it is. I can't help it. I love him but I don't want him happy like this.

This is not what he was really meant to be." And with that, this patient lands on what, for her, is the powerful force of the natural and appropriate, the boundary beyond which she cannot think, monitored by a force she names "what he was meant to be."

It seems to me that transsexuals present us clinically with what might be the most blunt conflict we will ever encounter between what a patient wants and what we might feel "s/he was meant to be"; that is, between a patient's sexual "appetite" and what we might feel to be his/her appropriate sexual "nature." The patient declares that the very possibility of sexual satisfaction depends upon the radical—surgical—transformation of the material structure—the "nature"—of the sexual apparatus.

Here then, before anything else, the work demanded of mind by virtue of its attachment to body is that the body be fundamentally—materially—reconfigured before any further psychic work can even begin. This demand will likely be heard by many of "us" as a demand not merely for reconfiguration, though, but also, in violation of the appropriate and the natural, a demand for deformation and destruction; that is, the demand made by an appetite gone awry, one whose sincere self-accounts cannot be treated as reliable. And in turn, our hearing it this way will, in all likelihood, itself be heard as the expression of our own appetite—in this case, an appetite for the natural, say—gone awry and turned foul.

In what follows, I will present two radically different ways of looking at a transsexual person, a person who presents us, in extremis, with an irreconcilable and undeniable opposition between the claims of "appetite" and the givens of "nature."

The first comes via Kimberly Pierce's popular 1999 film, *Boys Don't Cry*. The film is based on the true story of the rape and murder of a transsexual person. Decisively, and interestingly, Pierce locates the irreconcilable conflict between appetite and nature not in the transsexual herself, but rather in the minds of the men who murder her. In effect, Pierce moves the boundary over, placing trans-sexualism in the zone of the "natural." She then illuminates the unchecked work-ings of appetite in the form of the maddened minds of those driven to obliterate this unbearable object, this "unnatural monster."

The second comes via Danielle Quinodoz's two seminal psychoanalytic papers (1998, 2002). In these, the nature-appetite boundary maintains its traditional position. For Quinodoz, it is the transsexual himself who, under the threat of being driven mad by the claims of nature, denies the authority of those claims and undergoes a vaginoplasty.

In both looks, then, erotic appetite obliterates an unbearable object.

I begin with Pierce's film. *Boys Don't Cry* was provoked by the 1993 rape and murder of Teena Brandon/Brandon Teena, a 21-year-old transsexual. Brandon was killed in rural Nebraska, to which he had fled from Lincoln, where, Pierce sketchily, and light-heartedly, informs us, life had been laced with the intermittent pleasures and steady difficulties of trying to live as though a boy. Once relocated, Brandon won the friendship of a number of the town's young men, and the love of one of its most desired young women. When Brandon's neurotic penchant for acting out leads to yet another brief stay in a local jail, personal history and biological gender combine to expose her. This exposure eventually leads to her rape and murder.

Pierce, a New Yorker, dropped everything to attend the murder trial and, for months afterwards, lived among people who had constituted Brandon's last circle of intimates. The film, then, is a kind of case report. But rather than primarily studying Brandon's transsexuality, the film presents her transsexual inclinations as a series of euphoric conquests. The film focuses on a range of anxious reactions to her transsexuality. Its strategy is comparable, perhaps, to using the particulars of the Dora case not for what they might reveal about female hysteria, but for what they might reveal about misogyny. The internal anguish wrought by and determining Brandon's sexual confusion is mostly left for the viewer to imagine and fill in. This gap will be particularly noticeable to a clinically inclined viewer. As viewers, we are given only intermittent glimpses into the costs of Brandon's daily sexual transgressions. These glimpses seem meant to remind us of the costs of our own daily economies of transgression and compliance.

In her film, Pierce inserts the unconventional problems of transsexuality into a conventional narrative structure. Throughout the film, Brandon is presented as a doomed though beguiling and beautiful rascal, recognizably located in the lineage of well-known cinematic bad-boys like James Dean, Steve McQueen and Paul Newman. Like these predecessors, Brandon's heroic stature derives from her unwillingness to compromise her identity. Unlike them, though, the identity in question is in an unremitting and overt "sexual crisis." Pierce presents Brandon's struggles against biological determinism as the struggles of a dignified renegade.

Brandon's exhilarated state breaks down rarely in the film. The most poignant moments come when she is about to be revealed as a girl, or, more precisely, as a person with female genitals. Her euphoria is protected only while she can hide, and jeopardized only when her genitals might be seen by attacking men, by an examining doctor, or by her lover. These encounters between two different kinds of reality—one insistent upon hiding and one upon exposure—bring home the enormity of Brandon's crisis. The film presents these crises as taking place in a transitional zone. Rather than focus on the problems of Brandon's isolated, private, and tortured sexual identity, Pierce highlights the culture-wide problems associated with separating sexual identity from genital anatomy.

The weight of Brandon's masquerade does not break her. We see her manage it strategically—tampons stolen from a drug store and carefully placed out of sight, her body "strapped and packed" for every encounter. From the standpoint of the film, what demands accounting for is not her "masquerade," but rather the indignation and, finally, the murderous rage that the masquerade provokes.

In the most thoroughgoing psychoanalytic encounters, as our patients recount their more or less effective efforts to mitigate what Freud called "the bitter experience of life," we painfully bear witness to the eventual capitulation of appetite-driven fantasies to the counterforce of what seems like material necessity. We bear similar witness when watching Pierce's film. Pierce presents Brandon as the incarnation of the elementally Utopian, and classically tragic, hope in the triumph of psychic over material reality. Bearing such helpless witness, whether as clinicians or citizens, compels us to think of our own complicity in the usually latent violence by which cultural order is maintained and its renegades punished. In the film, then, the figure of Brandon takes on martyred status. Her death seems, in effect, a consequence of our sins, as the Paul Newman character's is in *Cool Hand Luke,* or the Jack Nicholson character in *One Flew Over the Cuckoo's Nest.*

Once Brandon makes it out of Lincoln to rural Nebraska, the film focuses on his relationships with five people there: two male friends, a female lover, the lover's mother and a female friend. When Brandon, whom the five have all warmly received as a boy, is discovered to have a female body, each of the relationships is put into crisis. The varying responses seem intended to mark out a full range of possibilities. The female friend feels betrayed but remains sympathetic, perhaps pitying. The female lover remains adamant; no matter the genital particulars, for her, Brandon was, is, and will always be a boy. The mother is disgusted; the figure she once adored as so "handsome" is now transformed into someone "sick" and despicable; she is indifferent to his fate. The two male friends feel they have been lied to, deceived; they react vengefully, furiously, first with rape, and then, when Brandon informs the police, with murder. These are the reactions that the audience must work to comprehend.

Brandon's erotic fluidity unearths the violence in these men. Anything but erotically fluid themselves, they each seem, instead, to be stuck in extremely restrictive prototypical versions of masculinity. For both, erotic competence is lived out lock-step, primarily in the form of a preening, aggressive meanness—a competence grounded in resentful submission to the way things have to be. Meanness and resentment provide contact points for mutual identification and an effective cover for mutual love. Men are the primary audience for other men's preening. They alone are endowed with the power to judge each other's claim to be "real" men. The film vividly illuminates this in a rodeo scene where men ride the tailgates of careening pick-up trucks so as to demonstrate their heterosexual virility to other men. The scene conveys a circus atmosphere—masculine exhibi-tion, and an excited male audience. Women, meanwhile, occupy the position of mere coin in this barely concealed homoerotic economy. Brandon's erotic deftness, her capacities to "pass" the rodeo test and still remain tuned in to feminine desire, exposes both the restrictive and the homoerotic dimensions of the oppressive masculinity with which these men are saddled. They want to pay her back and do it on sexual terms. Together, each the other's witness, they rape her, in an act of violence that seems intended to simultaneously affirm and deny their erotic commitments to each other while teaching Brandon and her friends a female's proper place; when Brandon, by pressing charges, resists the lesson, they kill her.

Pierce uses these five relationships to interrogate the structural interrelations linking identity to normativity, power to desire, sexual fantasy to genital endow-ment, and truth to violence. The film is organized around the reactions to the discovery of Brandon's genital status. As such, the particular focus of the film's enormously dense agenda is on the contested relation between sexual authenticity and sexual masquerade. Pierce directs us, as viewers, away from the usual subject–object position underlying film spectatorship. We identify with Brandon, and with this, that traditional relation has been transformed into an identification. Dislodged from our customary position, we thus feel ourselves participating in the belief/delusion of Brandon's status as a boy. When we watch Brandon undress, we find ourselves believing, with her, that in spite of anatomy, we are seeing the body of a boy. And when anatomy makes its claims on our eyes, we wonder, with Brandon, how best to resist them. This internal conflict between perception and idea, in turn, reveals much about our assumptions concerning gender and gender prerogatives. Such is the driving effort of Pierce's film—to expose our desires and our hatreds even while the film protects Brandon's from more exacting scrutiny.

Brandon's life history, as presented by Pierce, leads us to again assess the shifting balance of forces underlying the relations between sexual identity and genital anatomy, psychic reality and material reality. For Pierce, none of the elements constituting those relations are fixed. This is made clear by her intense focus on the ongoing interpersonal elements that dog each transsexually laden encounter.

The film's material, then, both derives from and illuminates features of the contemporary debates on sexuality that are enlivening contemporary psychoanalysis and the culture at large. The ever-widening scope of this contemporary debate, instigated within psychoanalysis first by feminist and then by gay and lesbian activists, centers on the reading of the relations between sexual "difference" and sexual deviance. The debate, as presented by Pierce, coincides with and illuminates the two apparently irreconcilable promises of an ongoing debate within psychoanalysis.

One premise reads the periphery—difference and deviance—from the vantage point of a posited center. That posited center gives this reading its elemental point of stability and coherence. In principle, from this point of view, difference, as such, is distance from the center, and distance, when marked, is deviance. From here, the center is not the product of circumstance or convention; rather, it is the product of law, of necessity. Within psychoanalysis, a most articulate spokesperson of this point of view is Janine Chasseguet-Smirgel.

The other premise reads the center from the point of view of the periphery. The center, then, becomes merely a "center," a construction. From here, the pertinent task is not, primarily, a critical assessment of deviance, but rather a critical assessment of the center's claims—its metaphysical sense of itself, and of the norms grounded in this metaphysics—phallocentrism, logocentrism, Eurocentrism, etc. From the periphery, the center ought not to serve as theory's source, but rather as theory's object. Difference, in principle, is to be read as a marker of multiplicity rather than of deviance. Here, we might locate the representative voices of Thomas Ogden, say, and Jessica Benjamin.

This contemporary debate, with all of its baroque postmodern turns, is a continuation of the one from which Freud extracted the elementary tenets of clinical psychoanalysis a century ago. It is one measure of the merit of *Boys Don't Cry* that both the problems it addresses and the rhetorical and narrative strategies it employs bear comparison to the problems faced and the strategies he used in writing his foundational text, "Three essays on the theory of sexuality" (Freud 1905).

Freud's "Three essays on the theory of sexuality" are a marvel of rhetorical cunning. They invite the reader to participate in what seems a traditional and conservative approach to the so-called "sexual deviations." But Freud finally, and subtly, turns the entire classificatory project around on itself. Essays that begin by accepting the established divide between the classifying subject and the deviant object end by asserting a covert relation binding deviation to normality. While the traditional strategy of classification leads to a localization and externalization of deviance, Freud's leads to a universalization and internalization of it. If the deviant is enacting what the classifiers fantasize, then the direct classification of manifest sexual deviance will correspond to an indirect classification of neurotic fantasy. Freud's essays have the effect of moving his reader from the secure position of disinterested subject to the less secure one of implicated object.

Like Freud's "Three essays on the theory of sexuality," *Boys Don't Cry* is a rhetorically sophisticated look at sexual deviance. The film's sophisticated structure, like Freud's, is grounded in its reversal of normative premises. Traditionally, transsexuals are situated as "cases," people whose problematic sexuality potentially assists us in our ongoing effort at mapping the relations between sexuality and gender, mind and body, fantasy and reality. Like Freud, Pierce inverts the framing question. Freud established sexuality as the independent, and universal, variable and charted its formal variations in subjects and objects. Pierce presents transsexuality as a kind of unloosed sexuality, a sexuality apparently shorn of material constraint, and of all the signifiers that usually clothe it in reasonableness. She then charts the formal variations this wild card provokes in affected subjects and objects.

As did Freud, Pierce directs our attention not to an interrogation of the unbound sexual constant, but rather of its bound, and inconstant, variations. She wants us to ask: given the disruptions of an unadorned, tyrannical sexuality, what are the determinants that provoke disgust here, hatred there, violence there, love here; an affirmation of psychic over material reality here, its reverse there? As did Freud, Pierce uses such questions to illuminate the fault lines that undermine our every sense of sexual certainty. After all, Pierce seems to suggest, leaning this time on both Flaubert and Freud, for all of us, to the extent that we are all sexual, *"Teena Brandon/Brandon Teena, c'est nous."*

And now, the Quinodoz papers. These are the only two papers in the mainstream psychoanalytic literature to report on a traditional psychoanalytic treatment of a transsexual patient. The aim of the papers is to interrogate the familiar categories of sexuality, psychopathology, transference and counter-transference, as each is illuminated through a sustained clinical encounter with a very unfamiliar category of patient. Quinodoz's central clinical point—her orienting way of looking—is to see the ostensibly unfamiliar as a disguised variant, a masquerade, of the familiar.

For Quinodoz, transsexualism represents a local, and rare, expression of a more fundamental, and more general, phenomenon that she calls "heterogeneity." Heterogeneity is the familiar category; transsexualism is the unfamiliar, but structurally typical, example. Heterogeneity refers to people who cannot bear the co-existence of incompatible psychic parts, and who, therefore, are burdened with an elemental fear of going mad. Such patients have no confidence in the possibility of either an internal or external integrative object—one through which these parts could be integrated. The only imaginable solution, then, is to rid themselves, via expulsion or obliteration, of at least one of the incompatible parts. Quinodoz, then, sees in the transsexual this incompatibility finding expression at the manifest level of sexual identity. The part to be obliterated is located in the sexual apparatus, per se. This location leads to the exigent wish to obliterate and transform primary and secondary characteristics; appetite's aim is to find, or re-find, a condition in which the mix of parts is bearable.

For Quinodoz, then, transsexualism represents merely one possible expression of a more general, and more familiar, problem: an elemental incapacity to tolerate contradictory psychic elements. As such, for her, transsexualism is best thought of as, in effect, *apparent transsexualism*—notwithstanding its manifest material presentation. For Freud, of course, "First and foremost, the ego is a body ego." Quinodoz inverts this orienting phrase. For her, in conditions of heterogeneity, first and foremost the body is an ego body, that is, the mind will use the body to reconfigure itself. Here, Quinodoz positions the body in service to the mind. The body, that is, does the work of self-sacrifice that the mind cannot do on its own. The mind outsources work to the body and the body then speaks, in effect, as mind's proxy.

With its sense of conceptual certainty and its material focus, transsexualism, for Quinodoz, might be categorized as akin to, say, anorexia. Each mounts a sustained assault on the body. Each claims the assault to be grounded in an exigent, reality-based appetite. And each, for the analyst, can be understood as a symptomatic expression of a set of interpretable psychic determinants, emanating, fundamentally, at the frontier between body and mind: Both the anorexic and the transsexual declare, in effect, "I cannot begin to satisfy the demands of mind unless I radically—even violently—transform the given/natural contours of my body."

Here is the first obvious point of both contact and contrast between Pierce and Quinodoz. In transsexualism, analyst and director each sees violent assault; Pierce focuses on the assault originating outside, Quinodoz on the one originating inside. Each views the assault as the inevitable outcome of an incapacity to tolerate an unbearable mix of sexual elements. For Quinodoz, it is the transsexual who cannot bear the mix and then, driven to transform the mix into something bearable, targets her/his given body. For Pierce, it is the outsider who cannot bear the mix and targets the transsexual's transformed body. The transsexual avoids the threat of madness by willing his/her unbearable sexual body from something fixed to something plastic; the outsider avoids the threat of madness by obliterating the transsexual's plastic sexual body and affirming the necessity of it, and all bodies, remaining fixed in their given, natural, condition.

In both cases, violence rules.

The radical—psychoanalytic—turn that Quinodoz takes is to look at the body of the transsexual as the material site on which a fundamental psychic fault finds expression. For Quinodoz, the incapacity to bear one's given body provides a relatively coherent picture. This picture offers what feel like psychic facts, a set of coherent problems, and a vision of a solution. For Quinodoz, this coherent picture disguises the incoherence encountered by a mind unable to integrate itself into a bearable unit; Quinodoz says, in effect, "where unbearable incoherence was, there bearable coherence will be."

In effect, then, for Quinodoz, transsexualism belongs in the category of "conversion symptom." Like hysterical conversion, transsexualism organizes and converts otherwise unrepresentable psychic elements into representable elements located in and on the body. The coherent narrative of hysterical conversion—my body is numb—both satisfies and disguises unacceptable wishes. The coherent narrative of the transsexual, no matter how steep its costs, satisfies the vital need for integration while protecting the mind from catastrophic breakdown.

Quinodoz "looks" at the transsexual's exigent relation to her unacceptable body and "sees" a disguised picture of a bracketed off and disavowed "heterogeneous" mind. Pierce "looks" at the killers' enraged and exigent masculinity and "sees" her version of a comparable heterogeneity—a mind unable to bear itself when presented with a certain kind of body. Quinodoz locates heterogeneity in the mind of the transsexual. Pierce locates its analog in the mental structure of brittle masculinity. For each, the body functions as the site on which an organized coherent picture can emerge. For each, this picture displaces and obscures an unbearable and unrepresentable mental state. This constructed picture leads to violence, of course, but, within the economic terms of heterogeneity or of brittle masculinity, the violence is worth it. Violence is a coherent expenditure. It targets an organized object. Incoherence, on the other hand, has no viable economy. The object it generates, and the violence this object provokes, spawns a coherent economy, sanity's minimal requirement. Stressed beyond its integrative capacities, lacking a represented object and the violent organization that defines a relation to that object, both heterogeneous mind and brittle masculinity fall apart.

The question now is whether these two monocular ways of looking can be brought together binocularly. Can we focus not only on the distinctive difference between the two—violence inside vs violence out—but also on what we can see at the point where the two images converge?

I think that if we look binocularly, we will see not only the violent contests played out on the body of the transsexual, but also the less directly violent, but nonetheless forceful, contests played out on the bodies of everyone. These contests have a transformative effect. Listen for a moment to this 63-year-old male patient, in a long, four-day-per-week analysis:

> You button the top button of your shirt. Don't do it for my sake. I want to make fun of it. It's what I used to do in school. I was the only boy to keep my

top button buttoned. I wouldn't undo it. It was me. I'd be getting ready for school and my mother would say how neat it looked, how proper, how proud she was of me. And then I'd get there and they'd tease me about it. They'd wait for me after school. It was me, though. I wasn't going to change. It was me and my mother. I was a momma's boy. It drove them crazy. I was the exception. I wouldn't give in. I still won't. I don't care. You say I dress like a boy. I am a boy. So what? If I could be a man just like that, no waiting, no going through anything, maybe I'd take it. But I'm not about to give up what I have in order to maybe get something everyone else has. I won't do it.

This man does his best to keep his body and its presentation boyish. He maintains himself as a "momma's boy." He says he cannot bear the uncertainty associated with any passage toward adult masculinity. In effect, he works against the demands of "nature," insisting that his body be maintained as that of a boy's. And with this, he preserves a coherent, simplified, and exceptional connection to his mother, and also preserves a sense of sanity: "This is me. Stop being me and I stop being sane. I know it sounds crazy. Maybe it is crazy. That doesn't matter. To me, it's sane."

He suffers violence. He is still taunted. He feels himself in permanent exile from what he calls "your world." He has no friends. He has never been in love. He feels himself unable to think, to interact, to connect. And yet, he steadily communicates a kind of pride, arrogance even, a sense that his is a heroic mission, one aimed at the preservation of what he calls his "dignity" no matter the costs.

Sacrifice in the name of dignity—I think the phrase is not only pertinent to this patient but also bluntly describes the basic orientation we have when we work interpretively with all patients. That is, we are constantly wondering what makes our patients' manifest sacrifices worth their price. And, in effect, when we think of sacrifice's worth, we invariably think of the preservation of something vital, something, that is, linked to "dignity." And it is this—the pursuit of erotic "dignity"—that I think comes into stark focus when one looks binocularly at the minds and bodies of transsexual patients. How can it be worth it, we wonder. And this, of course, is the question we are always asking, with all of our patients, men and women. We ask it most overtly precisely at the moment when we sense erotic appetite to have gone awry. How can it be worth it—those tattoos, that surgery, that inhibition, that pain, etc.? This, our ongoing and universal question, becomes more obvious the more severe the sacrifice. With transsexuals, where the sacrifice seems particularly severe, the question, therefore, erupts with particular force.

How can it be worth it? Once we ask the question, we begin to see the effort, inside and out, to maintain and preserve a sense of integrity, dignity in the face of incompatible appetitive demands. Of course, neither "integrity" nor "dignity" is a psychoanalytic concept. But, what they each get at, I think, is the work of making oneself into a person who can be simultaneously sexual and sane.

This work, thought of psychoanalytically, consists of three parts: 1) regulating the intense and incompatible demands of bodily grounded drives; 2) maintaining an organized mental structure; and 3) preserving an attachment to crucial objects.

In my patient, and in the subjects of Pierce's and Quinodoz's work, the cost of this three-pronged effort is dramatically high, the sacrifices enormous, the violence brutal and undeniable.

But, using binocular vision, one can see and think of the analogous costs incurred by all those men whose "dignity"—like the transsexuals', like my patient's—demands an ever-vigilant renunciation of possibility, a renunciation whose violence may be more indirect, somehow tucked away into psychic structure via repression, but nonetheless must be accepted in the name of regulating drives, maintaining structure, and preserving objects. Like transsexuals, like my patient, these men have undergone and continue to undergo self-administered "sex change operations" in the name of dignity and integrity, in the name, that is, of keeping the psychic, and erotic, operations going.

Chapter 10

War stories[1]

What follows began as a contribution to an edited book entitled *First Do No Harm*, a group of essays taking up issues arising from the interface of psychoanalysis and war. The issue I landed on was "war stories"—the loves and ideals they spawn, the bonds they create, the harm they may do. Like many boys, I played at war as a child: games with "guns," "killing," "dead guys," "bad guys"; games of real stealth and make-believe violence. I also read war comics, saw war movies and documentaries, heard about relatives killed in the Holocaust, saw footage of liberated camps, watched *The World at War* every week on TV, saw a slew of Westerns in which Indians were slaughtered, talked to friends about war, wondered what combat would be like, what it would take to really kill somebody, and—most of all—listened to my father tell me about war, about his war, 19 months of infantry combat from Normandy until V-E Day.

My father's war stories were peculiar. He started telling them to me when I was a boy and continued telling me the same stories until I left home. Thirty years later, I was interviewing him, aiming to construct a biography. During the interviews, he told me one of his war stories, one I had heard many times before. What was peculiar was that he seemed to have forgotten that he had ever told me this story. He introduced it hesitantly, as he always had—"just this once," he would say—and, indeed, said again in the interview. Apparently, he had to keep telling it, always as though for the first time, as though perhaps this time would be the cathartic one, the last one necessary. It never was the last one necessary. This time, though, it was the last one.

Of course, in his story, as in the others, all the warriors in all the wars were men. There is nothing idiosyncratic about this fact. For me, and, I think, for so many other boys and young men, the relation between masculinity and war cannot be ignored. Saturating the cultural air we breathe is the claim that the warrior is the realization of the masculine. Of course, this claim can be rejected, can be countered,

---

1 Material from this chapter first appeared in Moss, D. (2010c) "War stories," in A. Harris and S. Botticelli (eds) *First Do No Harm: The Paradoxical Encounters of Psychoanalysis, Warmaking and Resistance*, London: Routledge. Used with permission.

can be critiqued, can be taken up in a wide variety of ways. However, the claim is too deep, too infiltrative, too insistent to be ignored or pushed aside. The hard-muscled body, the determined face, the loyal comrade, the willingness to take on, and kill, the deadly enemy—these features set one bar that, I think, few, if any, men can evade.

Of course, there are other bars as well. But this one, I think, has a special status. For me and for my male patients—to a one, in my view—who were fortunate enough to have stayed out of combat, we are left with a sense of unease and disquiet about how we would have fared in war and whether or not we can now claim equal standing with those men who, either through choice or conscription, have had real versions of the war experiences that we have only been able to imagine.

War stories are an essential vehicle for communicating the ideological link between the warrior and the man. In what follows, I mean to communicate some of what went on in my repeatedly hearing my father's war stories and some of what continues to go on as his stories reverberate through me and get picked up by one of my sons. Like the other first-person narratives in this book, this one seems to me, in spite of its peculiar particularities, representative of the work men do as they try to position themselves in relation to the wars and war stories bequeathed to them in the stories told by and about their fathers, their fathers' generation, and the line of fathers who preceded them.

***

I sit down. The shades are drawn in the windows across the street. Everyone, silent and somber, is at work on a text: everyone, every American adult. The country has taken a pause. All of us have been given the same assignment. Our writing, compiled and preserved, will constitute a monument to a citizenry thinking about war and harm. We will be remembered for this. We will have interrupted history.

This fiction lasts a second.

A shade opens. A woman appears on her terrace. The heating contractor knocks on the door. There will be no large compilation, no major monument.

I'm doing this alone, then. I want to stop more than I want to continue. I pause. I don't have to do this, I think. Yes I do. It's an obligation. It's about being a Jew, this obligation. You must keep telling about what was done, about what remained, about what came next. You do this, you keep telling, and it hooks you in. You find your place. Telling holds your place for you. You listen, you tell, you listen, you tell.

I once went to Terezin. Down the road from the concentration camp were the ovens. I walked there alone. You walk into an innocuous brick building and there they are: two ovens. The ovens were exactly like ovens, only mammoth. The doors of the ovens were open. You stand in front of the open doors, looking in. For me, "ovens" had been a metaphor for the Holocaust. But here, the metaphor collapsed. But not all the way. Though these ovens looked exactly like ovens, what most impressed was my incapacity to experience them as the actual ovens they apparently were; they remained likenesses. I couldn't actually achieve concreteness in front of them. There was a gap I couldn't navigate. I couldn't get real people into these particular ovens. I stared at them but no matter what I tried, they kept being "ovens," as though they were models, somehow, of other ovens into which people had been put, as though this were an exhibit, a rendering, of the ovens at Terezin. I stayed there a long time. I was surprised at this incapacity. I kept working to diminish the gap between what I was seeing and what was there. But I didn't really know what kind of work to do. After an hour or so, I think, I saw a small, torn, piece of paper on the floor next to one of the ovens. On the paper, written in Hebrew, was a prayer: "Sh'ma Yisrael . . ." ["Hear, O Israel: the Lord is our God, the Lord is one"]. The paper had been left there by a Jew who had been there before me. Whether yesterday or forty years earlier didn't matter. What mattered was that the torn paper opened up a time channel for me. I held the paper in my hand. This paper was concrete. The prayer was concrete. Neither was a likeness. Holding the paper and reading the prayer placed me in a historical line: me here now, and the person who wrote this before me, and all the others before both of us. The paper put me in contact with all the others. The contact was not a likeness to contact. This contact was concrete and overwhelming. What had been a feeling of insufficiency turned immediately into excess. The intensity was too much. I had to leave. I walked out and stayed away for a few minutes. When I came back, the gap reappeared. Although the ovens were still "ovens," I now felt like I had achieved contact with the people for whom they were designed. The gap had narrowed.

That text in Terezin not only did no harm, it transformed harm—helpless disidentification—into connection. For now, here, that prayer written on torn paper is my exemplary text, the one that opens up a time channel and narrows the disidentificatory gap. The exemplary text binds reader to writer and each to a lineage of shared predecessors. How to write my own?

I was going to write about contemporary films about the Iraq war: *Stop Loss, Jarhead, In the Valley of Elah*. It seemed similar to writing about newspaper reports from a year or two ago: an inert project.

I was going to write about some books, comparing first-hand reports of the Iraq war with similar reports from Vietnam and from the Second World War. I knew there would be differences—the moral high ground vanishing over the decades—and also knew I could make little of them.

I was going to write about a recently published surgical textbook filled with grim, nearly unbearable photos of traumatized people in Iraq and the recommended treatment procedures. I had read reviews of this book. The reviews said that it succeeded where most war writing did not; that it conveyed, more directly, what it is like, or what, from my point of view, I might imagine it must be like. The book left me cold: surgical treatments of generic gore. Nothing for me to say.

I was going to write about 9/11, about feeling frightened, crying, enraged, vengeful, about what I had already written, but I've already said what I can.

How to write here, lacking a sense that there is something I know, something ready. The task, then, is to look, see what I can find. Whatever my method, the aim will be to keep the lever arm short: no confessions, conclusions, or conceptualizations.

Start with an inventory.

This war, old wars, my father at war, Vietnam, the next war, new wars, just wars, torture, restraint, reason, Freud, civilization, my kids, war games, video games, murder rates, the death penalty, doctors in war, doctors against war, evading the draft, my father killing people and telling me about it, war and telling it, what happens when you tell it, when you show it, when you think it, when you do it, when you wonder about it, what do you wonder about, what's the harm, where's the harm, why's the harm, war as a fact like time is a fact, all the books and pictures, the films, all the showing terrible, clever, sad, brilliant, enraged, heroic, resistant, courageous, all the ones who have wanted us to see, and all the killers and the killed, the dramas, the stories, the memories, centuries of them, no memory without war, there's always a war, war like an illness, an infection, a death cell, a terror, gathering stories to tell, no harm in that, is there? How to know, really, what harm is, the need to remember, the harm of remembering, the harm of forgetting, which is it, being a psychoanalyst, remembering, forgetting, telling, not telling, staying silent, moving on, visiting, staying away, what to do, why, with whom, someone comes into the house and kills everyone and leaves and that's it, and my father did that, well there you are, and who do you tell, and why, and you hear about this, and who do you tell, and why?

There's a finding: my father, his war stories. I'll start with him.

The entrance wound

> And I'll only say this one once. We didn't have time to fuck with prisoners. Five minutes before they were prisoners, they were killing us. My captain used to say things like "take these prisoners back to the prisoner dump," which would be eight miles or ten miles back, "and be back in five minutes." So we would be back in five minutes.
>
> Anyway, I really can't talk about some of that stuff. It's forty-five years. Perhaps I can. There were two, one instance still haunts me, two instances I can talk about, one maybe. We were foot troops and we would clean up any pockets. And we're running along trying to stay below the windows and guys behind us are trying to cover the windows here on the other side of the street. I don't know if I can talk . . . Jesus, fifty years, I'd think I'd be over it. We went underneath the window and we heard noises in a window. Now all the Germans knew. I mean they knew what we were doing. So, I pulled two grenades out and I tossed them both in the window, over my head. And then you wait for the blast. And I think the door was locked but we blew the door

open and ran in and evidently there was a nursery and there had to be I don't
know how many—maybe six, maybe three—babies in bassinets blew all over
the room. At the time, I didn't think. I remember maybe I might have said 'oh
shit' and I got out of there.

We had pot-bellied stoves. I was evidently warming up and this German
officer pulls himself up and gives a Nazi salute. And he says "I'm a German
officer and I demand Geneva rights." Rominick is a Polack. There's all these
dead people scattered around. Rominick kneed him twice with his 45
automatic and the guy is lying there. And Rominick announced to the people
standing there, including me, which made me deathly afraid of Rominick from
then on, "first man touches him, I'll kill him." Nobody bothered him.

One of the things that makes it hard, one of the first things was the delight
I felt, I remember feeling, in shooting things, in killing things, now not those
babies, that was, Jesus Christ. But, I would volunteer to snipe, which is a, even
now is kind of a sneaky way of doing anything. And if you played with it a
little bit, if you were careful, got the windage, how much wind there was, from
what direction, how far your target was away, you could lay a bullet in, if
you've got time. And I used to like that. I'd catch a guy, he'd be going to the
can to take a shit. I mean, a guy might be thinking of his fraulein, going home,
so far removed from the war, and I'd kill that poor fucker, or at least I'd hit
him, and enjoy it, Jesus, Donald, I enjoyed it.

The passage through, the infiltration

The strangest feature of this story—"And I'll say this only once"—is that my father,
in fact, told this story to me 50–60–70 times. And each time, just like this one—
the second-to-last—he would hesitate, resist, be unable to continue, be overcome.
And then, always as though for both the first and last time, he would find a way to
say it, to tell me about those babies, and those prisoners and the captain and the
guy going to the can to take a shit. So each time, then, the real force of the story
lay in the fact that my father had once again and for the first time, found the
strength, the narrative muscle, to get the telling out. Each time he told it, the telling
turned him into a hero, as if it weren't the deeds that were difficult and it certainly
wasn't the hearing that was difficult, but only, really, the telling. As though I were
witnessing something like a self-surgery he were performing, an extraction of a
bullet, say, or an amputation. And I, each time, never an exception, felt exactly in
accord with his premise. It was, for me too, always both the first and last time. I
was always the only witness. I never said, never quite thought even, that he was
doing this again, that we were doing this again. And yet, also, I always knew,
always thought, that yes, here we are again, doing this again.

The telling began, I think, before I was 10 years old. It ended the year he died.
He told it to me once more after this. I was 54 then. More than forty-four years of
this story, of this doing together what no one but us really knew. It was not exactly
a secret. The information was not meant to be held in private. I never thought it

mattered much who knew. I used to tell people. I was neither ashamed nor proud of what he had done. But, like him, I knew that, yes, I'd tell someone and enjoy it. Jesus. I enjoyed it. He never told me he enjoyed telling me, but I know he did. I never told him about my enjoyment either, in the hearing or in my own tellings. Whatever he had done, years before, served as a means for what he/we were doing then and what I, with this writing, am doing now. And of this I never spoke, except for now, and, in the face of it all, yes, even now, I can say, like him, and with him, I'm enjoying it.

It wasn't, finally, information that was being transmitted; it wasn't trauma either. It was excitement—his and mine. Those babies, prisoners, the guy on the can, the captain—they were never quite the point. My father and I put the stories to our use. That—the stories' use—was the point. And that use had something to do with a shared sense that, in each telling, those blown-up babies, murdered prisoners, wasted shitter and tortured officer were the price we willingly were paying. He—and I—as the tellings went on, would, we each knew, have it all happen again, knowing we could make this out of it. That was our secret. Given the chance, he would do it again, and I would want him to.

One terrible part of this secret is that both of us would deny its truth had either of us tried to expose it. Therefore, now, when I write that it was a secret, I wonder whether I am writing an exculpatory fiction and whether it may have been I alone for whom both the deeds and the tellings were a means to a treasured end—the treasure consisting of the discovery, the repetition, and the deep enjoyment of this inverted fairy tale—in which the worst that can happen does happen and that only because it happened can you enjoy an intimacy that all of civilization aims to forbid: the pleasures and excitements of telling it. I know he was in on it. I know it. I also have my doubts. What kind of knowledge is this? It's madness to be certain of a mind not your own. But I know it.

So this, then, is, I guess, one of the harms engendered by war stories. Maybe all war stories are told by fathers to sons. You can't know that. When you encounter the admonition to "first do no harm," you are meant to know, as a matter of course, what harm is. But here, in these stories my father told me, in my housing them now, in my telling them, I cannot distinguish pleasure from harm. I know with certainty that he told me too much, that I, like any child, was, in some sense, harmed by hearing what I heard, by knowing what I knew. But only in some sense. I also feel that the stories were a gift providing pleasures unrivalled to this day. And I also know that the fact of those pleasures is, in large measure, what is meant by the stories doing harm to me. I've heard people speak this way about shooting up cocaine. They speak of an intensity of pleasure that they know the rest of the world will never provide. They speak, then, of the harm done to them by pleasure. This is what I am trying to do now: speak of the harm done to me by pleasure. But the contradiction knocks me off my feet. I don't feel on firm ground as I write this. I know there is harm. I know there is pleasure. But I'm writing from a zone in which both are absent. I don't think it would be possible to write from the zone in which either—meaning both—were present.

I remember hearing of some Navajo soldiers who, under no circumstances, would ever speak of war to either their wives or children. Instead of war stories, there was silence. I wonder about the impact of that silence. Is it a way of telling a war story? I remember my admiration of these Navajo and of the forces that allowed them to retain what they knew, to remain silent. Admiration and reason saluted their self-control, their commitment to do no further harm to those who depended on them, those who would have had to listen if they had spoken. That's what home is, what I was—the place where the others (at least one other, I think) have to listen to you. But admiration and reason actually did not, and do not, penetrate, do not disrupt, the flow and impact of these stories. The stories take on an admirable glow themselves, precisely because they are so shameful, their telling such a sign of helplessness and neglect, such a refusal, such an overflow, of all the constraints and limits established by the mere demands of being decent. The babies are blown apart and so is the mind of the child who hears of it. The story is a grenade, thrown this time with secret foreknowledge. Okay, you play the soldier, I'll play the babies. Let's do it again and again. Actually, as I write this, I realize that the roles are not as clear as that. Yes, let's do it again and again. But, let's really be in on it together, each of us the soldier, each of us the babies, each of us telling each of us, without it mattering really who appears to be telling, who listening. Let's go beneath differences like that. Let's tap into force, into the joy, power and energy pulsing through and destroying all those arbitrary differences. Here it is, then, the impact of those stories—they eliminate difference and make it impossible to distinguish pleasure from harm. For a moment, then, the title of the book may seem like it could just as well have been *First Do No Pleasure*. This is hard-won: the sense that the difference between the two is not fundamental, that it is the product of some activity. Knowing that, or thinking you know it, is itself both a marker of harm done and pleasure taken.

The moment you use a phrase like "eliminate difference," you have abandoned the project. The project is not to conceptualize an effect. The project is to tell an effect, show an effect, affect an effect. It's to do what my father did, to do it as his son, to find a listener, and to expose a pulse, an artery, just this once, that carries and transports these stories, these tellings. The tellings are immortal. The father's tellings are injected, not like venom but like syrup. No, the tellings are not injected. They do not penetrate. They are opportunistic, like water. The tellings flow. They slide in through an opening that can't be seen. They slide in at a point of attachment, a kind of umbilical attachment, binding father to son. "Binding" is not right. "Umbilical" is not right. Binding is a side effect. Perhaps the stories bind, but before that, the point of attachment is cool and open, a point through which things flow, back and forth, father to son, son to father. The son can make the father sick if what flows from son to father presents father with a mismatch or an excess. And for the son, the flow is, at the beginning, unremarkable; as the lungs attach all of us to the air and, therefore, to the planet so this point, this opening, attaches son to father. The opening changes character when these stories flow through. The opening takes on muscle and force; here, then, the point of attachment begins to bind. I write this and of course think of bodies, male bodies, hard, muscular, forceful, binding. But this, too, this package of thoughts, of associations, seems a side effect, a flight more than a realization. First comes the point of attachment. It precedes. Whatever you try to say about it, it precedes that, too. The point of attachment, the place where the stories come in, then, is behind you, behind what you can be conscious of. You can only be conscious of the tellings once they have arrived inside of you.

The stories leave from in front. I can direct them, aim them. What I can't do is tame them, turn them into words, into ideas, concepts, tell you about them. The stories are made up of primal words. They are disguised as words. The harm they do includes providing undeniable evidence that the primal is real and the word part is being put to use. They do harm by infiltrating all your efforts at thought, love, order, and reason with the fragrance of uncertainty. You, too, the stories affirm, you, too. Fragrance is not right. Umbilical is not right. There is nothing like a cord, a conduit. You cannot catch the stories in passage. The stories are, in the hearing, the air you are breathing. You breathe the stories through a mouth or nose you cannot see and do not know you have. The stories are a heat or pain. They are a temperature.

The partial exit, the passage out: the return of the sniper

Tomorrow is Inauguration Day. Today our dog was diagnosed with lymphoma. The diagnosis was sudden and devastating. The dog now has a year or so to live. Late in the evening, I was sitting with our 12-year-old son, trying to console him about the dog. I found nothing to say. He wouldn't let me touch him.

We were both silent for a few minutes—he, I think, focused on the dog, me focused on him.

Suddenly, my son asked me what I thought the odds were of Obama being assassinated. He wanted the odds on an assassination tomorrow, not those on the entire Obama presidency. He clearly felt I knew enough to answer his question. "No idea" would not suffice. I said, uncertain why, that the odds might be about a million to one. My son said he thought they were less, closer to one thousand to one, maybe less than that.

All you need, he said, is to sit two miles away with a high-powered sniper rifle and have a clear line of sight. Do that, he said, and Obama's dead.

Enjoying it: the harm transfigured

One of the things that makes it hard, one of the first things was the delight I felt, I remember feeling, in shooting things, in killing things, now not those babies, that was, Jesus Christ. But, I would volunteer to snipe, which is a, even now is kind of a sneaky way of doing anything. And if you played with it a little bit, if you were careful, got the windage, how much wind there was, from what direction, how far your target was away, you could lay a bullet in, if you've got time. And I used to like that. I'd catch a guy, he'd be going to the can to take a shit. I mean, a guy might be thinking of his fraulein, going home, so far removed from the war, and I'd kill that poor fucker, or at least I'd hit him, and enjoy it, Jesus, Donald, I enjoyed it.

So here it is, I thought. Here's my father's war story, being told to me, with variations, by my 12-year-old. My 12-year-old imagines the sniper and identifies with the victim. He's blown away by the technology—his version of "if you played with it a little bit." It somehow helps him out to get in touch with this, helps him deal with his dog's terminal illness. The story moves my son from the position of helpless object of an inexplicable disease to the position of an excited object of a determined man's capacity.

My dad's is a story about being a sniper, about how he liked it, and I wondered how that story is filtering through me to my 12-year-old. I know I've told him about sniper rifles like the one he imagines. In fact, I like hearing about these rifles, and until last night, I never thought about the line formed by that liking, the line binding me to my father, and my son to my father's son. My father's sniper bullet goes through that guy on the can and then continues through the assassinations of the 60s and 70s until it comes to a moment's rest in my son's question about the odds of Obama's being killed today. He told me that the DC police have arrested many people today who had threatened Obama's life. I told him that people say a lot of things. And what he said was, yes, but some people do them. There, I think, there, my father's bullet, and his "Jesus, Donald, I liked it" come to momentary rest.

Epilogue

In my first year of elementary school, we were taught a new song each week. From the start, we were told that, at the end of the year, we would each be given a chance to lead the class in singing our favorite, which we were to keep secret. As the year went on, a kind of drama emerged: speculation, teasing and play; who would choose what, which song would be the winner. For me there was no doubt what my choice was going to be. The only song I loved was the lullaby "When at night I go to sleep," from *Hansel and Gretel*. We learned it in early autumn. This meant I got to keep my secret for months. I remember the pleasure of being certain for all those months. Knowing that none of the newer songs had a chance, I could bluff and create illusions: this one's great, I could say, or I really like that one.

But mine was, and would always be, the most beautiful song I had ever heard. This I knew. I sang it to myself every night. I'd always had trouble sleeping and easily went into a panic while lying in bed, imagining the disaster of never sleeping—days, weeks, months of it, and finally being sent away when it was decided that nothing could be done. This lullaby was precious to me. It worked where nothing else had. "When at night I go to sleep, 13 angels watch to keep . . ." Throughout the fall and winter, the angels would come when called, watching me, keeping me, keeping me safe, letting me sleep. They were neither dream come true, nor wish come true. They were, instead, an astonishing appearance, an absolute surprise. At first, I didn't love the song because it brought me the angels. I loved it for its sounds. I had never heard anything like it. I knew only rhyming songs, kids' songs, bouncy and fun Yiddish melodies. But nothing like this, nothing that both respected and lifted a child's sadness. I hadn't thought it possible. Sadness, I thought, was shameful, heavy and permanent.

A night or two after I learned the song, the angels came. Here they were, exactly like the song said: two above me, two below me, two on my right side, two on my left. Before them, the lights went, I closed my eyes, and there was nothing. With them, the lights went out, I closed my eyes, and I could sleep.

Mine was not a childhood of wishes coming true. Mine had been the reverse. In my childhood, wishing was something you were caught at. Wishes were meant to be exposed; they were a version of lying. After all, when you wished for something, you were trying to make what was in front of you fade; you were saying to yourself that what was in front of you was insufficient or wrong and, because of that, wasn't good enough. And because it wasn't good enough, it might not be quite true, at least not permanently true. In wishing, you had the idea that something else might be even more true than what was in front of you. You had the idea that what was better might be truer. This is what made wishing a kind of lie. In order to wish for more than you had, you had to believe that the idea of more was at least as real as the idea of what you had. Wishing put the lie to what you had. Wishing could only set you up for disappointment. In my childhood, wishing, then, was a way of hurting yourself. Stop lying, stop wishing, stop hurting yourself. It was simple to think that way but difficult to make that kind of thinking real. I was taught that contending with that difficulty constituted the task of growing up.

Strangely enough, even though wishing was a kind of lying, it was still a good thing to do. Wishing was the only way you could really learn. This was so because not getting what you wished for taught you what real life was. Wishing taught you that real life was right in front of you, whatever it was. This was all there was, all there ever would be. You'd wish for something different and, in that moment, you would be creating a gap between what you had and what you wanted. Real life demanded that you eliminate that gap. That's what time was, really—days and nights, minutes and hours—giving you what it had and nothing more. You weren't meant to be grateful, you weren't meant to be disappointed; you were meant to proceed, to keep going, to be carried along by time. This is what growing up meant: first this, and after that, the next, and then the next, and next, and next. And that is what wishing was good for: to help you get oriented to real time; to help you dig in, to ride it out, day and night, minute by minute, hour by hour, to ride it out.

To teach you this was what parents were for, particularly what my father was for. He made it clear to me that that's what he was doing: riding his time out. You'd never catch him doing what he wanted to do. That was never in the picture. He'd been to the Army, to the war; he'd come back tired, married, and now with a kid— me. So he woke up early, delivered diapers, came home, slept, and did it again. My mother was never really in the picture, neither for him nor for me. She was part of what each of us had to do; we had to deal with her. That's what I was meant to do, and that's what I did: wake up early, go to school, deal with my mom, and become like my dad, if not immediately, then soon, the quicker the better.

Any gap, any wanting it otherwise, and my father would show it to me, point out how I was lagging behind, waiting for what wasn't coming. His job was to show me what I wanted and to make it clear to me that whatever it was, not getting it was life's most reliable fact. This was part of what he had to do: teach me. We were of one mind on this: he would clarify the situation, mark out its terms, put the whole thing in perspective. He would help me to eliminate the fairy tale, the soft landing, the "maybe next time," the "we'll see what can happen."

I loved my father for all of this, the sacrifice, the duty. He was helping me out, setting me straight, immunizing me against disappointment. Keep hopes minimal and expectations close to zero—and then, get to work. I thought I was getting ready. This is how it had been for him and how it was going to be for me.

Days were fine. Reading, numbers, physical things: you didn't have to wish for any of this; it was here, present, and you could put it to use, you could have fun with it. It was available before you had the chance, or need, to wish for it. Nights, though, were a big problem. The lights went out and everything vanished. No persons, no things. There was nothing to hold on to and, of course, nothing to wish for. That's when I'd panic.

In the morning, when I'd wake up, I'd feel gratitude to both the song and to its angels. At first, this gratitude was enormous; it was infiltrated with amazement. I had what I never thought I'd have. Slowly, the amazement diminished. I came to expect the angels. They had no cause to refuse me. Just as they were mine, I was theirs. They had taken me on; I had given myself over. Each night was an affirmation of the nights preceding. Things would continue. Nothing would change. There was never a ceremony; I certainly never said anything to anyone about this.

I'd wake up as though nothing exceptional had taken place, nothing exceptional had been done for me. I got used to angels around me every night, like the way you might feel when the plane lands or the mail comes, a background recognition that you are being taken care of, but nothing to be that excited about. It was simple: the angels now took care of me. They were never concrete figures in my mind; they had no color, no wings, no faces; they made no sound. They never really appeared, not really. They were neither invisible nor visible. They were out of sight, elsewhere, just on the other side, guarding the room I was in, guarding the body I was in. Were they to have had faces, their faces would have been turned out, like the faces of Secret Service agents. They established a perimeter that nothing could penetrate. As long as I could locate myself within the perimeter, I was fine.

My grandfather would chant a prayer each morning, giving thanks for waking up, for being brought back to life from the death of sleep. I never could pray like he did. Prayer was for old people, I thought, people born in Europe. But I could give thanks to my angels. I'd open my eyes, feel that morning was near enough, and I'd get out of bed, long before my parents. I'd go to the TV and turn on the test pattern. I'd stare at the pattern for a while—it was always the same—and then place my cheek against the warm machine. It was a comfort to me. I'd wait there until light came or my father, whichever was first. The angels and the TV got me through night after night. Once it was light outside, I could relax. There seemed little to worry about. My days were good. The nights had been bad, though, and now the angels were carrying me through.

So, as the months passed, not only did I know what my favorite song was, I also knew that, when I would announce it and lead everyone in singing it, this would represent a moment of appreciation, a public declaration of love and gratitude to the angels that were saving me. It would be a chance to pay off some of my accumulating debt. I kept all of this secret: the song, the angels, my terror at night, the TV, all of it. It was mine. I loved my angels. They loved me.

It was late spring when I got my chance to lead the class in singing for and about my angels. Called upon, I walked to the front of the class. I was pleased that no one knew what I was about to do. The teacher asked me what song I had chosen. I began to tell her: "It's the lullaby . . ." But immediately, out of the corner of my eye, I saw the reaction of the boys in the front row. Their faces were lighting up, in shock. They were looking at each other. Until then, I hadn't even considered these boys, except for the certainty that my choice would surprise, that my secret had been kept intact.

But, as I began to speak to the teacher, as I saw the faces of these boys, I knew, knew in a way that was immediate, clear and certain, that what I was about to do, the song I was about to choose, the declaration that I was about to make, represented an enormous, and irrevocable error. I must not do it. The boys were telling me that. I must not. The moment was instantaneous. There were no words. Don't go down that alley. Don't walk alone on that street. Don't. You will regret it for the rest of your life if you do that. The boys, the eyes of the boys, took over. They got in between me and my angels. I had no time to think. No time to wonder what this was. It just was. It was a moment of certainty. Don't go down that alley. And there I was. It was the boys, now, and not the angels, who were saving my life. Don't speak of angels, the boys were telling me, don't speak of lullabies. Bury this. Silence this. Let it never again appear. And my gratitude now went out to the boys. I wanted to thank them. But that too would have to be silenced. The lesson they were teaching me could never be acknowledged. I was never to show that I had needed this lesson. No, what the boys were teaching me was that I was to know now, and to have always known, that "When at night I go to sleep" could not be my favorite song, that a lullaby had no place here, that something else was called for, had always been called for, would always be called for. In a flash, in an act of gratitude not to my angels, but to my boys, I changed my selection. I smiled at the teacher, told her I was just kidding, told her I would now lead the class in singing the "Marines' Hymn": "From the Halls of Montezuma to the shores of Tripoli. . ."

Yes, this was my favorite song. Of course. It had always been my favorite song. We finished. There was applause. I went back to my seat. For a little while, I was confused. But by late morning, when we had gone outside, the boys and I, when we had all played, run, enjoyed each other, I was happy.

That night I thought I could no longer call upon my angels, that I had betrayed them and that they would turn away from me. But they didn't. I could still sing to them, they would still come, I could still sleep. But I stopped being able to do it. I stopped being able to sing the song, to call them. The angels became something I used to do, used to use, something I could remember.

I stopped singing my favorite lullaby. It had once been okay, but now it would be a mistake. I vowed to myself not to do it again and I didn't.

And at night, I again couldn't sleep. I'd try a trick my dad told me about. Tell my toes to relax, and then my ankles, my calves, my knees. Work my way up, and by the time I'd reach my head, I would already be asleep. But I could never really do it. A little ways up my body, I would start to get too frightened to continue, too worried about what would happen if I got to my face and I still wasn't sleeping. That, I thought, would be the end of it, and, who knew, maybe the end of me.

In my memory, my first spoken words arrived there, in front of the class, when I backed off from the angels and turned to the marines. My first remembered words, then, were a kind of lie. Before then, I remember others speaking, saying things, presenting me with themselves in their various ways: my grandfathers, my uncles, my dad, but I have no sense that I spoke back, or ever initiated something with words.

This book can be thought of as an extended effort to unpack that moment in front of the class and, indirectly, to apologize to the angels for my treachery. I was unfaithful to them. I renounced them in public and continued to do so for decades. Their love for me was unconditional. It remains unconditional. They ask for no explanation. They demand no apology. They are still there, those angels, I know it. My love for them is another of those that dare not speak its name. In fact, even if it dared, what name would it have, that love of protective angels?

Of course, my love of these angels is likely linked, strangely enough, with the forbidden love of boys—strange, since it was the love of boys that catalyzed my renunciation of the angels. There is something backward, then, about the commonsensical reading of this incident. The commonsensical reading: a boy loves his angels so much and is, therefore, a kind of sissy. The more immediate, and, for me, more trustworthy, reading: a boy loves boys so much that, in the name of that love, in fear of their rejection, he renounces his angels, the loves of his life. He then turns outward, now in the company of boys like himself, and searches for new "angels"—cute girls, say—melancholically aware that what he is "really" doing in that fateful turning outward is simultaneously preserving and betraying his original love of angels, affirming and denying his new love of boys; after all, now he and the boys are joined together in looking elsewhere for the angels they might have all once had.

Bibliography

Adorno, T.W., Frenkel-Brunswik, E., Levinson, D. and Nevitt Sanford, N. (1950) *The Authoritarian Personality*, abr. edn, New York, NY: Norton, 1982.

Antelme, R. (1957) *L'espece humaine [The human race]*, trans. J. Haight and A. Mahler, Evanston, IL: Marlboro Press/Northwestern.

Ashbery, J. (1992) "From Palookaville," in *Hotel Lautréaumont,* New York, NY: Knopf, 46–48.

Beckett, S. (1978) "Malone dies," in *Three Novels,* New York, NY: Grove Press.

Bersani, L. (1988) "Is the rectum a grave?" in D. Crimp (ed.), *AIDS: Cultural Analysis, Cultural Activism*, Cambridge, MA: MIT Press.

Bion, W. (1961) *Experiences in Groups*, London: Tavistock Publications Limited.

Bird, B. (1957) "A consideration of the etiology of prejudice," *Journal of the American Psychoanalytic Association,* 5: 490–513.

Boys Don't Cry (1999) [Film] Directed by Kimberly Pierce. USA: Fox Searchlight.

Butler, J. (1990) *Gender Trouble,* New York, NY: Routledge.

Cool Hand Luke (1967) [Film] Directed by Stuart Rosenberg. USA: Warner Brothers.

Crimp, D. (ed.) (1988) *AIDS: Cultural Analysis, Cultural Activism*, Cambridge, MA: MIT Press.

Freud, S. (1900) "The interpretation of dreams," in James Strachey *et al.* (eds), *The Standard Edition of the Complete Works of Sigmund Freud*, Vol. 5, London: The Hogarth Press and the Institute of Psychoanalysis, 1953–74.

—— (1905) "Three essays on the theory of sexuality," in James Strachey *et al.* (eds), *The Standard Edition of the Complete Works of Sigmund Freud*, Vol. 7, London: The Hogarth Press and the Institute of Psychoanalysis, 1953–74, 130–243.

—— (1911) "Psychoanalytic notes on an autobiographical account of a case of paranoia," in James Strachey *et al.* (eds), *The Standard Edition of the Complete Works of Sigmund Freud*, Vol. 12, London: The Hogarth Press and the Institute of Psychoanalysis, 1953–74.

—— (1913) "Totem and taboo," in James Strachey *et al.* (eds), *The Standard Edition of the Complete Works of Sigmund Freud*, Vol. 13, London: The Hogarth Press and the Institute of Psychoanalysis, 1953–74.

—— (1915a) "The unconscious," in James Strachey *et al.* (eds), *The Standard Edition of the Complete Works of Sigmund Freud*, Vol. 14, London: The Hogarth Press and the Institute of Psychoanalysis, 1953–74.

—— (1915b) "Instincts and their vicissitudes," in James Strachey *et al.* (eds), *The Standard Edition of the Complete Works of Sigmund Freud*, Vol. 14, London: The Hogarth Press and the Institute of Psychoanalysis, 1953–74, 117–140.

—— (1920a) "Beyond the pleasure principle," in James Strachey *et al.* (eds), *The Standard Edition of the Complete Works of Sigmund Freud*, Vol. 18, London: The Hogarth Press and the Institute of Psychoanalysis, 1953–74.

—— (1920b) "The psychogenesis of a case of homosexuality in a woman," in James Strachey *et al.* (eds), *The Standard Edition of the Complete Works of Sigmund Freud*, Vol. 18, London: The Hogarth Press and the Institute of Psychoanalysis, 1953–74, 145–172.

—— (1921a) "Group psychology and the analysis of the ego," in James Strachey *et al.* (eds), *The Standard Edition of the Complete Works of Sigmund Freud*, Vol. 18, London: The Hogarth Press and the Institute of Psychoanalysis, 1953–74, 65–144.

—— (1921b) "Mass psychology and analysis of the 'I'," in J. A. Underwood (trans.), A. Phillips (ed.), *Mass Psychology and Other Writings,* London: Penguin Books, 2004, 15–106.

—— (1923) "The ego and the id," in James Strachey *et al.* (eds), *The Standard Edition of the Complete Works of Sigmund Freud*, Vol. 19, London: The Hogarth Press and the Institute of Psychoanalysis, 1953–74, 12–66.

—— (1924) "The loss of reality in neurosis and psychosis," in James Strachey *et al.* (eds), *The Standard Edition of the Complete Works of Sigmund Freud*, Vol. 19, London: The Hogarth Press and the Institute of Psychoanalysis, 1953–74.

—— (1926) "Inhibitions, symptoms and anxiety," in James Strachey *et al.* (eds), *The Standard Edition of the Complete Works of Sigmund Freud*, Vol. 20, London: The Hogarth Press and the Institute of Psychoanalysis, 1953–74, 87–174.

—— (1927) "The future of an illusion," in James Strachey *et al.* (eds), *The Standard Edition of the Complete Works of Sigmund Freud*, Vol. 21, London: The Hogarth Press and the Institute of Psychoanalysis, 1953–74, 5–56.

—— (1929) "Civilization and its discontents," in James Strachey *et al.* (eds), *The Standard Edition of the Complete Works of Sigmund Freud*, Vol. 21, London: The Hogarth Press and the Institute of Psychoanalysis, 1953–74, 64–145.

—— (1937) "Analysis terminable and interminable," in James Strachey *et al.* (eds), *The Standard Edition of the Complete Works of Sigmund Freud*, Vol. 23, London: The Hogarth Press and the Institute of Psychoanalysis, 1953–74, 216–253.

Hildebrand, H.P. (1992) "A patient dying of AIDS," *International Review of Psycho-Analysis,* 19: 457–471.

Junger, S. (2010) *War,* New York, NY: Twelve Hatchett Book Group.

Kafka, Franz (1948) [first published 1919] "In the penal colony," in *Metamorphosis: In the Penal Colony and Other Stories*, New York, NY: Schocken Books, 191–231.

Klein, M. (1957) *Envy and Gratitude*, London: Tavistock Publications.

Lacan, J. (1953) "The function of language in psychoanalysis," in A. Wilden (ed.), *The Language of the Self*, Baltimore, MD: Johns Hopkins University Press, 1968.

—— (1956) "On a question preliminary to any possible treatment of psychosis," in A. Sheridan (trans.), *Écrits: A Selection*, New York, NY: W.W. Norton & Co., 1977.

—— (1966) "The mirror stage as formative of the function of the I as revealed in psychoanalytic experience," in A. Sheridan (trans.), *Écrits: A Selection*, New York, NY: W.W. Norton & Co., 1977.

—— (1977) *The Four Fundamental Concepts of Psycho-Analysis,* New York, NY: Norton.

Laplanche, J. and Pontalis, J.B. (1968) "Fantasy and the origins of sexuality," *International Journal of Psychoanalysis,* 49(1): 1–18.

Lewes, K. (1988) *The Psychoanalytic Theory of Homosexuality,* London and New York, NY: Quartet Books.

—— (1992) "Homophobia and the heterosexual fear of AIDS," *American Imago* 49: 343–357.

—— (2009) *Psychoanalysis and Male Homosexuality: 20th Anniversary Edition,* London, New York, NY: Jason Aronson.

Licensed to Kill (1998) [Film] Directed by Arthur Dong. USA: PBS POV.

Loffreda, B. (2000) *Losing Matt Shepherd,* New York, NY: Columbia University Press.

Moss, D. (1989) "From the treatment of a nearly psychotic man: A Lacanian point of view," *International Journal of Psychoanalysis,* 70: 275–286.

—— (1992) "Hating in the first person plural: The example of homophobia," *American Imago,* 49: 277–293.

—— (1997) "On situating homophobia," *Journal of the American Psychoanalytic Association,* 45: 201–215.

—— (2001) "On hating in the first person plural: Thinking psychoanalytically about racism, homophobia, and misogyny," *Journal of the American Psychoanalytic Association,* 49: 1315–1334.

—— (2002) "Internalized homophobia in men: Wanting in the first person singular, hating in the first person plural," *Psychoanalytic Quarterly,* 71: 21–50.

—— (2006) "Masculinity as masquerade," *Journal of the American Psychoanalytic Association,* 54(4): 1187–1195.

—— (2008) "Immaculate attachment/intelligent design," *Constellations,* 15(8), No. 8.

—— (2010a) "All I wish to say," *Cousin Corinne's Reminder,* No. 1.

—— (2010b) "Like drives, cultural products exert a demand on the mind for work: An introduction to two exemplary essays," *Psychoanalytic Quarterly,* 79: 159–170.

—— (2010c) "War stories," in A. Harris and S. Botticelli (eds) *First Do No Harm: The Paradoxical Encounters of Psychoanalysis, Warmaking and Resistance,* London: Routledge.

—— (2011a) "It's Oedipal all the way down," *Fort/Da,* 17: 42–52.

—— (2011b) "Sensuous personal identity vs. conceptual universal reason: Competing claims on the analyst while listening to sexually charged material," *DIVISION/Review,* Fall 2011.

Moss, D. and Zeavin, L. (1999) "The female homosexual: C'est nous," in R. Lester and E. Schoenberg (eds) *That Obscure Subject of Desire: Freud's Female Homosexual Revisited,* London: Routledge.

Nacho Libre (2006) [Film] Directed by Jared Hess. USA: Paramount Pictures.

New York Times, July 17, 2006, A4.

Nunokawa, J. (1992) "Homosexual desire and the effacement of the self in *The Picture of Dorian Gray,*" *American Imago,* 49: 311–323.

One Flew Over the Cuckoo's Nest (1975) [Film] Directed by Milos Forman. USA: United Artists.

Proust, M. (1913) *Swann's Way,* trans. L. Davis, New York, NY: Viking Penguin, 2003.

Quinodoz, D. (1998) "A fe/male transsexual patient in psychoanalysis," *International Journal of Psychoanalysis,* 79: 95–111.

—— (2002) "Termination of a fe/male transsexual patient's analysis: An example of general validity," *International Journal of Psychoanalysis*, 83: 783–796.

Ricoeur, P. (1970) *Freud and Philosophy: An Essay on Interpretation*, trans. D. Savage, New Haven, CT: Yale University Press.

Riviere, J. (1929) "Womanliness as a masquerade," *International Journal of Psychoanalysis*, 10: 303–310.

Rubin, G. (1975) "The traffic in women: Notes on the 'political economy' of sex," in R. Reiter (ed.), *In Toward an Anthropology of Women*, New York, NY: Monthly Review Press.

Selby, H. (1957) *Last Exit to Brooklyn*, New York, NY: Grove Press.

Servicemembers Legal Defense Network (SLDN) (2000) *Conduct unbecoming: The 6th annual report on "Don't Ask, Don't Tell, Don't Pursue, Don't Harrass"* [online] Available at: http://www.sldn.org/pages/sldn-report-6 [Accessed November 30, 2011].

Stevens, W. (1982) *The Collected Poems*, New York, NY: Vintage Books.

Treichler, P. (1988) "AIDS, homophobia, and biomedical discourse: An epidemic of signification," in D. Crimp (ed.), *AIDS: Cultural Analysis, Cultural Activism*, Cambridge, MA: MIT Press, 31–71.

Wings of Desire (1987) [Film] Directed by Wim Wenders. Germany: Road Movies FilmProduktion.

Winnicott, D. (1950) "Transitional object and transitional phenomena," in *Through Pediatrics to Psychoanalysis: The Collected Papers of D.W. Winnicott*, New York, NY: Basic Books, 1975.

Index

Ogden, Thomas 122
omnipotence 112
outrage 23, 30, 34

passivity 15, 108
pathos 55
penis envy 111
perversion 25, 27, 28
phallus 38–39, 99; Lacan's theorization of
the 6; phallic disappointment 100–1,
102
phobias 86, 94
Pierce, Kimberley 119–23, 125, 127
polio 42–8
Pontalis, J. B. 100
power 76
prejudice 52–3, 94, 95
primary process 25, 26, 27–8, 112
Proust, Marcel 4–6
psychoanalysis viii, xvii; AIDS 83;
disappointment 107; female genital 85;
as grandiose conceit 29; homosexuality
51–3, 54–6, 87, 88; identification 14;
ideology 4, 5; Little Richard 116;
malignant forces 83–4; with men who
don't wish 22–6; phobias 86;
renunciation of 77–8; repudiations of
homosexuality 3; sexuality 53–5, 56,
101, 102, 105–6; tilt away from
neutrality 58; transsexuals 123–4;
writing ix–x, 9–10; see also Freud
psychosis 25, 27, 28, 31, 35–6

Quinodoz, Danielle 119, 123–7

racism 86, 94, 95, 96
rape 119, 120, 121
reason 6, 61
repression 34, 89
revenge 30, 33, 38, 77
Ricoeur, Paul 39–40
Riviere, Joan xii
Roughton, Ralph 66–7, 78
Rubin, Gayle 75

sacrifice 54, 55, 126
sadness 39

satisfaction xx, 26–8, 92, 93, 104
schizophrenia 34
Schreber case 35–6, 96
secondary process 25, 26, 27–8
Selby, Hubert 69–71
self-analysis x
self-concept 66, 78
self-hatred/self-loathing ix, 63, 64
self-sufficiency 30, 31, 35, 36, 112
sensuousness 60–1, 62
sexual difference xii, xiii, xiv, 98, 122
sexual problems 19–20
sexuality 2, 30, 52–6, 101–2, 114;
clinical agenda 88; excessive parental
78–9, 80; Freud's "female homosexual"
107, 112; Freud's "Three essays on
the theory of sexuality" 123; genital
adequacy 107–8; incorprojection 96;
infant/caregiver relationship 104, 105;
irrational xxii; male and female 102–3;
melancholy element of 32; misplaced
92; phallic disappointment 100–1,
102; phobic object 97; repudiation of
femininity 93, 94, 95–6; symptomatic
expression of 76; theorizing 105–6;
see also heterosexuality;
homosexuality
shame 63, 66
silence, clinical 88–9
sincerity 101–3, 104, 105–6, 108, 114
social structure 83, 84
somatic identity 41
Stevens, Wallace xiii, xvi
subject/object relations 26–7, 36, 90
substitutes 27
sucking 105
suicide 29, 33, 35, 69
superego 37, 74, 87
symbols 39–40

taboo 75
tattoos 117–18
Terezin 129–30
terror 34
theory 88, 102–3, 104, 105, 106, 114
time 42
transference 31